Objective-C for Absolute Beginners

iPhone, iPad, and Mac Programming Made Easy
Second Editon

Gary Bennett
Mitch Fisher
Brad Lees

Apress®

Objective-C for Absolute Beginners: iPhone, iPad, and Mac Programming Made Easy, Second Edition

ISBN-13 (pbk): 978-1-4302-3653-5

ISBN-13 (electronic): 978-1-4302-3654-2

President and Publisher: Paul Manning
Lead Editors: Michelle Lowman and Matthew Moodie
Technical Reviewer: James Bucanek
Editorial Board: Steve Anglin, Mark Beckner, Ewan Buckingham, Gary Cornell,
    Morgan Engel, Jonathan Gennick, Jonathan Hassell, Robert Hutchinson,
    Michelle Lowman, James Markham, Matthew Moodie, Jeff Olson, Jeffrey Pepper,
    Douglas Pundick, Ben Renow-Clarke, Dominic Shakeshaft, Gwenan Spearing,
    Matt Wade, Tom Welsh
Coordinating Editor: Kelly Moritz
Copy Editor: Scribendi, Inc.
Compositor: MacPS, LLC
Indexer: BIM Indexing & Proofreading Services
Artist: SPi Global
Cover Designer: Anna Ishchenko

Distributed to the book trade worldwide by Springer Science+Business Media, LLC., 233 Spring Street, 6th Floor, New York, NY 10013. Phone 1-800-SPRINGER, fax (201) 348-4505, e-mail orders-ny@springer-sbm.com, or visit www.springeronline.com.

For information on translations, please e-mail rights@apress.com or visit www.apress.com.

Apress and friends of ED books may be purchased in bulk for academic, corporate, or promotional use. eBook versions and licenses are also available for most titles. For more information, reference our Special Bulk Sales–eBook Licensing web page at www.apress.com/bulk-sales.

Any source code or other supplementary materials referenced by the author in this text is available to readers at www.apress.com. For detailed information about how to locate your book's source code, go to http://www.apress.com/source-code/.

I'd like to dedicate this book to the two people who had the biggest impact on my career: my dad, Don W. Bennett, and Steve Jobs. Both passed away this year. Thanks for inspiring me to work in the field where I can have fun, make a difference, be creative, and live the American Dream.

—Gary Bennett

I would like to thank my family and friends who have always supported my endeavors. I would especially like to thank Heather, Matthew, and my two children Eric and Jade for patiently living without me for the many nights and forever-busy weekends. I would also like to thank my friends Gary and Brad for all the help they provided. It's been great working with them again.

—Mitch Fisher

I would like to thank my wife Natalie and my kids for the support and time they have given me to work on this book. I am also grateful for good friends who persuade me to take on crazy endeavors.

—Brad Lees

Contents at a Glance

Contents

About the Authors

Gary Bennett is president of xcelMe.com. xcelMe.com provides iPhone/iPad programming courses online. Gary has taught thousands of students how to develop iPhone/iPad apps, and has several very popular apps in the iTunes App Store. Gary's students have some of the best-selling apps in the iTunes App Store. Gary also worked for 25 years in the technology and defense industries. He served 10 years in the US Navy as a nuclear engineer aboard two nuclear submarines. After leaving the Navy, Gary worked for several companies as a software developer, CIO, and president. As CIO, he helped take VistaCare public in 2002. Gary also coauthored *iPhone Cool Projects* for Apress. He lives in Scottsdale, Arizona, with his wife Stefanie and their four children.

Mitch Fisher is a software developer in the Phoenix, Arizona, area. He was introduced to PCs back in the 1980s when 640 KB was considered more memory than anyone could ever use. Over the last 25 years, Mitch has worked for several large and medium-sized companies as a software engineer, software architect, and software manager, and has led teams of developers on multimillion-dollar projects. Mitch now divides his time between writing iOS applications, creating server-side UNIX technologies, and teaching iOS development at xcelMe.com.

Brad Lees has more than 14 years of experience in application development and server management. He has specialized in creating and initiating software programs in real estate development systems and financial institutions. Highlights of his professional career include his positions as information systems manager at The Lyle Anderson Company, product development manager for Smarsh, vice president of application development for iNation, and information technology manager at The Orcutt/Winslow Partnship, the largest architectural firm in Arizona. A graduate of Arizona State University, Brad resides in Phoenix with his wife Natalie and their five children.

About the Technical Reviewer

 **James Bucanek** has spent the past 30 years programming and developing microcomputer systems. He has experience with a broad range of technologies, from embedded consumer products to industrial robotics. James currently focuses on Macintosh and iPhone software development. When not programming, James indulges in his love of the arts. He earned an associate degree in classical ballet from the Royal Academy of Dance, and occasionally teaches at Adams Ballet Academy.

Acknowledgments

We would like to thank Apress for all their help in making this book possible. Specifically, we would like to thank Kelly Moritz, our coordinating editor, for helping us stay focused and overcoming many obstacles. Without Kelly, this book would not have been possible.

Special thanks to Matthew Moodie, our development editor, for all his suggestions during the editorial review process to help make this a great book. Thanks to Chandra Clarke and Scribendi, Inc., the copy editors who made the book look great.

We would also like to thank the Alice Community and Carnegie Mellon University for developing Alice and making learning object-oriented programming fun and easy!

Introduction

Over the last three years, we've heard the following countless times:

- ▧ "I've never programmed before, but I have a great idea for an iPhone/iPad app."
- ▧ "Can I really learn to program the iPhone or iPad?"

We always answer, "Yes, but you have to believe you can." Only you are going to tell yourself you can't do it.

For the Newbie

This book assumes you may have never programmed before. The book is also written for someone who may have never programmed before using object-oriented programming (OOP) languages. There are many Objective-C books out there, but all of these books assume you have programmed before and know OOP and computer logic. We wanted to write a book that takes readers from knowing little or nothing about computer programming and logic to being able to program in Objective-C. After all, Objective-C is the native programming language for the iPhone, iPad, and Mac.

Over the last three years, we have taught well over a thousand students at xcelMe.com to be iPhone/iPad (iOS) developers. Many of our students have developed some of the most successful iOS apps in their category in the iTunes App Store. We have incorporated what we have learned in our first two courses, Introduction to Object-oriented Programming and Logic and Objective-C for iPhone/iPad Developers, into this book.

For the More Experienced

Many developers who programmed years ago or programmed in a non-OOP language need a background in OOP and Logic before they dive into Objective-C. This book is for you. We gently walk you through OOP and how it is used in iOS development to help make you a successful iOS developer.

Why Alice: An Innovative 3D Programming Environment

Over the years, universities have struggled with several issues with their computer science departments:

- ▧ High male-to-female ratios
- ▧ High drop-out rates

■ Longer than average time to graduation

One of the biggest challenges to learning OOP languages like Java, C++, or Objective-C is the steep learning curve from the very beginning. In the past, students had to learn the following topics all at once:

■ Object-oriented principles
■ A complex Integrated Development Environment (IDE), i.e., Xcode, Eclipse, Visual Studio
■ The syntax of the programming language
■ Programming logic and principles

As a result, Carnegie Mellon University received a grant from the US government and developed Alice. Alice, an innovative 3D programming environment, makes it easy for new developers to create rich graphical applications. Alice is a teaching tool for students learning to program in an OOP environment. The software uses 3D graphics and a drag-and-drop interface to facilitate a more engaging, less frustrating first programming experience.

Alice enables students to focus on learning the principles of OOP without having to focus on learning a complex IDE and Objective-C principles all at once. You get to focus on each topic individually. This helps students feel a real sense of accomplishment as they progress.

As drag-and-drop programming, Alice removes all the complexity of learning an IDE and programming language syntax. You'll see programming is actually fun, and you can develop very cool and sophisticated apps in Alice.

After we introduce the OOP topic and readers feel comfortable with the material, we then move into Xcode, where you get to use your new OOP knowledge in writing Objective-C applications. This way, you can focus on the Objective-C syntax and language without having to learn OOP at the same time.

Learning Objective-C Without Alice

More than a thousand xcelMe.com students have used this book to become successful iOS developers. At the end of each course, we ask our students if the Alice sections in the first four sections were useful. More than half of the students thought using Alice at the beginning of the first four chapters to introduce the chapter was critical to their success. However, some of the students didn't feel they needed the Alice examples at the beginning of the first four chapters.

We have laid out the first four chapters of this book with the first part of each chapter introducing the OOP topic with Alice; the remaining part of the chapter introduces the topic using Objective-C. Thus, you can skip the Alice material if you feel comfortable with the topic.

How This Book Is Organized

You'll notice that we are all about successes in this book. We introduce the OOP and Logic concepts in Alice and then move those concepts to Xcode and Objective-C. Many students are visual or learn by doing. We use both techniques. We'll walk you through topics and concepts with visual examples and then take you through step-by-step examples reinforcing the concepts.

We often repeat topics in different chapters to reinforce what you have learned and apply these skills in new ways. This enables new programmers to reapply development skills and feel a sense of accomplishment as they progress. Don't worry if you feel you haven't mastered a topic. Keep moving forward!

The Formula for Success

Learning to program is an interactive process between your program and you. Just like learning to play an instrument, you have to practice. You must work through the examples and exercises in this book. Understanding the concept doesn't mean you know how to apply it and use it.

You will learn a lot from this book. You will learn a lot from working through the exercises in this book. *However, you will really learn when you debug your programs.* Spending time walking through your code and trying to find out why it is not working the way you want is an unparalleled learning process. The downside of debugging is a new developer can find it especially frustrating. If you have never wanted to throw your computer out the window, you will. You will question why you are doing this, and whether you are smart enough to solve the problem. Programming is very humbling, even for the most experienced developer.

Like a musician, the more you practice the better you get. By practicing, we mean programming! You can do some amazing things as a programmer. The world is your oyster. Seeing your app in the iTunes App Store is one of the most satisfying accomplishments. However, there is a price, and that price is time spent coding and learning.

Having taught more than a thousand students to become iOS developers, we have put together a formula for what makes students successful. Here is our formula for success:

- Believe you can do it. You'll be the only one who says you can't do this. So don't tell yourself that.
- Work through all the examples and exercises in this book.
- Code, code, and keeping coding. The more you code, the better you'll get.
- Be patient with yourself. If you were fortunate enough to have been a 4.0 student who can memorize material just by reading it, this will not happen with Objective-C coding. You are going to have to spend time coding.
- You learn by reading this book. You really learn by debugging your code.
- Use the *free* xcelMe.com webinars and YouTube videos explained at the end of this chapter.
- Don't give up!

The Development Technology Stack

We will walk you through the process of understanding the development process for your iOS apps and what technology you need. However, briefly looking at all the pieces together is helpful. For a sample iPhone app in a Table View, see Figure 1.

Figure 1. *The iPhone/iPad technology stack*

Required Software, Materials, and Equipment

One of the great things about Alice is it available on the three main operating systems used today:

- Windows
- Mac
- Linux

The other great thing about Alice is it is free! You can download Alice at www.Alice.org.

Operating System and IDE

Although you can use Alice on many platforms, the Integrated Development Environment (IDE) that developers use to develop iOS apps is Xcode. You have to use *an Intel-based Mac to use Xcode and submit apps!* Xcode is free and is available in the Mac App Store.

Software Development Kits

You will need to register as an iOS developer. You can do this at
http://developer.apple.com/iphone.

When you are ready to upload your app to the iTunes App Store, you will need to pay
$99/year.

Dual Monitors

We recommend developers have a second monitor connected to their computer. It is great to
step through your code and watch your output window and iPad simulator at the same time on
dual independent monitors. Apple hardware makes this easy. Just plug your second monitor into
the display port of any Intel-based Mac, with the correct Mini DisplayPort adapter of course, and
you have two monitors working independently of one another. See Figure 2. Note that dual
monitors are not required. You will just have to organize your open windows to fit on your screen
if you don't.

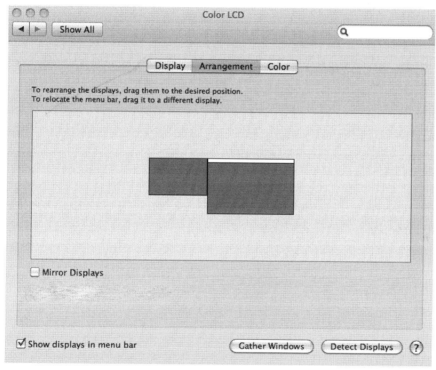

Figure 2. *Dual monitors*

Free Live Webinars, Q&A, and YouTube Videos

Nearly every Wednesday night at 7:30 p.m. Pacific daylight time, we have live webinars and
discuss a topic from the book or a timely item of interest. These webinars are free, and you can
register for them at www.xcelme.com/free-webinars.php.

At the end of the webinars, we do a Q&A. You can ask a question on the topic discussed or
any topic in the book.

Additionally, all these webinars are recorded and available on YouTube.

Make sure you subscribe to the YouTube channel so you are notified when new recordings are uploaded.

Figure 3. *Free Objective-C webinars and YouTube videos*

Free Book Forum

We have developed an online forum for this book at http://forum.xcelme.com, where you can ask questions while you are learning Objective-C and get answers from the authors. You will also find answers to the exercises and additional exercises to help you learn. See Figure 3.

You can also access answers to exercises and discover helpful links to help you become a successful iPhone/iPad developers and create great apps. See Figure 4. So let's get started!

TOPICS	REPLIES	VIEWS
Registration is now required to post by gary.bennett • Tue Sep 21, 2010 12:33 pm	1	178
A-Book Information by gary.bennett • Mon Aug 16, 2010 9:49 pm	3	497
B-Introduction by gary.bennett • Sat Aug 14, 2010 3:14 pm	4	361
Chapter 1 : Becoming a Great iPhone/iPad or Mac Programmer by gary.bennett • Sat Aug 14, 2010 3:17 pm	8	1073
Chapter 2 : Programming Basics by gary.bennett • Sat Aug 14, 2010 3:21 pm	4	499
Chapter 3 : It's All About the Data by gary.bennett • Sat Aug 14, 2010 3:29 pm	21	741
Chapter 4 : Making Decisions About...and Planning Program Flow by gary.bennett • Sat Aug 14, 2010 3:31 pm	36	2061
Chapter 5 : Object Oriented Programming with Objective-C by gary.bennett • Sat Aug 14, 2010 3:32 pm	7	538
Chapter 6 : Introducing Objective-C and Xcode by gary.bennett • Sat Aug 14, 2010 3:33 pm	8	622
Chapter 7 : Objective-C Classes, Objects, and Methods by gary.bennett • Sat Aug 14, 2010 3:34 pm	19	817
Chapter 8 : Programming Basics in Objective-C by gary.bennett • Sat Aug 14, 2010 3:38 pm	32	1050
Chapter 9 : Comparing Data by gary.bennett • Sat Aug 14, 2010 3:36 pm	4	234
Chapter-10: Creating User Interfaces with Interface Builder by gary.bennett • Sat Aug 14, 2010 3:43 pm	9	306
Chapter-11: Memory, Addresses, and Pointers by gary.bennett • Sat Aug 14, 2010 3:45 pm	3	152
Chapter-12: Debugging Programs with Xcode by gary.bennett • Sat Aug 14, 2010 3:45 pm	1	106
Chapter-13: Storing Information by gary.bennett • Sat Aug 14, 2010 3:47 pm	2	148
Chapter-14: Protocols and Delegates by gary.bennett • Sat Aug 14, 2010 3:48 pm	1	132
Free Weekly Q&A Webinars every Weds by gary.bennett • Sun Sep 26, 2010 10:28 pm	1	504

Figure 4. *Reader Forum for accessing answers to exercise and posting questions for authors*

Chapter 1

Becoming a Great iOS or Mac Programmer

Now that you're ready to become a software developer and have read the Introduction of this book, you need to become familiar with several key concepts. Your computer program will do exactly what you tell it to do—no more and no less. It will follow the programming rules that were defined by the operating system and programming language. Your program doesn't care if you are having a bad day or how many times you ask it to perform something. Often, what you think you've told your program to do and what it actually does are two different things.

> **KEY TO SUCCESS:** If you haven't already, take a few minutes to read the Introduction of this book. The Introduction shows you where to go to access the free webinars, forums, and YouTube videos that go with each chapter. Also, you'll better understand why we are using the Alice programming environment and how to be successful in developing your iOS and Mac apps.

Depending on your background, working with something absolutely black and white may be frustrating. Many times, programming students have lamented, "That's not what I wanted it to do!" As you begin to gain experience and confidence programming, you'll begin to think like a programmer. You will understand software design and logic, and you will experience having your programs perform exactly as you want and the satisfaction associated with this.

Thinking like a Developer

Software development involves writing a computer program and then having a computer execute that program. A **computer program** is the set of instructions that we want the computer to perform. Before beginning to write a computer program, it is helpful to list the steps that we want our program to perform, in the order we want them accomplished. This step-by-step process is called an **algorithm**.

If we want to write a computer program to toast a piece of bread, we would first write an algorithm. This algorithm might look something like this:

1. Take the bread out of the bag.

2. Place the bread in the toaster.

3. Press the toast button.

4. Wait for the toast to pop up.

5. Remove the toast from the toaster.

At first glance, this algorithm seems to solve our problem. However, our algorithm leaves out many details and makes many assumptions. For example,

1. What kind of toast does the user want? Does the user want white bread, wheat, or some other kind of bread?

2. How does the user want the bread toasted? Light or dark?

3. What does the user want on the bread after it is toasted: butter, margarine, honey, or strawberry jam?

4. Does this algorithm work for all users in their cultures and languages? Some cultures may have another word for toast or not know what toast is.

Now, you might be thinking we are getting too detailed for just making a simple toast program. Over the years, software development has gained a reputation of taking too long, costing too much, and not being what the user wants. This reputation came to be because computer programmers often start writing their programs before they have really thought through their algorithms.

The key ingredients to making successful applications are **design requirements**. Design requirements can be very formal and detailed or as simple as a list on a piece of paper. Design requirements are important because they help the developer flush out what the application should do and not do when complete. Design requirements should not be completed in a programmer's vacuum, but should be produced as the result of collaboration between developers, users, and customers.

NOTE: If you take anything away from this chapter, take away the importance of considering design requirements and user interface design before starting software development. This is the most effective (and least expensive) use of time in the software development cycle. Using a pencil and eraser is a lot easier and faster than making changes to code because you didn't have others look at the designs before starting to program.

Another key ingredient to your successful app is the **user interface (UI)** design. Apple recommends that you spend over 50% of the entire development process focusing on the UI design. The design can be simple pencil-and-paper layouts created using the *iPhone Application Sketch Book or the iPad Application Sketch Book* by Dean Kaplan (Apress, 2009) or on-screen layout created with the Omni Group's OmniGraffle (www.omnigroup.com) software application with the Ultimate iPhone Stencil plug-in (www.graffletopia.com). Many software developers start with the UI design, and after laying out all the screen elements and having many users look at paper mock-ups, they then write out the design requirements from their screen layouts.

After you have done your best to flush out all the design requirements, laid out all the user interface screens, and had the client(s) or potential customers look at your design and give you feedback, coding can begin. Once coding begins, design requirements and user interface screens can change, but the changes are typically minor and easily accommodated by the development process. See Figures 1–1 and 1–2.

Figure 1–1 shows a mock-up of a mobile banking app screen prior to development using OmniGraffle. Developing mock-up screens along with design requirements forces developers to think through many of the applications usability issues before coding begins. This enables the application development time to be shortened and makes for a better user experience and better reviews on the iTunes App Store. Figure 1–2 shows how the view for the mobile banking app actually appears when completed.

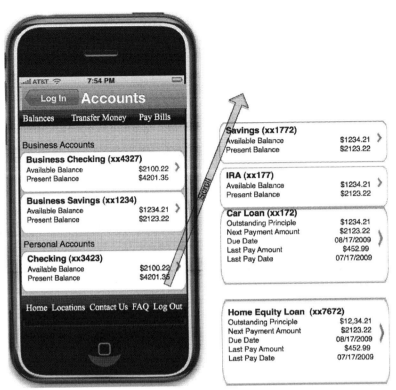

Figure 1–1. *This is a User Interface (UI) mock-up of the Account Balance screen for an iPhone mobile banking app before development begins. This UI design mock-up was completed using OmniGraffle.*

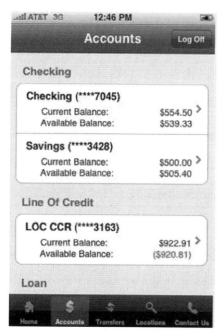

Figure 1–2. *This screenshot shows a completed iPhone mobile banking application as it appeared on the iTunes App Store. This app is called Woodforest Mobile Banking.*

Completing the Development Cycle

Now that we have our design requirements and user interface designs and have written our program, what's next? After programming, we need to make sure our program matches the design requirements and user interface design and ensure that there are no errors. In programming vernacular, errors are called **bugs**. Bugs are undesired results of our programming and must be fixed before the app is released to the App Store. The process of finding bugs in programs and making sure the program meets the design requirements is called **testing**. Typically, someone who is experienced in software testing methodology and who didn't write the app performs this testing. Software testing is commonly referred to as **Quality Assurance (QA)**.

> **NOTE:** When an application is ready to be submitted to the iTunes App Store, Xcode gives the file an `.app` extension, for example, `appName.app`. That is why iPhone, iPad, and Mac applications are called **apps**. We will use "program," "application," and "app" to mean the same thing throughout this book.

During the testing phase, the developer will need to work with QA staff to determine why the application is not working as designed. The process is called **debugging**. It requires the developer to step through the program to find out why the application is not working as designed. Figure 1–3 shows the complete software development cycle.

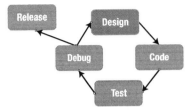

Figure 1–3. *The typical software development cycle*

Frequently during testing and debugging, changes to the requirements (design) must occur to make the application more usable for the customer. After the design requirements and user interface changes are made, the process begins over again.

At some point, the application that everyone has been working so hard on must be shipped to the iTunes App Store. Many considerations are taken into account when this happens:

- Cost of development
- Budget
- Stability of the application
- Return on investment

There is always the give-and-take between developers and management. Developers want the app perfect and management wants to start realizing revenue from the investment as soon as possible. If the release date were left up to the developers, the app would likely never ship to the App Store. Developers would continue to tweak the app forever, making it faster, more efficient, and more usable. At some point, however, the code needs to be pried from the developers' hands and uploaded to the App Store so it can do what it was meant to do.

Introducing Object Oriented Programming

As discussed in detail in the Introduction, Alice enables us to focus on **object oriented programming (OOP)** without having to cover all the Objective-C programming syntax and complex Xcode development environment in one big step. Instead, we can focus on learning the basic principles of OOP and using those principles quickly to write our first programs.

For decades, developers have been trying to figure out a better way to develop code that is reusable, manageable, and easily maintained over the life of a project. OOP was designed to help achieve code reuse and maintainability while reducing the cost of software development.

OOP can be viewed as a collection of objects in a program. Actions are performed on these objects to accomplish the design requirements.

An **object** is anything that can be acted on. For example, an airplane, person, or screen/view on the iPad can all be objects. We may want to act on the plane by making the plane bank. We may want the person to walk or to change the color of the screen of an app on the iPad. Actions are all being applied to these objects; see Figure 1–4.

Figure 1–4. *These are two objects in an Alice application, a Dropship and Fighter. Both objects can have actions applied—takeoff and landing, turn right and turn left..*

Alice will run a program, such as the one shown in Figure 1–4, for you if you click the play button. When we run our Alice applications, the user can apply actions to the objects in our application. Similarly, Xcode is an **Integrated Development Environment (IDE)** that enables us to run our application from within our programming environment. We can test our applications on our computers first before running them on our iOS devices by running the apps in Xcode's simulator, as shown in Figure 1–5.

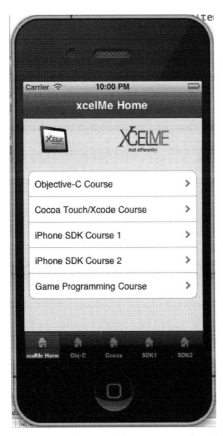

Figure 1–5. *This sample iPhone app contains a table object to organize a list of courses. Actions such as "rotate left" or "user did select row 3" can be applied to this object.*

Actions that are performed on objects are called **methods**. Methods manipulate objects to accomplish what we want our app to do. For example, for our jet object in Figure 1–4, we might have the following methods:

```
goUp
goDown
bankLeft
turnOnAfterBurners
lowerLandingGear
```

Our table object in Figure 1–5 is actually called UITableView when we use it in a program, and it could have the following methods:

```
loadView
shouldAutorotateToInterfaceOrientation
numberOfSectionsInTableView
cellForRowAtIndexPath
didSelectRowAtIndexPath
```

All objects have data that describes those objects. This data is defined as **properties.** Each property describes the associated object in a specific way. For example, the jet object's properties might be as follows:

```
altitude = 10,000 feet
heading = North
speed = 500 knots
pitch = 10 degrees
yaw = 20 degrees
latitude = 33.575776
longitude = -111.875766
```

For our UITableView object in Figure 1–5, the following might be our properties:

```
backGroundColor = Red
selectedRow = 3
animateView = No
```

An object's properties can be changed at any time when our program is running, when the user interacts with the app, or when the programmer designs the app to accomplish the design requirements. The values stored in the properties of an object at a specific time are collectively called the **state of an object**.

State is an important concept in computer programming. When teaching students about state, we ask them to go over to a window and find an airplane in the sky. We then ask them to snap their fingers and make up some of the values that the plane's properties might have at that specific time. Those values might be

```
altitude = 10,000 feet
latitude = 33.575776
longitude = -111.875766
```

Those values represent the state of the object at the specific time that they snapped their fingers.

After waiting a couple minutes, we ask the students to find that same plane, snap their fingers again, and record the plane's possible state at that specific point in time.

The values of the properties might then be something like

```
altitude = 10,500 feet
latitude = 33.575665
longitude = -111.875777
```

Notice how the state of the object changes over time.

Working with the Alice Interface

Alice offers a great approach in using the concepts that we have just discussed without all the complexity of learning Xcode and the Objective-C language at the same time. It takes only a few minutes to familiarize oneself with the Alice interface and begin writing a program.

The Introduction of this book describes how to download Alice. After it's downloaded and installed, you need to open Alice. It will look like Figure 1–6.

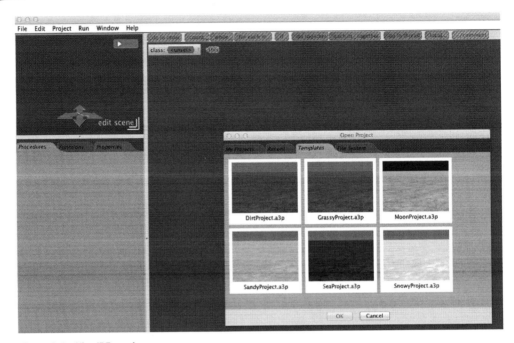

Figure 1–6. *Alice IDE running*

Technically speaking, Alice is not a true IDE like Xcode, but it is pretty close and much easier to learn than Xcode. A true IDE combines code development, user interface layout, debugging tools, documentation, and simulator/console launching for a single application; see Figure 1–7. However, Alice offers a similar look, feel, and features to Xcode. This will serve you well later when we start writing Objective-C code.

Figure 1–7. *The Xcode integrated development environment (IDE) with the iPhone Simulator*

In the next chapter, you will go through the Alice interface and write your first program.

Summary

Congratulations, you have finished the first chapter of this book. It is important that you have an understanding of the following terms because they will be reinforced throughout this book:

- Computer program
- Algorithm
- Design requirements
- User interface
- Bug
- Quality assurance (QA)
- Debugging
- Object oriented programming (OOP)

- Object
- Property
- Method
- State of an object
- Integrated development environment (IDE)

Exercises

- Answer the following questions:
    - Why is it so important to spend time on your user requirements?
    - What is the difference between design requirements and an algorithm?
    - What is the difference between a method and a property?
    - What is a bug?
    - What is state?
- Write an algorithm for how a soda machine works from the time a coin is inserted until a soda is dispensed. Assume the price of a soda is 80 cents.
- Write the design requirements for an app that will run the soda machine.

Chapter 2

Programming Basics

This chapter will focus on the building blocks that are necessary to become a great Objective-C programmer. This chapter is going to go over how to use the Alice user interface, how to write our first Alice program, how to write our first Objective-C program, and explore some new OOP terms.

> **NOTE:** We want to introduce new concepts in Alice and later, in this chapter, enable you to use these concepts in Objective-C. We have used this approach for the last 3 years and know, from personal experience, that this approach helps you learn the concepts quickly, without discouragement, and gives you a great foundation to build upon.

Taking a Tour with Alice

Alice's 3D programming environment makes it easy to write your first program, as it applies some of the principles that you have learned in Chapter 1. First, you need to learn a little more about Alice's user interface. When we first launch Alice, we are presented with a screen that looks like Figure 2–1.

You can start with the default blue sky and green grass template or pick another template with a different background. Feel free to explore and have fun. This is where we will spend most of our time and write our first Alice application.

The Alice user interface is set up to help us efficiently write our applications. The user interface is very similar in form and function to the Xcode IDE. We will now explore the major sections of Alice.

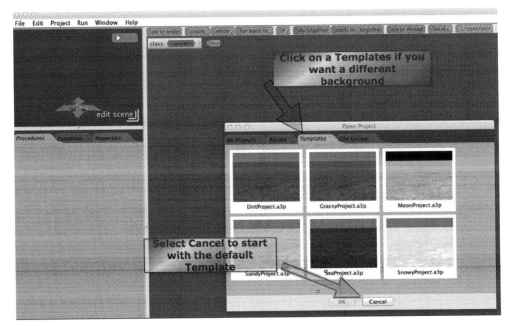

Figure 2-1. *Opening screen in Alice*

Navigation Menu

The Navigation menu, shown in Figure 2-2, enables us to open and close files, set our application preferences, and view world statistics, text output, and the error console. We can also access example worlds and Alice Help from the Navigation menu.

> **NOTE:** It is important that you save your program frequently when using Alice. If Alice crashes and you haven't saved your work, you will lose all your code or changes since you last saved. Additionally, we recommend that you close Alice completely and reopen it when you want to open a new Alice program.

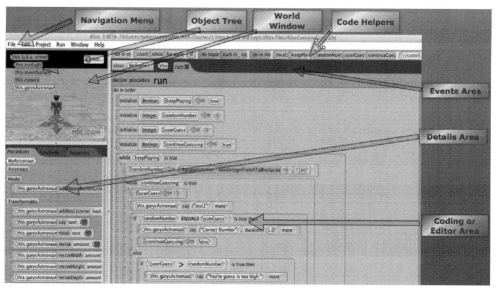

Figure 2–2. *This shows the Alice's user interface's main sections Take some time to explore the user interface. You will see in this chapter how it compares with Xcode and how it will help us learn Objective-C.*

World Window

The World window shows what our virtual world will look like when it runs. This window is similar to the iPhone/iPad simulator that we will use later to run our apps. The World window enables us to take advantage of Alice's 3D user interface to model our application.

In the World window, we can move the camera around and place it where we want for the viewing prospective we desire. Moving the three arrow tools in Figure 2–3 enables incredible flexibility for bringing our applications to life.

It is important to learn how to move the camera around your world in order to get the view you want the users to see.

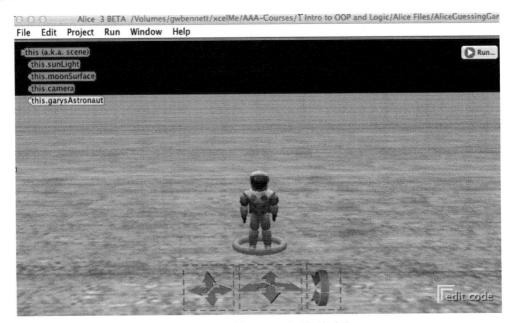

Figure 2–3. *Camera manipulation arrows to control the camera in World window.*

One of the most important Alice controls is the **Edit Scene** control. See Figure 2–4. When we click the Edit Scene button in the bottom-right corner of the World window, we launch Alice's **Scene Editor**.

Figure 2–4. *The Edit Scene button in the World window is outlined with a box and is one of the most important controls. This button will launch Alice's Scene Editor and enable us to add objects to our Alice World.*

Take a minute to familiarize yourself with the Scene Editor shown in Figure 2–5. The Scene Editor enables us to:

■ Add objects to our world from the gallery.

■ Add objects to our world from the Internet.

■ Position the objects in our world.

■ Adjust the camera for viewing our world.

We will spend a lot of time adding objects and setting the camera in our worlds by using the Scene Editor.

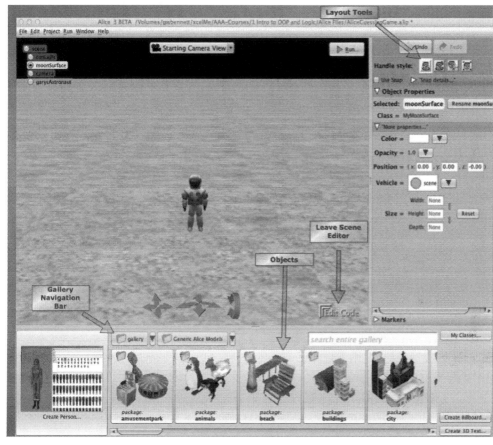

Figure 2–5. *Alice's Scene Editor*

Classes, Objects, and Instances in Alice

A group of objects with the same properties and same methods (actions) are called a **class**. For example, we could have a class called `Airplane`. In this class, we could have five objects:

```
boeing747
lockheedSR71
boeing737
citation10
f18Fighter
```

These objects are nearly identical. They are from the same `Airplane` class. They all have the same following methods:

```
land()
takeOff()
lowerLandingGear()
raiseLandingGear()
bankRight()
bankLeft()
```

The only thing that differentiates the objects is the values of their properties. Some of the properties of the values might be:

```
wingLength = 20ft
maxThrust = 200,000lbs
numberOfEngines = 2
```

In your world, you may have two objects that are exactly the same. You may want two Boeing 737s in your view. Each copy of a class is called an **instance**. Adding an instance of a class to our program is called **instantiation**.

Object Tree

The **Object Tree** (see Figure 2–6) enables us to view all of the objects in our Alice world. Additionally, if the object has subparts, you can view these subparts by clicking the plus sign, or collapse the subparts by clicking the minus sign.

Figure 2–6. *The Object Tree*

Many of the Alice worlds come with several built-in objects that we will need for our apps. The world in Figure 2–6 comes with the Camera, Light, and Ground objects.

Editor Area

The Editor Area, the largest area of the Alice interface, is where we write our code. With Alice, we don't have to actually type code; we can drag and drop our code to manipulate our objects and properties.

> **NOTE:** Don't forget the top of the Editor Area. The top contains a row of control and logic tiles for looping, branching, and other logical structures that we can use to control the behavior of our objects.

Details Area

The **Details Area** of the Alice interface contains the tabs for properties, procedures, and functions that make up the object that is selected in the Object Tree.

- **Properties** contain the specific information of our selected object (e.g., weight, length, and height).

- **Procedures (Methods)** perform actions upon the object (e.g., take off and land).

- **Functions** and methods are similar. In Alice, the difference between the two is that a method does not return a value. A function will return a value.

Events Area

The Events Area of the Alice interface contains a listing of all the existing events used by our app, and provides us with the opportunity to create new events. **Events** are conditions that trigger our methods. Methods (or procedures) that react to these events are called **event handlers**. When a specific event occurs, it **triggers** a signal that the event handler receives and handles.

Some examples would be the user touching a button on an iPhone. The touching or swiping triggers events and the methods that handle these events act on objects in our app. See Figure 2–7.

Figure 2–7. *Phonics Easy Reader 1, by Rock 'n' Learn, is running on the iPad Simulator in the left landscape orientation. Tapping the "Read to me" or "Let me try" button triggers events that methods receive and act on—in this example, reading to the child or having the child read the words of a sentence.*

Creating an Alice App—To the Moon Alice

We have covered some new terms and concepts, and now, it is time to do what programmers do—write code. It is customary for new developers to write a **Hello World** app as their first program. We will do something similar, but Alice makes it more interesting. We will then follow up our first Alice app with our first Objective-C app.

This Alice app will have three objects on the screen, the lunar lander object and two astronauts. One astronaut will say, "The Eagle has landed." The other astronaut will say, "That's one small step for man, one giant leap for mankind."

Alice really makes apps like this easy and fun to do. Make sure you follow these steps:

1. Click **File** and then **New**.

2. Click the **Template** tab.

3. Choose the **MoonProject.a3p Template**, and click the **Open** button. See Figure 2–8.

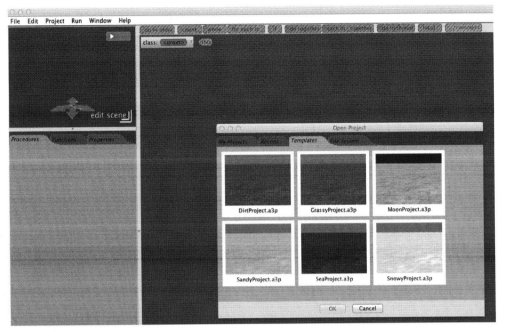

Figure 2–8. *Select the Space Template.*

4. Now, we need to add our objects. Click **Edit Scene**. It was the important button in the World window shown in Figure 2–4.

5. In the Object Gallery, select the **Space Class from the Generic Alice Models**.

6. Right-click the **Lunar Lander** to view some of the information about the object. See Figure 2–9. We can click **"OK"** to add our objects to our world, or we can drag and drop them from the gallery to the world.

> **NOTE:** You can see in this example why an instance is a copy of an object. We are making a copy of the object and putting it in our world. *Instantiation* is a big word for the process of making a copy of and initializing our object.

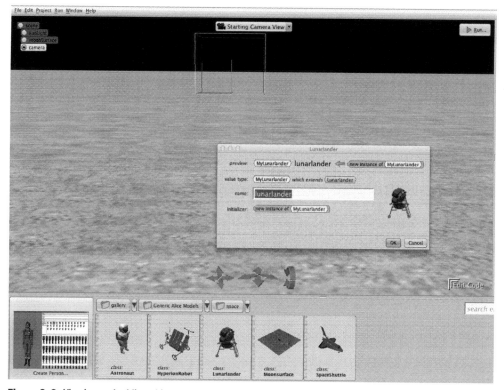

Figure 2–9. *Viewing and adding objects to our world from Step 6.*

7. Click the Astronaut class twice to add our two astronauts to our world.

8. Use the **Camera Adjustment** and **Objects Adjustment** tools, outlined in boxes in Figure 2–10, to achieve the look and perspective you desire.

> **TIP:** Sometimes when you add two objects, Alice places one object over the other. Drag the top astronaut to the side of the other astronaut if this occurs. Your world should look like Figure 2–10.

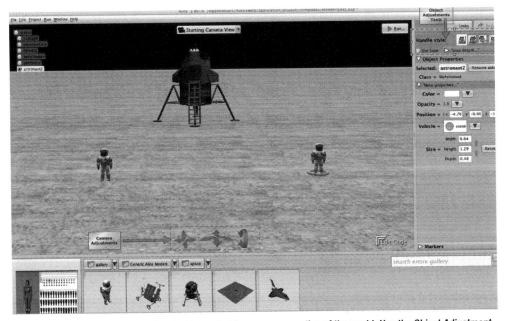

Figure 2–10. *Use the Camera Adjust tool to control the user perspective of the world. Use the Object Adjustment tools to shape and orientate your objects in your world.*

9. At the top right corner are the **Object Adjustment** tools. Hover the mouse over each tile to discover what each tile tool will do to the object. Notice the Object Tree in Figure 2–10. The ground, `lunarLander`, `astronaut`, and `astronaut2` objects are in the Object Tree.

10. Click the **Edit Code** button at the bottom right of the screen. This will return us to the editor view.

11. Click the left astronaut in the World window. Make sure the **Procedures tab** is selected in the Details Area.

12. We are now going to make our astronauts say something. Remember actions to objects require methods. Drag the **Astronaut2|turn** tile from the Details Area to our Editor. Select **turn left**, **0.25 rotation** from the parameter list. See Figure 2–11. When we run our app, the left astronaut will turn to their left one-quarter of a rotation and face the other astronaut.

Figure 2–11. *The left Astronaut's methods and parameters.*

13. Let's do the same thing for the other astronaut. Click the right astronaut. Drag the **Astronaut|turn** tile from the Details Area to our Editor. **Select turn right, 0.25 rotation** from the parameter list.

14. A **parameter** is the information a method needs to act upon the object. A method may need one or more parameters for a method. Click the right astronaut, drag the **Astronaut2|say tile** to the editor, **select other**, and then type **The Eagle has landed.** See Figure 2–12.

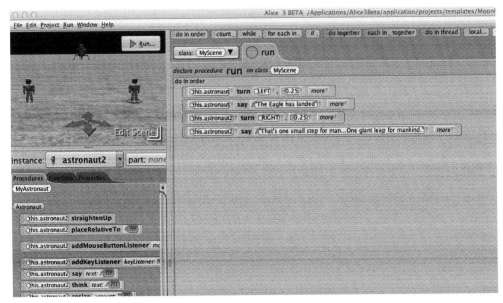

Figure 2–12. *Your Editor should have these methods within the listed parameters.*

15. Click the right astronaut. Drag the **astronaut|say** tile to the editor, **select other**, and type, **That's one small step for man. . . One giant leap for mankind.** Your app should look like Figure 2–12.

16. Let's run our first program by clicking **Play**. If you have completed everything correctly, your app should look like Figure 2–13 when it runs. If not, you have some debugging to do.

17. Save the app as toTheMoonAlice.a3p. We will be using this app later. Click File ➤ Save World, or File ➤ Save World As.

Figure 2–13. *From the top portion of the World Running window, we can rerun our program, pause, resume, restart, stop, and take a picture of our app. We can also speed up or slow down our app, depending on how slow or fast our application is running.*

Your First Objective-C Program

Now that you have learned a little about OOP, and have your first Alice program completed, it's time to write your first Objective-C program and begin to understand the Objective-C language, Xcode, and syntax. First, we have to install Xcode. Xcode is the IDE that we use when developing Objective-C apps. It is equivalent to Alice's interface.

Launching and Using Xcode 4.2

Xcode 4.2 is available for download from the Mac App Store for free. See Figure 2–14, and from the iOS Dev Center, see Figure 2–15 and Figure 2–16.

Figure 2–14. *Xcode 4.2 is available for download from the Mac App Store for free.*

NOTE: This package has everything we need to write Objective-C and Mac apps. To develop iPhone apps, you will need to apply for the iPhone Developer Program, pay $99 (when ready to test on your iOS device), and download the iPhone SDK from Apple at
`http://developer.apple.com/iphone`.

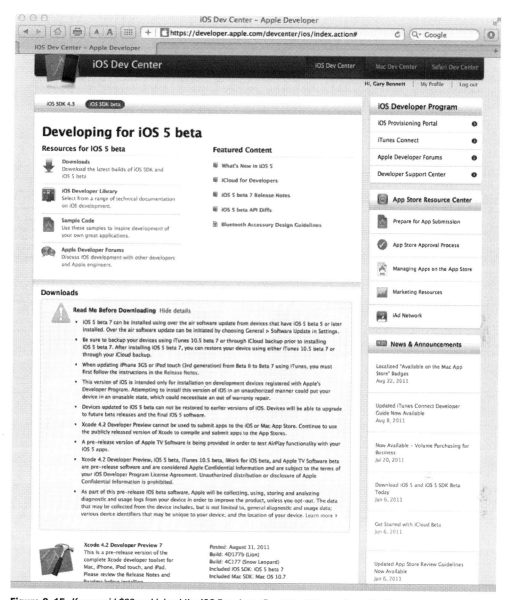

Figure 2–15. *If you paid $99 and joined the iOS Developer Program, beta versions, like the example above, of Xcode and the iOS SDK, are available to download.*

Now that we have installed Xcode, we need to begin writing Objective-C applications; so let's get started. After launching Xcode, follow these steps:

1. Click **Create a new Xcode Project**. See Figure 2–16.

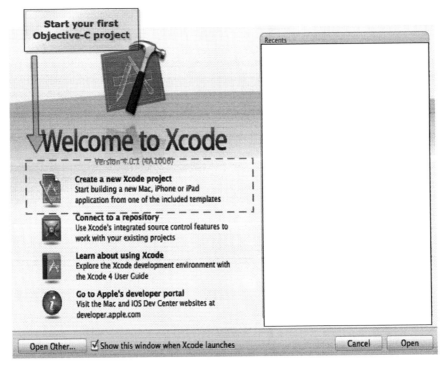

Figure 2–16. *Creating our first Objective-C project.*

IMPORTANT: This is where many beginners get stuck, depending on their version of Xcode, and if they have the iPhone SDK installed. In Figure 2–17, you can see that we have the iOS SDK installed. We also have the Lion version of Xcode installed. If you don't have these installed, that is OK. Just navigate in the left pane of your template options, click on **Applications,** and look for the Command Line Tool.

2.   Select **Applications** on the left-side pane, select the **Command Line Tool** template, and then press **Next**. See Figure 2–17.

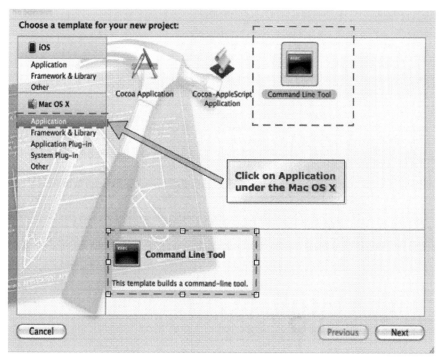

Figure 2–17. *Select the Command Line Tool. You may have to navigate to an equivalent screen with other versions of Xcode. The bottom line is to navigate to the Command Line Tool.*

3. Let's name our app **HelloWorld** and select **Foundation** as the application type, as shown in Figure 2–18. Then press **Next,** and save your app in the directory of your choice.

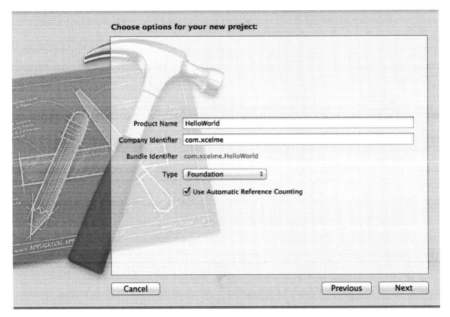

Figure 2–18. *Name your app HelloWorld, and select the Foundation as the App Type.*

4. In the **Project Navigator**, click on the *main.m* file. See Figure 2–19

Xcode does a lot of work for us and creates a directory with files and code ready for us to use. That is what Xcode templates do—they save us a lot of time.

We need to become familiar with the Xcode IDE. Let's look at two of the most often used features (see Figure 2–19):

- The Navigator area.
- The Editor area.

These sections should look similar to what we used in Alice. The **Navigator** area contains files needed to build our apps. It will contain our classes, methods, and resources.

The **Editor** area is the business end of the Xcode IDE; where our dreams are turned into reality. The editor section is where we write our code. You will notice that as you write your code it will change color. Sometimes, Xcode will even try to auto-complete words for you. The colors have meanings that will become apparent as we use the IDE. The Editor area will also be the place where we debug our apps.

> **NOTE:** Even if we've mentioned it already, it is worth saying again: you will learn Objective-C programming by reading this book, but you will *really* learn Objective-C by debugging your apps. Debugging is where developers learn and become great developers.

The **Run** button turns our code from plain text to an .app that our Macs, iPhones, or iPads know how to execute. With our Alice interface, we used the play button to run our Alice app.

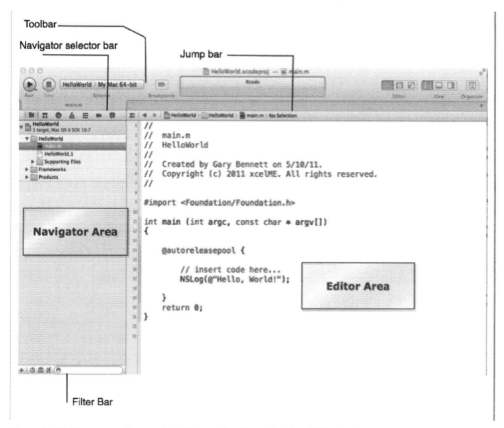

Figure 2–19. *You can run the app right after creating the project by clicking the Run button and seeing,* **Hello World!** *printed out in the console.*

To run our first program, simply click the **Run** button. Xcode checks our code syntax, compiles our app, and if no errors are found, makes an .app file and runs it. This application runs in a console (also known as a terminal).

When the app runs, it prints out **Hello World** in the console. Also, in the console window, we can see if the application terminated and why it terminated. In this case, it terminated normally. We can see this with the message, Program ended with exit code: 0, which means our app didn't crash. See Figure 2–20.

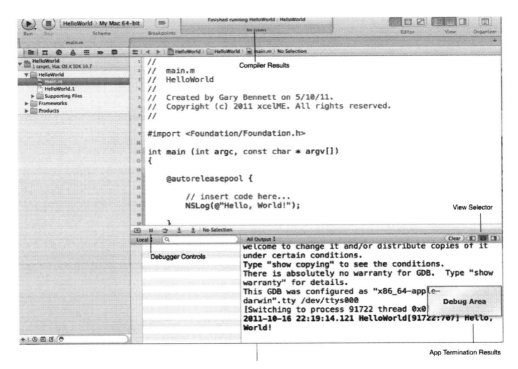

Figure 2–20. *Our app executing in the Debugger Console.*

Let's modify our application to do what we did with our astronauts:

1. Navigate to the *main.m* file.

2. Change lines 17 and 18 to be shown as in Figure 2–21.

3. We are going to intentionally misplace a semicolon at the end of line 8.
    This will cause a compiler error.

4. Click the **Run** button.

You can see that something will go wrong when we try to compile and run our app. We have a compiler error, a red pointer, and the notices in the Xcode IDE denote this. See Figure 2–21.

When we write Objective-C code, everything is important—even semicolons, capitalization, and parentheses. The collection of rules that enable our compiler to compile our code to an executable app is called **syntax**.

NSLog is a function that will print out the contents of its parameters in the console.

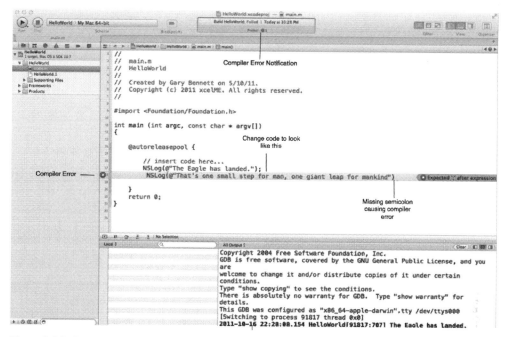

Figure 2–21. *Our app with a syntax error caught by our Objective-C compiler.*

Now, let's fix our app by adding the semicolon at the end of line 18. Building and running the app will enable us to see the output to the debug console. See Figure 2–22.

Feel free to play around and change the text that is printed out. Have fun!

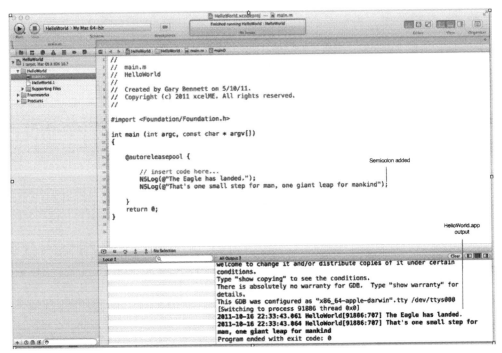

Figure 2–22. *Our app compiled with no compiler errors, and completion executed successfully with the output we wanted.*

Summary

In this chapter, we have built our first Alice app. We also installed Xcode and compiled, debugged, and ran our first Objective-C app together. We also covered new OOP terms that are key to our understanding of Objective-C.

KEY TO SUCCESS: As mentioned in the Introduction, visit www.xcelme.com and click on the Free Videos tab to view related videos on this chapter. Also visit http://forum.xcelme.com to ask questions on these chapters, and see answers to common mistakes.

The terms that you should understand are as follows:

- Classes
- Objects
- Methods
- Parameters
- Instances
- Instantiation

Exercises

- Extend your toTheMoonAlice.a3p Alice app. Place another object of your choosing in the world and have the object say something to the two astronauts, when they have finished speaking.

- Extend your Objective-C HelloWorld.app by adding a third line of code that prints any text of your choosing to the console.

Chapter **3**

It's All About the Data

As you probably know, data is stored as zeros and ones in your computer's memory. However, zeros and ones are not very useful to developers or app users, so we need to know how our program uses data and how data is stored on our computer.

In this chapter, we will look at how data is stored on computers and how we can manipulate that data. Then we'll write a fun Alice app illustrating data storage and then write the same Alice app in Objective-C. So let's get started!

Numbering Systems Used in Programming

Computers work with information differently than do humans. This section covers the various ways information is stored, tallied, and manipulated by devices such as your Mac, iPhone, and iPad.

Bits

A **bit** is defined as the basic unit of information used by computers to store and manipulate data. A bit has a value of either **0** or **1**. When computers were first introduced, transistors and microprocessors didn't exist. Data was manipulated and stored by vacuum tubes being turned on or off. If the vacuum tube was on, the value of the bit was 1 and if the vacuum tube was off, the value was 0. The amount of data a computer was able to store and manipulate was directly related to how many vacuum tubes the computer had.

The first recognized computer was called the Electronic Numerical Integrator And Computer (ENIAC). It took up more than 136 square meters and had 18,000 vacuum tubes. It was about as powerful as your handheld calculator.

Today, computers use transistors to store and manipulate data. The power of a computer processor depends on how many transistors are placed on its chip or CPU. Like the vacuum tube, transistors have an off or on state. When the transistor is off, its value is 0. If the transistor is on, its value is 1. At the time of this writing, the A5 processor that comes in the iPhone 5 and iPad 2 has a dual core ARM processor with over 200 million transistors, up from 149 million transistors on the A4 processor that was in iPhone 4 and the first iPad. See Figure 3–1.

Figure 3–1. *Apple's proprietary A5 processor*

Moore's Law

The number of transistors on your iPhone's or iPad's processor is directly related to your device's processing speed, memory capacity, and the sensors (accelerometer, gyroscope) available in the device. The more transistors, the more powerful your device is.

In 1965, the cofounder of Intel, Gordon E. Moore, described the trend of transistors in a processor. He observed that the number of transistors in a processor doubled every 18 months from 1958 to 1965 and would likely continue "for at least 18 months." The observation became famously known as "Moore's Law" and has proven accurate for more than 55 years. See Figure 3–2.

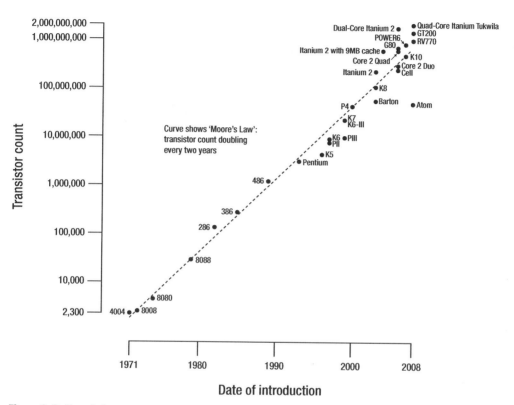

Figure 3–2. *Moore's Law*

> **NOTE:** There is a downside to Moore's Law and you have probably felt it in your pocket book. The problem with rapidly increasing processing capability is that it renders technology obsolete quickly. So when your iPhone's two-year cell phone contract is up, the new iPhones on the market will be twice as powerful as the iPhone you had when you signed up. How convenient for everyone!

Bytes

A byte is another unit used to describe information storage on computers. A **byte** is composed of 8 bits and is a convenient power of 2. Whereas a bit can represent up to two different values, a byte can represent up to 2^8 or 256 different values. A byte can contain values from 0–255.

> **NOTE:** In Chapter 13, we discuss Base-2, Base-10, and Base-16 number systems in more detail. However, it is necessary to have an introduction to these systems in this chapter in order to understand data types.

The **binary** number system represents numerical symbols 0 and 1. To illustrate how the number **71** would be represented in binary, we will use a simple table of 8 bits (1 byte), with each bit represented as a power of 2. To convert the byte value **01000111** to decimal, simply add the on bits. See Table 3–1.

Table 3–1. *The number 71 represented as a byte*

Power to 2	2^7	2^6	2^5	2^4	2^3	2^2	2^1	2^0
Value for "**on**" bit	128	64	32	16	8	4	2	1
Actual bit	0	1	0	0	0	1	1	1

To represent the number **22** in binary, turn on the bits that add up to 22 or **00010110**. See Table 3–2.

Table 3–2. *The number 22 represented as a byte*

Power to 2	2^7	2^6	2^5	2^4	2^3	2^2	2^1	2^0
Value for "**on**" bit	128	64	32	16	8	4	2	1
Actual bit	0	0	0	1	0	1	1	0

To represent the number **255** in binary, turn on the bits that add up to 255 or **11111111**. See Table 3–3.

Table 3–3. *The number 255 represented as a byte*

Power to 2	2^7	2^6	2^5	2^4	2^3	2^2	2^1	2^0
Value for "**on**" bit	128	64	32	16	8	4	2	1
Actual bit	1	1	1	1	1	1	1	1

To represent the number **0** in binary, turn on the bits that add up to 0 or **00000000**. See Table 3–4.

Table 3–4. *The number 0 represented as a byte*

Power to 2	2^7	2^6	2^5	2^4	2^3	2^2	2^1	2^0
Value for "**on**" bit	128	64	32	16	8	4	2	1
Actual bit	0	0	0	0	0	0	0	0

Hexadecimal

Often, it will be necessary to represent characters in another format that is recognized by computers, namely a hexadecimal format. You will encounter hexadecimal numbers when you are debugging your apps. The **Hexadecimal** system is a base-16 number system. It uses 16 distinct symbols, 0–9, to represent values zero to nine and A, B, C, D, E, and F to represent values 10 to 15. For example, the hexadecimal number 2AF3 is equal in decimal to $(2 \times 16^3) + (10 \times 16^2) + (15 \times 16^1) + (3 \times 16^0)$, or 10,995. Figure 3–3 shows the ASCII table of characters. Because 1 byte can represent 256 characters, this works well for Western characters. For example, hexadecimal 20 represents a space. Hexadecimal 7D represents a "}".

Dec	Hx	Oct	Char		Dec	Hx	Oct	Html	Chr	Dec	Hx	Oct	Html	Chr	Dec	Hx	Oct	Html	Chr
0	0	000	NUL	(null)	32	20	040	&#32;	Space	64	40	100	&#64;	@	96	60	140	&#96;	`
1	1	001	SOH	(start of heading)	33	21	041	&#33;	!	65	41	101	&#65;	A	97	61	141	&#97;	a
2	2	002	STX	(start of text)	34	22	042	&#34;	"	66	42	102	&#66;	B	98	62	142	&#98;	b
3	3	003	ETX	(end of text)	35	23	043	&#35;	#	67	43	103	&#67;	C	99	63	143	&#99;	c
4	4	004	EOT	(end of transmission)	36	24	044	&#36;	$	68	44	104	&#68;	D	100	64	144	&#100;	d
5	5	005	ENQ	(enquiry)	37	25	045	&#37;	%	69	45	105	&#69;	E	101	65	145	&#101;	e
6	6	006	ACK	(acknowledge)	38	26	046	&#38;	&	70	46	106	&#70;	F	102	66	146	&#102;	f
7	7	007	BEL	(bell)	39	27	047	&#39;	'	71	47	107	&#71;	G	103	67	147	&#103;	g
8	8	010	BS	(backspace)	40	28	050	&#40;	(	72	48	110	&#72;	H	104	68	150	&#104;	h
9	9	011	TAB	(horizontal tab)	41	29	051	&#41;	)	73	49	111	&#73;	I	105	69	151	&#105;	i
10	A	012	LF	(NL line feed, new line)	42	2A	052	&#42;	*	74	4A	112	&#74;	J	106	6A	152	&#106;	j
11	B	013	VT	(vertical tab)	43	2B	053	&#43;	+	75	4B	113	&#75;	K	107	6B	153	&#107;	k
12	C	014	FF	(NP form feed, new page)	44	2C	054	&#44;	,	76	4C	114	&#76;	L	108	6C	154	&#108;	l
13	D	015	CR	(carriage return)	45	2D	055	&#45;	-	77	4D	115	&#77;	M	109	6D	155	&#109;	m
14	E	016	SO	(shift out)	46	2E	056	&#46;	.	78	4E	116	&#78;	N	110	6E	156	&#110;	n
15	F	017	SI	(shift in)	47	2F	057	&#47;	/	79	4F	117	&#79;	O	111	6F	157	&#111;	o
16	10	020	DLE	(data link escape)	48	30	060	&#48;	0	80	50	120	&#80;	P	112	70	160	&#112;	p
17	11	021	DC1	(device control 1)	49	31	061	&#49;	1	81	51	121	&#81;	Q	113	71	161	&#113;	q
18	12	022	DC2	(device control 2)	50	32	062	&#50;	2	82	52	122	&#82;	R	114	72	162	&#114;	r
19	13	023	DC3	(device control 3)	51	33	063	&#51;	3	83	53	123	&#83;	S	115	73	163	&#115;	s
20	14	024	DC4	(device control 4)	52	34	064	&#52;	4	84	54	124	&#84;	T	116	74	164	&#116;	t
21	15	025	NAK	(negative acknowledge)	53	35	065	&#53;	5	85	55	125	&#85;	U	117	75	165	&#117;	u
22	16	026	SYN	(synchronous idle)	54	36	066	&#54;	6	86	56	126	&#86;	V	118	76	166	&#118;	v
23	17	027	ETB	(end of trans. block)	55	37	067	&#55;	7	87	57	127	&#87;	W	119	77	167	&#119;	w
24	18	030	CAN	(cancel)	56	38	070	&#56;	8	88	58	130	&#88;	X	120	78	170	&#120;	x
25	19	031	EM	(end of medium)	57	39	071	&#57;	9	89	59	131	&#89;	Y	121	79	171	&#121;	y
26	1A	032	SUB	(substitute)	58	3A	072	&#58;	:	90	5A	132	&#90;	Z	122	7A	172	&#122;	z
27	1B	033	ESC	(escape)	59	3B	073	&#59;	;	91	5B	133	&#91;	[	123	7B	173	&#123;	{
28	1C	034	FS	(file separator)	60	3C	074	&#60;	<	92	5C	134	&#92;	\	124	7C	174	&#124;	|
29	1D	035	GS	(group separator)	61	3D	075	&#61;	=	93	5D	135	&#93;	]	125	7D	175	&#125;	}
30	1E	036	RS	(record separator)	62	3E	076	&#62;	>	94	5E	136	&#94;	^	126	7E	176	&#126;	~
31	1F	037	US	(unit separator)	63	3F	077	&#63;	?	95	5F	137	&#95;	_	127	7F	177	&#127;	DEL

Source: www.LookupTables.com

128	Ç	144	É	161	í	177	▒	193	┴	209	╤	225	ß	241	±
129	ü	145	æ	162	ó	178	▓	194	┬	210	╥	226	Γ	242	≥
130	é	146	Æ	163	ú	179	│	195	├	211	╙	227	π	243	≤
131	â	147	ô	164	ñ	180	┤	196	─	212	╘	228	Σ	244	⌠
132	ä	148	ö	165	Ñ	181	╡	197	┼	213	╒	229	σ	245	⌡
133	à	149	ò	166	ª	182	╢	198	╞	214	╓	230	µ	246	÷
134	å	150	û	167	º	183	╖	199	╟	215	╫	231	τ	247	≈
135	ç	151	ù	168	¿	184	╕	200	╚	216	╪	232	Φ	248	°
136	ê	152	ÿ	169	⌐	185	╣	201	╔	217	┘	233	Θ	249	∙
137	ë	153	Ö	170	¬	186	║	202	╩	218	┌	234	Ω	250	·
138	è	154	Ü	171	½	187	╗	203	╦	219	█	235	δ	251	√
139	ï	156	£	172	¼	188	╝	204	╠	220	▄	236	∞	252	ⁿ
140	î	157	¥	173	¡	189	╜	205	═	221	▌	237	φ	253	²
141	ì	158		174	«	190	╛	206	╬	222	▐	238	ε	254	■
142	Ä	159	ƒ	175	»	191	┐	207	╧	223	▀	239	∩	255	
143	Å	160	á	176	░	192	└	208	╨	224	α	240	≡		

Source: www.LookupTables.com

Figure 3–3. *ASCII Characters*

Unicode

Representing characters with a byte worked well for computers until about the 1990s, when the personal computer became widely adopted in non-Western countries where languages have more than 256 characters. Instead of a 1-byte character set, Unicode can have up to a 4-byte character set.

In order to facilitate faster adoption, the first 256 code points are indicial to the ASCII character table. Unicode can have different character encodings. The most common encoding used for Western text is called UTF-8. As an iPhone developer, you will probably use this character encoding the most.

Data Types

Now that we've discussed how computers manipulate data, we need to cover a very important concept called **data types**. Humans can generally just look at data and the context in which it is being used to determine what type of data it is and how it will be used. Computers need to be told how to do this. The programmer needs to tell the computer the type of data it is being given. For example,

$2 + 2 = 4.$

The computer needs to know you want to add two numbers together. In this example, they are integers. You might first believe that adding these numbers is obvious to even the most casual observer, let alone a sophisticated computer. However, it is common for users of iPhone apps to store data as a series of characters, not a calculation. For example, a text message might read

```
"Everyone knows that 2 + 2 = 4".
```

In this case, we are using our previous example in a series of characters called a **string**. A **data type** is simply the declaration to our program that defines the data we want to store. A **variable** is used to store our data and is declared with an associated data type. All data is stored in a variable and the variable has to have a variable type. For example, in Objective-C, the following are variable declarations with their associated data types.

```
int x = 10;
int y = 2;
int z = 0;
char prefix = 'c';
NSString *submarineName  = @"USS Nevada SSBN-733";
```

Data types cannot be mixed with one another. You cannot do the following.

```
z = x + submarineName;
```

Mixing data types will cause either compiler warnings or compiler errors and your app will not run.

Most data you will use in your programs can be classified into three different types— Booleans, numbers, and objects. We will discuss how to work with numbers and object data types in the remainder of this chapter. In Chapter 4, we will talk more about Boolean data types when we write apps with decision-making.

> **NOTE:** Localizing your app is the process of writing your app so users can buy and use it in their native language. This process is too advanced for this book, but it is a simple one to complete when you plan from the beginning. Localizing your app greatly expands the total number of potential customers and revenue for your app without your having to rewrite it for each language. Be sure to localize your app. It is not hard to do and can easily double or triple the number of people who buy it.

Using Variable and Data Types with Alice

Now that we have learned about data types, let's write an Alice app that adds two numbers and displays the sum using an object and methods.

1. Open Alice and select File ➤ New World.

2. Select the Grass template and click Open. See Figure 3–4.

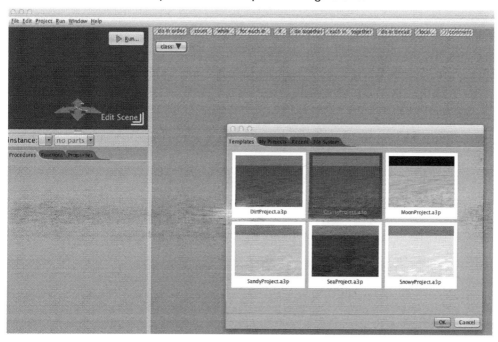

Figure 3–4. *Choosing the Grass template*

Next, we need to make our variables and select the data types.

3. **Click and drag the local tile** on the top right of your editor

4. Name your first variable "**firstNumber**" and define the variable, as shown Figure 3–5.

5. The variable's data type is an integer. It is initialized with the value of 2.

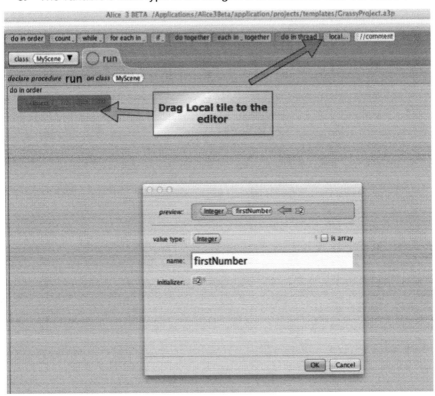

Figure 3–5. *Creating a new local variable*

It is always good programming practice to initialize our variables when they are declared.

6. Create another local variable called "**secondNumber**," as shown in Figure 3–6 and as done in step 5. The variable's data type is an integer and is initialized with the value of 3.

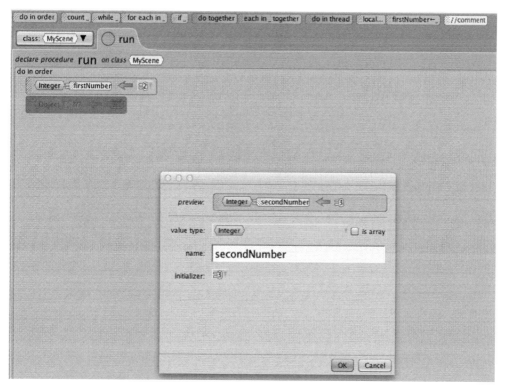

Figure 3–6. *Creating a second local variable*

7. Create another local variable called **"totalSum",** as shown in Figure 3–7 and as done in step 5. The variable's data type is an integer and is initialized with the value of 0. This local variable will eventually hold the sum of firstNumber and secondNumber.

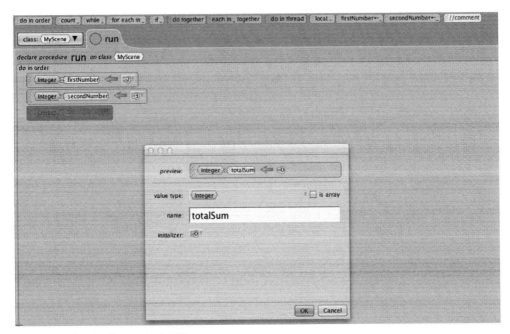

Figure 3–7. *Creating the variable totalSum*

8. Add your two variables together. Drag the totalSum tile to the last row. Right now, 0 is assigned to the local variable totalSum. **Click on the 0** and assign firstNumber to totalSum. See Figure 3–8.

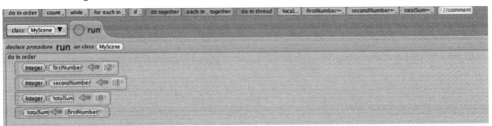

Figure 3–8. *Creating the variable totalSum*

9. Now that firstNumber is assigned to totalSum, click on the firstNumber tile.

10. Select secondNumber to add to firstNumber. See figure 3–9.

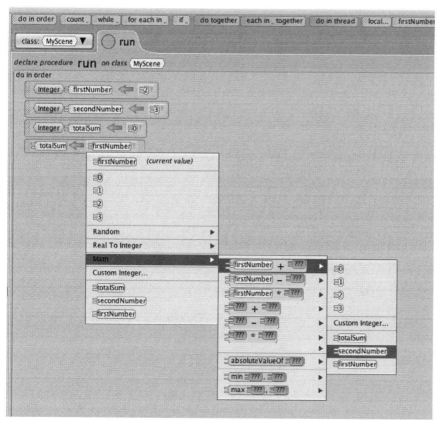

Figure 3–9. *Setting the value to math expressions*

11. totalNumber is now assigned to the total of firstNumber and secondNumber. See
    Figure 3–10.

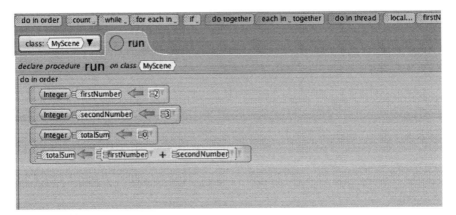

Figure 3–10. *Selecting totalSum*

Now we need to add a character to our world to display our total.

12. Click on Edit Scene and then add any object of your choosing from the Object Gallery at the bottom of the screen. We have selected a bunny. See Figure 3–11.

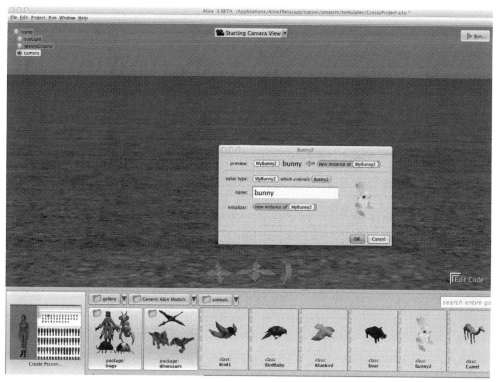

Figure 3-11. *Adding a bunny to our world*

We need to declare a variable of type **String**. The variable will hold the string, "**The sum of 2 + 3 is:5**".

13. Click "Edit Code" in the bottom right of the scene to go back to our Editor.

14. *Select the Bunny instance. From the Procedures Tab,* drag the this.bunny say text:??? procedure tile to the editor. See Figure 3-12.

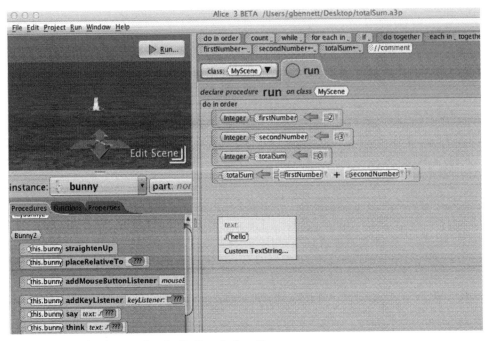

Figure 3–12. *Adding the procedure (method) say to the editor*

15. Click on Custom TextString and enter the string "The sum of 2 + 3 is:" as the parameter value. See Figure 3–13.

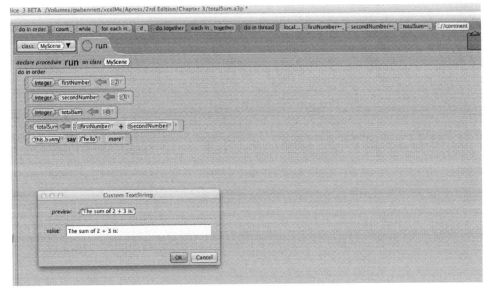

Figure 3–13. *Entering the string parameter*

16. Click OK and then click on the first parameter for the say procedure. Append the totalSum to our first parameter String. See Figure 3–14.

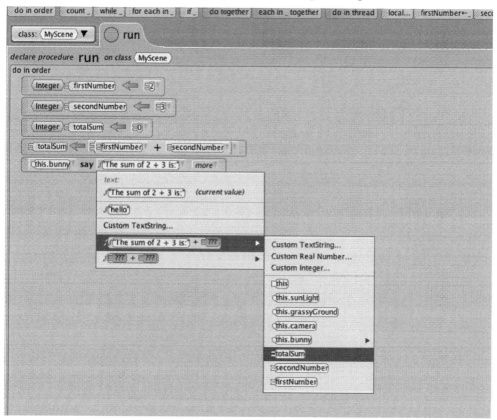

Figure 3–14. *Adding the totalNumber to our customized string to display to the user*

Alice did something very nice for us in the last step. It automatically converted the data type totalSum from an integer to a string when it appended its value to the "The sum of 2 + 3 is:". We will learn how to do this using Objective-C.

You can run the program now and will notice the customized string doesn't display for very long.

To increase the display time of our customized string, click on the option for a second parameter of the say procedure and change the duration to 2 seconds or any other value you like. See Figure 3–15.

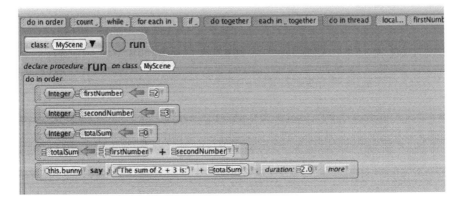

Figure 3–15. *The editor section*

17. Press the play button and if you've done everything correctly, your app should look like Figure 3–16 when it runs.

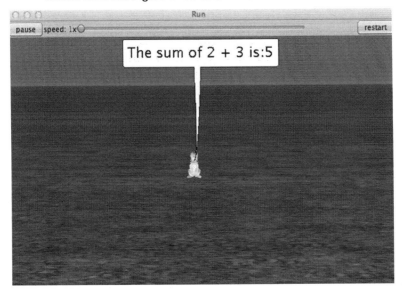

Figure 3–16. *The app has run successfully!*

Data Types and Objective-C

Now that we have covered the principles of data types and have written an Alice app to help show how these principles apply, let's write an Objective-C app that accomplishes what we just did in Alice.

In Objective-C, we have similar data types as we did in Alice. Some of the most frequently used data types for storing numbers are integers, doubles, floats, and longs.

Table 3–5 lists many of the basic data types. Many of these will be covered in later chapters.

Table 3–5. *Objective-C basic data types*

Type	Examples	Specifiers
char	'a', '0','\n'	%c
int	42, -42, 550 0xCCE0, 099	%i, %d,
unsigned int	20u, 101U, 0xFEu	%u, %x, %o
long int	13, -2010, 0xfefeL	%ld,
unsigned long int	12UL, 100ul, 0xffeeUL	%lu, %lx, %lo
long long int	0xe5e5e5LL, 501ll	%lld
unsigned long long int	11ull, 0xffeeULL	%llu, %llx, %llo
float	12.30f, 3.2e-5f, 0x2.2p09	%f, %e, %g, %a
double	3.1415,	%f, %e, %g, %a
long double	3.1e-5l	%Lf, %Le, %Lg, %La
id	Nil	%@

Our Objective-C app will add two integers and display their sum to the console. The app will also display the text "The program has successfully terminated." This will be fun and easy, so let's get started.

1. As iOS developers, Xcode is where we make our living, so open up Xcode and create a new project. To do this, select File ➤ **New project** and select the options shown in Figure 3–17. Click on Next.

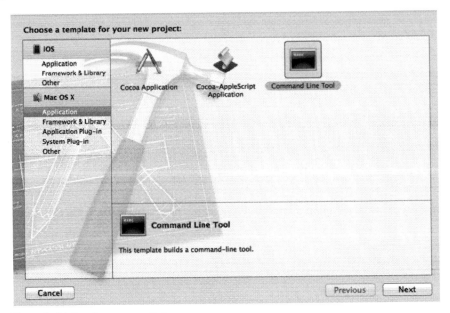

Figure 3–17. *Opening a new project*

> **NOTE:** One of the most common issues new students have when creating a command line app is finding the project in their version of Xcode. Figure 3–18 shows Xcode Version 4.2 on the Lion (10.7) operating system. Your version of Xcode may be newer or older and menus and selection options may be different. So, look around in the File ➤ New project settings for the equivalent options. If you have difficulty finding these options, visit our forum for this book at forum.xcelme.com and go to this chapter. We will be happy to answer your questions.

2. Save the Product Name as Chapter 3 (see Figure 3–18). Then select the directory to save your project and click on Next.

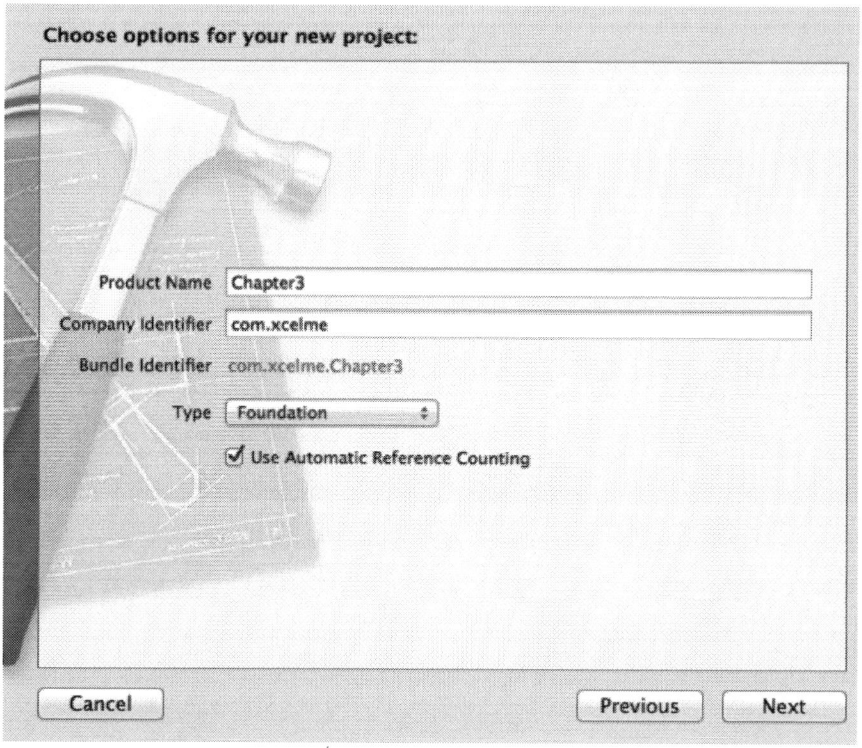

Choose options for your new project:

Product Name   Chapter3

Company Identifier   com.xcelme

Bundle Identifier   com.xcelme.Chapter3

Type   Foundation

☑ Use Automatic Reference Counting

Cancel   Previous   Next

Figure 3–18. *Project settings.*

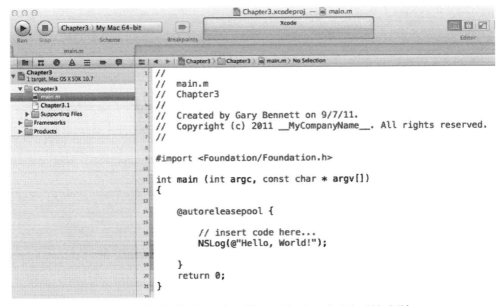

Figure 3–19. *When created, and selecting the main.m file, your Xcode project should look this*

> **3.** After you create the project, you need to open your source code file in your editor. Open the main.m source file. (see Figure 3–19)

If you haven't seen "//" used in computer programming before, it enables the programmer to comment about his or her code. Comments are not compiled by our applications and are used as notes for the programmer or, more importantly, for programmers who follow the original developer. Comments help both the original developer and follow-up developers understand how the app was developed.

Sometimes, it is necessary for comments to span several lines or just part of a line. This can be accomplished with the /* and the */. All the text between the /* and the */ are treated as comments and are not compiled.

In our example, we first need to declare and initialize our variables firstNumber and secondNumber. It is good practice to always initialize variables when they are declared or soon afterwards.

We'll then increment the variables firstNumber and secondNumber by 1. We'll print the sum of firstNumber and secondNumber.

Finally, we will print to the console, "The program has terminated successfully." See Figure 3–20

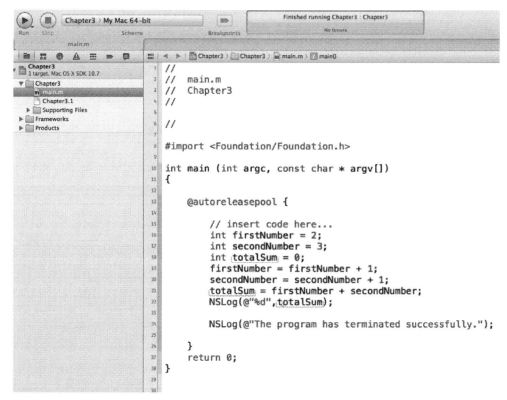

Figure 3–20. *Code for printing to the console*

NSLog is a function that can take one or more parameters. The first parameter is generally the string that is to be printed to the console. The @ symbol in front of the string tells the compiler this is an Objective-C type string and not a C++ string. The @ symbol is typically used in front of all your strings for iPhone apps. If you don't use the @ symbol, you will probably get a compiler error. NSLog is a very helpful function used by developers to test the execution of their code.

%d tells the compiler an integer will be printed and to substitute the value of the integer for the %d. See Table 3–5 for other NSLog formatting specifiers. Finally, our second parameter is the integer to be printed.

Figure 3–21 shows the completed executed output of our application.

To compile and run your application, click on the "Run" button on your toolbar. We can see that we printed out the NSLog string along with the notice at the end by the debugger saying the app's execution completed successfully.

> **NOTE:** If your editor doesn't have the same menus or gutter (the left-hand column that contains the line numbers of the program) you saw in the previous screenshots, you can turn these settings on in the Xcode preferences. You can open the Xcode Preferences by clicking on the Xcode menu in the menu bar and then selecting Preferences.

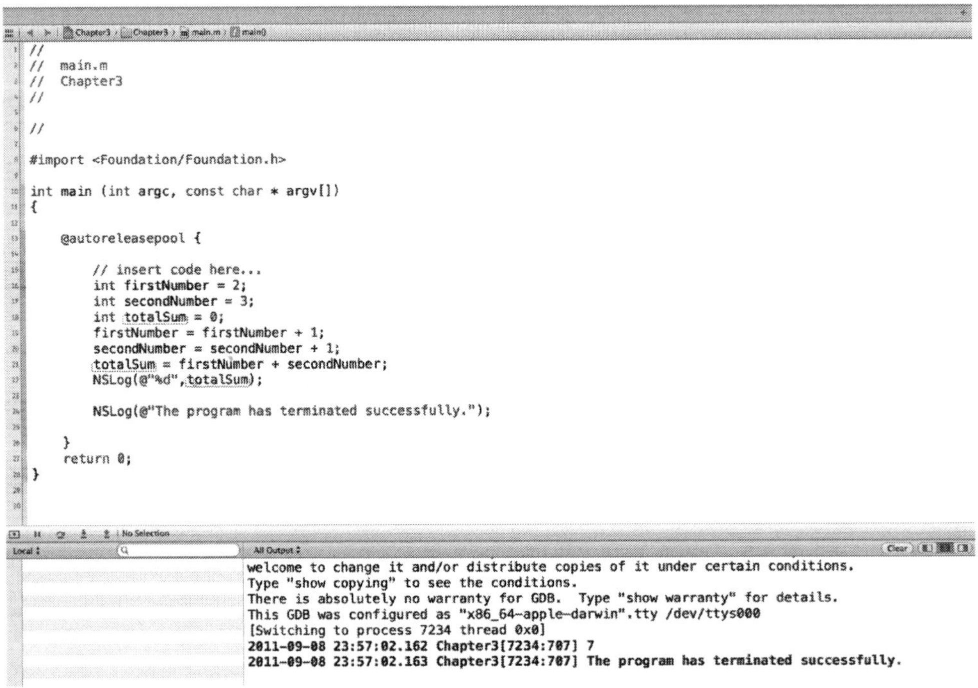

Figure 3–21. Console log displaying the results of our Objective-C app

Identifying Problems

Believe it or not, your program may not run the way you thought you told it to. The process of hunting down problems with your app is called **debugging**. In order to track down bugs in our apps, we can set breakpoints and inspect our variables to see the contents. To do this, simply click in the gutter where you want to set a breakpoint (see Figure 3–22). A breakpoint will stop our application from executing at that line and enable us to inspect our variables.

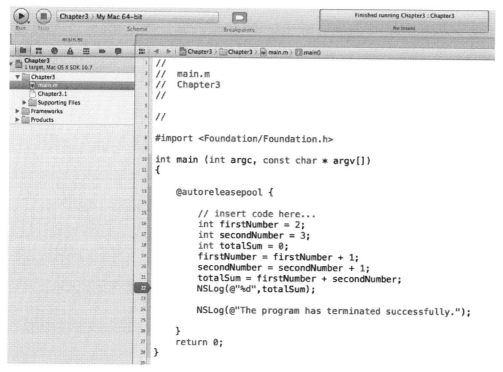

Figure 3–22. *Setting debugging "breakpoints"*

A blue pointer in the gutter of your editor denotes a breakpoint. When you run your application and your app hits a line of code that contains a breakpoint, your app will halt and display a blue line across the line of code with a breakpoint (see Figure 3–23). Additionally, you can inspect each variable by hovering over it with your mouse.

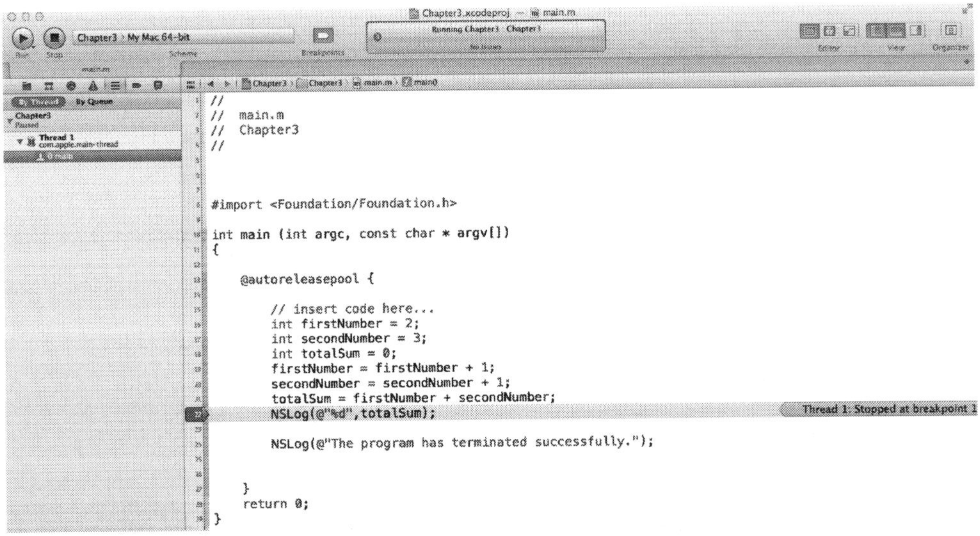

Figure 3–23. *Breakpoint hit*

We will talk more about debugging your apps in Chapter 14.

Summary

In this chapter, you learned about how data is used by our apps. You saw how to initialize variables and how to assign data to them. We explained that when variables are declared, they have a data type associated with them and that only data of the same type can be assigned to variables.

Finally, we showed you how to use variables in your first Alice app and finished by using variables with an Objective-C app.

Exercises

- Write an Objective-C console app (Command-Line Tool) that multiples two integers together and displays the result to the console.

- Write an Objective-C console app that squares a float. Display the resulting float in the console.

- Write an Objective-C console app that subtracts two floats, with the result being stored as an integer. Note that rounding does not occur.

Chapter 4

Making Decisions About…and Planning Program Flow

One of the cool things about being an iPhone/iPad/Mac developer is we get to tell our devices exactly what we want them to do and it will be done—our devices will do tasks over and over again without getting tired. That's because iPhones/iPads/Macs don't care how hard they worked yesterday, and they don't let feelings get in the way. These devices don't need hugs.

There is a downside to being developers: we have to think of all possible outcomes when it comes to our apps. Many students love having this kind of control. They enjoy focusing on the many details of their apps; however, it can be frustrating having to handle so many details. As we mentioned in the introduction to this book, there is a price to pay for developing apps . . . and that price is time. The more time you spend developing and debugging, the better you will get with all the details, and the better your apps will run. You have to pay this price to become a successful developer.

Computers are black and white; there are no shades of gray. Our devices produce results, many of which are based on true and false conditions.

In this chapter, you will learn about computer logic and controlling the flow of your apps. Processing information and arriving at results is at the heart of all apps. Your apps need to process data based on values and conditions. In order to do this, you need to understand how computers perform logical operations and execute code based on the information your apps have acquired.

Boolean Logic

Boolean logic is a system for logical operations. Boolean logic uses binary operators like AND, OR, and the unary operator NOT to determine if your conditions have been met.

Binary operators take two operands. Unary operators take one operand; AND and OR are binary operators, and NOT is a unary operator.

We just introduced a couple of new terms that can sound confusing; however, you probably use Boolean logic every day. Let's look a couple of examples of Boolean logic with the binary operators AND and OR in a conversation parents sometimes have with their teenage children.

"You can go to the movies tonight if your room is clean AND the dishes are put away."

"You can go to the movies tonight if your room is clean OR the dishes are put away."

Boolean operators' results are either TRUE or FALSE. In Chapter 3, we briefly introduced the Boolean data type. A variable that is defined as Boolean can only contain the values TRUE and FALSE.

```
BOOL seeMovies = FALSE;
```

In the preceding example, the AND operator takes two operands: one to the left and one to the right of AND. Each operand can be evaluated independently with a TRUE or FALSE.

For an AND operation to yield a TRUE result, both sides of the AND have to be TRUE. In our first example, the teenager has to clean his or her room AND have the dishes done. If either one of the conditions is FALSE, the result is FALSE—no movies for the teenager.

For an OR operation to yield a TRUE result, only one operand has to be TRUE, or both conditions can be TRUE to yield a TRUE result. In our second example, just a clean bedroom would result in the ability to go to the movies.

> **NOTE:** Behind the scenes, your iPhone/iPad/Mac defines a FALSE as a 0 and a TRUE as a 1. To be technically correct, a TRUE is defined as any non-zero value; so, values of 0.1, 1, and 2 would be evaluated as a TRUE when evaluated in a Boolean expression.

A NOT statement is a unary operator. It takes just one operand to yield a Boolean result. For example:

"You can NOT go to the movies."

This example takes one operand. The NOT operator turns a TRUE operand to a FALSE and a FALSE operand to a TRUE. Here, the result is a FALSE.

> **NOTE:** Performing a NOT operation is commonly referred to as *flipping-the-bit*, or *negating*. A TRUE is defined as a 1, a FALSE is defined as a 0, and zeros and ones are referred to as *bits*. A NOT operation turns a TRUE to a FALSE and a FALSE to a TRUE, hence *flipping-the-bit* or *negating* the result.

AND, OR, and NOT are three very common Boolean operators. Occasionally, you need to use more complex operators. XOR, NAND, and NOR are common operations for iPhone/iPad/Mac developers.

The Boolean operator XOR means *exclusive-or*. An easy way to remember how the XOR operator works is the XOR operator will return a TRUE result if only one argument is TRUE, not both.

Objective-C does not have these operators built in, but consider that NAND and NOR mean NOT AND and NOT OR. After evaluating the AND or the OR arguments and results, simply negate the results.

Truth Tables

Let's use a tool to help you evaluate all the Boolean Operators. A **truth table** is mathematical table used in logic to evaluate Boolean operators. They are helpful when trying to determine all the possibilities of a Boolean operator. Let's look at some common truth tables for AND, OR, NOT, XOR, NAND, and NOR.

In an AND truth table, there are four possible combinations of TRUE and FALSE.

- TRUE AND TRUE = TRUE
- TRUE AND FALSE = FALSE
- FALSE AND TRUE = FALSE
- FALSE AND FALSE = FALSE

Placing these combinations in a truth table results in Table 4–1.

Table 4–1. *An **AND** Truth Table*

A	B	A AND B
TRUE	TRUE	TRUE
TRUE	FALSE	FALSE
FALSE	TRUE	FALSE
FALSE	FALSE	FALSE

An AND truth table only produces a TRUE result if both of its operands are TRUE.

Table 4–2 illustrates an OR truth table and all possible operands.

Table 4–2. *An OR Truth Table*

A	B	A OR B
TRUE	TRUE	TRUE
TRUE	FALSE	TRUE
FALSE	TRUE	TRUE
FALSE	FALSE	FALSE

An OR truth table produces a TRUE result if one or both of its operands are TRUE.

Table 4–3 illustrates a NOT truth table and all possible operands.

Table 4–3. *A NOT Truth Table*

NOT	RESULT
TRUE	FALSE
FALSE	TRUE

A NOT *flips-the-bit* or negates the original operand's Boolean value.

Table 4–4 illustrates an XOR (or exclusive-or) truth table and all possible operands.

Table 4–4. *An XOR Truth Table*

A	B	A XOR B
TRUE	TRUE	FALSE
TRUE	FALSE	TRUE
FALSE	TRUE	TRUE
FALSE	FALSE	FALSE

The operator XOR yields a TRUE result if only one of the operands is TRUE.

Table 4–5 illustrates a NAND truth table and all possible operands.

Table 4–5. *A **NAND** Truth Table*

A	B	A NAND B
TRUE	TRUE	FALSE
TRUE	FALSE	TRUE
FALSE	TRUE	TRUE
FALSE	FALSE	TRUE

Table 4–6 illustrates a NOR truth table and all possible operands.

Table 4–6. *A **NOR** Truth Table*

A	B	A NOR B
TRUE	TRUE	FALSE
TRUE	FALSE	FALSE
FALSE	TRUE	FALSE
FALSE	FALSE	TRUE

The easiest way to look at the NAND and NOR operators is to simply negate the results from the AND and OR truth tables, respectively.

Comparison Operators

In software development, the comparison of different data items is accomplished with **comparison operators**. These operators produce a logical TRUE or FALSE result. Table 4–7 shows the list of comparison operators.

Table 4–7. *Comparison Operators*

>	greater than
<	less than
>=	greater than or equal to
<=	less than or equal to
==	exactly equal to
!=	not equal to

> **NOTE:** If you're constantly forgetting which way the greater than and less than signs go, use a crutch I learned in grade school: If the greater than and less than signs represent the mouth of an alligator, the alligator always eats the bigger value. It may sound silly, but it works.

Designing Apps

Now that we've introduced Boolean logic and comparison operators, you can start designing your apps. Sometimes, it's important to express all or parts of your apps to others without having to write the actual code.

Writing out code helps a developer think out loud and brainstorm with other developers regarding sections of code that are of concern—this helps to analyze problems and possible solutions before coding begins.

Pseudo-Code

Pseudo-code refers to writing out code that is a high-level description of an algorithm you are trying to solve. Pseudo-code does not contain the necessary programming syntax for coding; however, it does express the algorithm that is necessary to solve the problem at hand.

Pseudo-code can be written by hand on paper (or a whiteboard) or typed on a computer.

Using pseudo-code, you can apply what you know about Boolean data types, truth tables, and comparison operators. Refer to Listing 4–1 for pseudo-code examples.

Listing 4–1. *Pseudo-Code Examples Using Conditional Operators in If-Then-Else Code*

```
int x = 5;
int y = 6;
isComplete  =  TRUE;
if ( x < y)
{
    //in this example, x is less than 6
    do stuff;
}
else
{
    do other stuff;
}

if  (isComplete == TRUE)
{
    //in this example, isComplete is equal to TRUE
    do stuff;
}
else
{
```

```
        do other stuff;
}
//another way to check isComplete == TRUE
if (isComplete)
{
    //in this example,  isComplete is TRUE
    do stuff;
}
//two ways to check if a value is false
if  (isComplete == FALSE)
{
    do stuff;
}
else
{
    //in this example, isComplete is TRUE so the else block will be executed
}
//another way to check isComplete == FALSE
if (!isComplete)
{
    do stuff;
}
else
{
    //in this example,  isComplete is TRUE so the else block will be executed
}
```

Note that the ! switches the value of the Boolean it's applied to; so, using ! makes a TRUE value into a FALSE, and a FALSE value into a TRUE.

Often, it is necessary to combine your comparison tests. A compound relationship test is one or more simple relationship tests joined by either the **&&** or the **||** (two pipe characters).

&& and **||** are verbalized as logical-and and logical-or, respectively. Pseudo-code in Listing 4–2 illustrates logical-and and logical-or operators.

Listing 4–2. *Using && and || Logical Operators*

```
int x = 5;
int y = 6;
isComplete  =  TRUE;
//using the logical and
if (x < y && isComplete == TRUE)
{
    //in this example, x is less than 6 and isComplete == TRUE
    do stuff;
}
if (x < y || isComplete == FALSE)
{
    //in this example, x is less than 6.
    //Only one operand has to be TRUE for an OR to result in a TRUE.
    //See Table 4-2 A OR Truth Table
    do stuff;
}
//another way to test for TRUE
if (x < y && isComplete)
```

```
{
    //in this example, x is less than 6 and isComplete == TRUE
    do stuff;
}
//another way to test for FALSE
if (x < y && !isComplete)
{
    do stuff;
}
else
{
    // isComplete == TRUE
    do stuff;
}
```

Design Requirements

As discussed in Chapter 1, the most expensive process in the software development life cycle is writing code. The least expensive process in the software development life cycle is gathering the requirements for your application; yet, this latter process is the most overlooked and least used in software development.

Design requirements usually begin by asking clients, customers, and/or stakeholders how the application should work and what problems it should solve.

With respect to apps, requirements can include long or short narrative descriptions, screen mockups, and formulas. It is far easier to open your word processor and change the requirements and screen mockups before coding begins than it is to modify an iPhone/iPad/Mac app. The following is the design requirement for one view of an iPhone mobile banking app:

- **View:** Accounts View

- **Description:** Displays the list of accounts the user has. The list of accounts will be in the following sections: Business Accounts, Personal Accounts and Car Loans, IRA, and Home Equity Loans.

- **Cells:** Each cell will contain the account name, the last four digits of the account, available balance, and present balance.

A picture is worth a thousand words. Screen mockups are helpful to developers and users because they can visualize how the views will look when they are completed. There are many tools that can quickly design mockups; one of these tools is OmniGraffle. See Figure 4–1 for an example of a screen mockup used for design requirements generated by OmniGraffle.

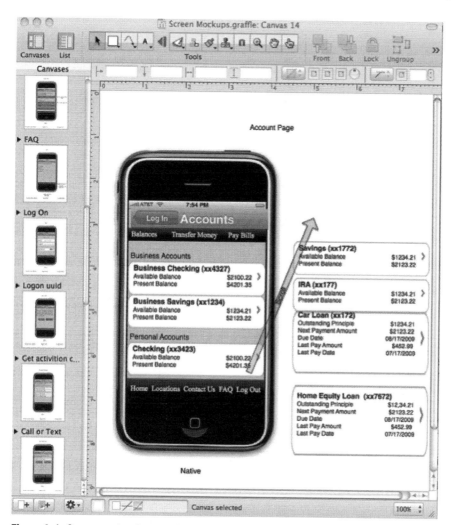

Figure 4–1. *Screen mockup for a mobile banking app using OmniGraffle and the Ultimate iPhone Stencil Plug-in*

Many developers believe that design requirements take too long and are unnecessary. There is a lot of information presented on the Accounts screen in Figure 4–1. Many business rules can determine how information is displayed to the user, along with all of the error handling when things go bad. When designing your app, working with all the business stakeholders at the beginning of the development process is critical to getting it right the first time.

Figure 4–2 is an example of all stakeholders being involved in your app's development. Having all stakeholders involved in every view from the beginning will eliminate multiple rewrites and application bugs.

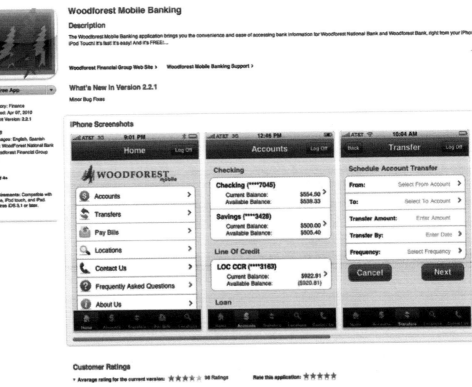

Figure 4–2. *Woodforest Mobile Banking app as it appears on the iTunes Connect app store; Compare with the app requirements Accounts screen in Figure 4–1.*

Additionally, Apple recommends that developers spend at least 50% of their development time on the user interface's design and development.

Apress's iPhone and iPad Sketch Books are also great tools for laying out your iOS app's look and feel on paper. See Figure 4–3.

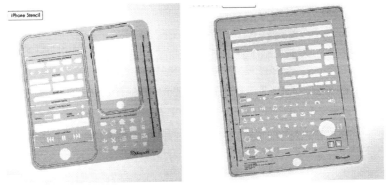

Figure 4–3. *Apress's iPhone Sketch Book Stencil and Apress's iPad Sketch Book Stencil*

Flowcharting

After design requirements are finalized, you can pseudo-code sections of your app to solve complex development issues. **Flowcharting** is a common method of diagramming an algorithm. An algorithm is represented as different types of boxes connected by lines and arrows. Developers often use flowcharting to express code visually. See Figure 4–4.

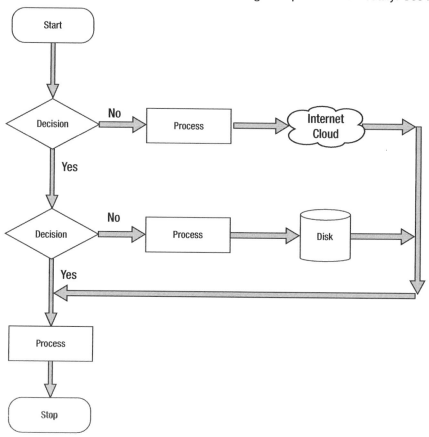

Figure 4–4. *Sample flowchart showing common figures and their associated names*

Flowcharts should always have a start and a stop. Branches should never come to an end without a stop. This helps developers make sure all of the branches in their code are accounted for and that they cleanly stop execution.

Designing and Flowcharting an Example App

We have covered a lot of information about decision making and program flow. It's time to do what programmers do best: write apps!

The app you have been assigned to write generates a random number between 0 and 100 inclusive, and asks the user to guess the number. The user has to do this until the number is guessed. You can use any object from the Alice gallery to ask the user for his or her guess, and you can also choose any world for your object to be in. The object will provide a visual queue for each high, low, and correct guess. The number that the user guesses will be displayed on the console. When the user guesses the correct answer, he or she will be asked if he or she wants to play again. See Figure 4–5.

Figure 4–5. *An astronaut object asking the user to guess a number between 0 and 100*

The App's Design

Using your design requirements, you can make a flowchart for your app. See Figure 4–6.

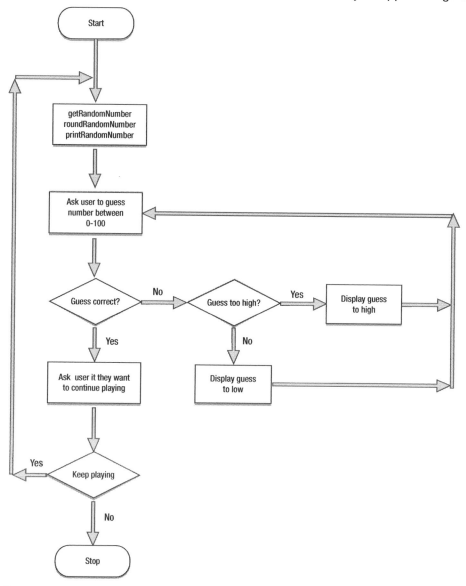

Figure 4–6. *Flowchart for guessing a random number app*

Reviewing Figure 4–6, you'll notice that as you approach the end of a block of logic in your flowchart, there are arrows that go back to a previous section and repeat that section until some condition is met. This is called **looping**. It enables you to repeat sections of programming logic—without having to rewrite those sections of code over—until a condition is met.

Using Loops to Repeat Program Statements

A **loop** is a sequence of program statements that is specified once, but can be repeated several times in succession. A loop can repeat a specified number of times (count-controlled) or until some condition (condition-controlled) occurs.

In this section, you'll learn about count-controlled loops and condition-controlled loops. You will also learn how to control your loops with Boolean logic.

Count-Controlled Loops

A count-controlled loop is a loop that repeats a specified number of times. In Objective-C and Alice, this is a **for loop**. A for loop has a counter variable. This variable enables the developer to specify the number of times the loop will be executed. See Listing 4–3.

Listing 4–3. *A Count-Controlled Loop*

```
int i;
for (i = 0; i < 10; i++)
{
      //repeat all code in braces 10 times
}
....continue
```

The loop in Listing 4–3 will loop 10 times. The variable i starts at zero and increments at the end of the } by one. The incrementing is done by the i++ in the *for* statement; i++, which is equivalent to $i = i +1$. i, is then incremented by 1 to 10 and then checked to see if it is less than 10. This for loop will exit when $i = 9$ and the } is reached.

> **NOTE:** It is common for developers to confuse the number of times they think their loops will repeat. If the loop started at 1 in Listing 4–3, the loop would repeat nine times instead of 10.

In Objective-C, for loops can have their counter variables declared in the for loop declaration itself. See Listing 4–4.

Listing 4–4. *Counter Variable is Initialized in For Loop Declaration*

```
for (int i = 0; i < 10; i++)
{
      //repeat all code in braces 10 times
}
....continue
```

Occasionally, you will need to repeat just one line of code in a for loop. This can be accomplished by not using any {}. The first line of code encountered after the for loop declaration is repeated, as specified in the for loop declaration. See Listing 4–5.

Listing 4–5. *Counter Variable is Initialized in the For Loop Declaration*

```
for (int i = 0; i < 10; i++)
    do this line of code 10 times;
....continue
```

Condition-Controlled Loops

Objective-C and Alice have the ability to repeat a loop until some condition changes. You may want to repeat a section of your code until a false condition is reached with one of your variables. This type of loop is called a **while loop**. A while loop is a control flow statement that repeats based on a given Boolean condition. A while-loop can be thought of as a repeating if statement. See Listing 4–6.

Listing 4–6. *An Objective-C While Loop Repeating*

```
BOOL isTrue = TRUE;
while (isTrue)
  {
    //do something;
     isTrue = FALSE; // a condition occurs that sometimes sets isTrue to FALSE
  };
....continue
```

The while loop in Listing 4–6 first checks if the variable isTrue is TRUE—which it is—so the {loop body} is entered where the code is executed. Eventually, some condition is reached that causes isTrue to become FALSE. After completing all the code in the loop body, the condition (isTrue) is checked once more, and the loop is repeated again. This process is repeated until the variable isTrue is set to FALSE.

Infinite Loops

An infinite loop repeats endlessly, either due to the loop not having a condition that causes termination or having a terminating condition that can never be met.

Generally, infinite loops can cause apps to become unresponsive. They are the result of a side effect of a bug in either the code or the logic.

Listing 4–7. *An Example of an Infinite Loop*

```
x = 0;
while (x  != 5)
  {
    do something;
    x = x + 2;
  };
....continue
```

Listing 4–7 is an example of an infinite loop caused by a terminating condition that can never be met. The variable x will be checked with each iteration through the while loop, but will never be equal to 5. The variable x will always be an even number because it was initialized to zero and incremented by 2 in the loop. This will cause the loop to repeat endlessly. See Listing 4–8.

Listing 4–8. *An Example of an Infinite Loop Caused by a Terminating Condition That Can Never Be Met*

```
while (TRUE)
 {
     do something;
};
....continue
```

Coding the Example App in Alice

Now that you have your design requirements and flowchart completed, and understand looping, you're ready to write your Alice application. See Figure 4–7.

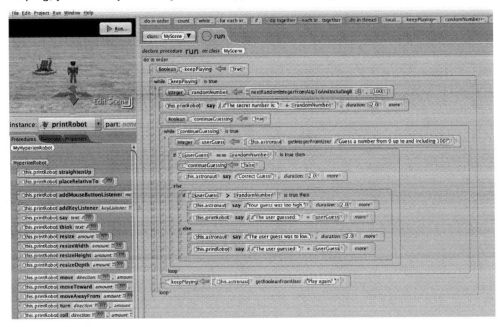

Figure 4–7. *Random number generator app*

It is not possible to list the source code for this Alice program in one screenshot. However, if you print out the source code in HTML, you can view all the code. See Figure 4–8.

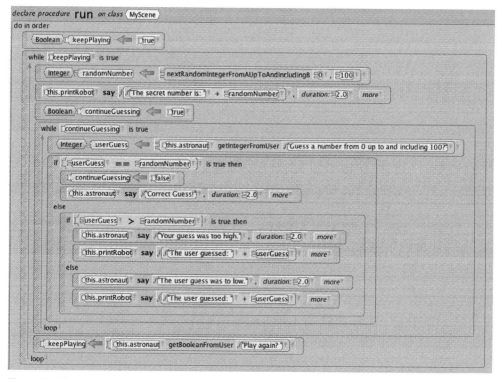

Figure 4–8. *Random number generator; complete program listing*

Figure 4–8 shows the entire program listing for your random number generator code.

> **NOTE:** You can download the complete random number generator app at forum.xcelme.com. The code will be under the Chapter 4 topic. There is also a video showing how to drag and drop all the tiles within the While and If code blocks in Alice.

Coding the Example App in Objective-C

Using your requirements and what you learned with your Alice app, try writing your random number generator in Objective-C.

Your Objective-C app will run from the command line, as it asks the user to guess a random number.

1. Open Xcode and start a New Project. Choose the Command Line Tool. See Figure 4–9.

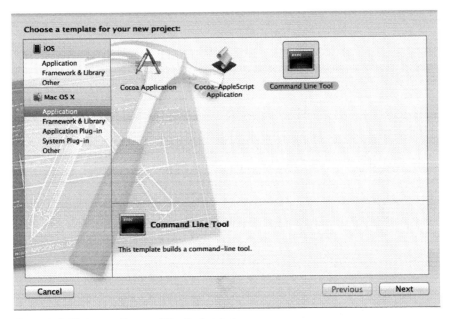

Figure 4–9. *Start a new Command Line Tool project.*

2. Call your project RandomNumber (see Figure 4–10). Select **Foundation** and make sure **Use Automatic Reference Counting** is checked. **Save** the project anywhere you prefer on your hard drive.

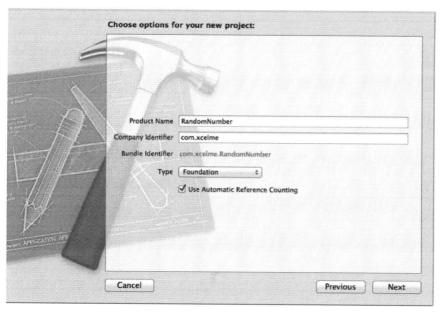

Figure 4–10. *Project options for RandomNumber*

Now, you need to open the implementation file in the Source group. This is where you will write your Objective-C code.

   3.   Open the main.m file. Delete the following line of code:

```
NSLog(@"Hello, World!");
```

   4.   You are ready to write your app. Start writing the code under

```
// insert code here...
```

See Figure 4–11.

```
#import <Foundation/Foundation.h>

int main (int argc, const char * argv[])
{

    @autoreleasepool {

        // insert code here...
        NSLog(@"Hello, World!");

    }
    return 0;
}
```

Figure 4–11. *The editor is now ready for you to write your code.*

Following your Alice code, you will write your random number generator app. You will notice that most of the code is very similar to your Alice app. See Listing 4–9.

Listing 4–9. *Source Code for Your Random Number Generator App*

```
11 int main (int argc, const char * argv[])
12 {
13
14 @autoreleasepool {
15
16 // insert code here...
17 int randomNumber = 1;
18 int userGuess = 1;
19 BOOL continueGuessing = TRUE;
20 BOOL keepPlaying = TRUE;
21 char yesNo = ' ';
22
23 while (keepPlaying)
24 {
25     randomNumber = (arc4random() % 101);
26     NSLog(@"The random number to guess is: %d",randomNumber);
27     while (continueGuessing)
28     {
29         NSLog (@"Pick a number between 0 and 100. ");
30         scanf ("%i", &userGuess);
31         fgetc(stdin);//remove CR/LF i.e extra character
32         if (userGuess == randomNumber)
33         {
34             continueGuessing = FALSE;
35             NSLog(@"Correct number!");
36         }
37         //nested if statement
38         else if (userGuess > randomNumber)
39         {
40             //user guessed too high
41             NSLog(@"Your guess is too high");
42         }
43         else
44         {
45             // no reason to check if userGuess < randomNumber. It has to be.
46             NSLog(@"Your guess is too low");
47         }
48         //refactored from our Alice app. This way we only have to code once.
49         NSLog(@"The user guessed %d",userGuess);
50     }
51     NSLog (@"Play Again? Y or N");
52
53     yesNo = fgetc(stdin);
54
55     if (yesNo == 'N' || yesNo == 'n')
56     {
57         keepPlaying = FALSE;
58     }
59     continueGuessing = TRUE;
60     }
61 }
62 return 0;
63 }
```

In Listing 4–9, there is new code that we haven't discussed before. The first new line of code (line 25) is

```
randomNumber = (arc4random() % 101);
```

This line will produce a random number between 0 and 100; `arc4random()` is a function that returns a random number. Although this will not generate a truly random number, it will work for this example.

The modulus operator is called `%`. This operator returns the remainder of its two operands; in this case, it's the remainder of `arc4random()` divided by 101.

The next line of new code is

```
scanf ("%i", &userGuess);
```

The function `scanf` reads a value from the keyboard and stores it in `userGuess`.

> **NOTE:** The source code for this Objective-C project is available for download at `forum.xcelme.com`. Additionally, there is a short video explaining the source code and the project.

Nested If Statements and Else-If Statements

Sometimes, it is necessary to **nest if statements**. This means that you need to have if statements nested inside an existing if statement. Additionally, it is sometimes necessary to have a comparison as the first step in the else section of the if statement. This is called an **else-if statement** (recall line 38 in Listing 4–9.

```
else if (userGuess > randomNumber)
```

Removing Extra Characters

Line 31 is another new line of code.

```
fgetc(stdin); //remove CR/LF i.e extra character
```

The function `scanf` can be difficult to work with. In this case, `scanf` leaves a remnant in your input buffer that needs to be flushed, so you can read a Y or N from the keyboard to determine if the user wants to play again.

Improving the Code Through Refactoring

Often, after you get your code to work, you examine the code and find more efficient ways to write it. The process of rewriting your code to make it more efficient, maintainable, and readable is called **code refactoring**.

As you were reviewing your code in Objective-C, you noticed that you could eliminate some unnecessary code. Your code had the following line repeated in the if-else statement:

```
//refactored from our Alice app. This way we only have to code once.
NSLog(@"The user guessed %d",userGuess);
```

> **NOTE:** As developers, we have found that the best line of code you can write is the line that you don't write—less code means less to debug and maintain.

Running the App

Press the Play button in your Objective-C project and run your app. See Figure 4–12.

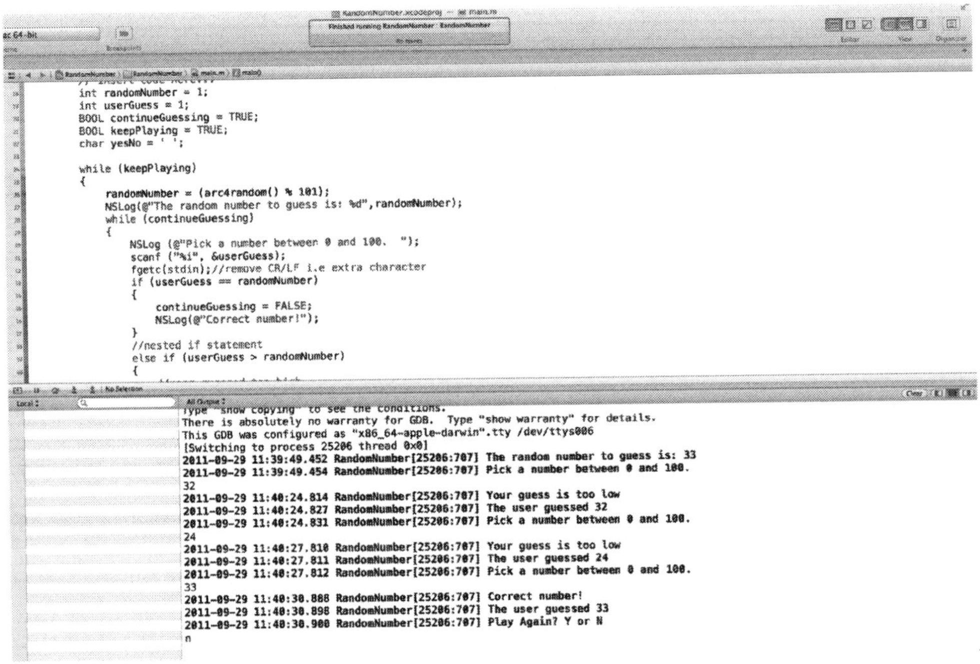

Figure 4–12. *The console output of the Objective-C random number generator app*

> **NOTE:** If you're not seeing the output console when you run your app, make sure you have selected (grayed) the same options at the top-right and bottom-right of the editor (see Figure 4–12).

Moving Forward Without Alice

You've used Alice to learn object-oriented programming. It has enabled you to focus on OOP concepts without having to deal with syntax and a compiler; however, it is necessary to become more familiar with the specifics of the Objective-C language. Alice has served you well and you can now focus on using Objective-C and Xcode for the remainder of the book.

Summary

In this chapter, you've covered a lot of important information on how to control your applications; program flow and decision-making are essential to every iPhone/iPad/Mac App. Make sure you have completed the Objective-C example in this chapter. You might review these examples and think you understand everything without having to write this app. This will be a fatal mistake that will prevent you from becoming a successful iPhone/iPad/Mac developer. You must spend time coding this example.

The terms in this chapter are very important. You should be able to describe the following:

- AND
- OR
- XOR
- NAND
- NOR
- NOT
- Truth tables
- Negation
- All comparison operators
- Application requirement
- Logical AND (&&)
- Logical OR (||)
- Flowchart
- Loop
- Controlled loops
- For Loop
- Condition-controlled loops
- Infinite loops
- While loops
- Nested if statements
- Code refactoring

Exercises

▨ Extend the random number generator app to print to the console how many times the user guessed before he or she guessed the correct random number. Do this in both Alice and Objective-C.

▨ Extend the random number generator app to print to the console how many times the user played the app. Print this value when the user quits the app. Do this in both Alice and Objective-C.

Object Oriented Programming with Objective-C

Over the past 15 years, the programming world focused on the development paradigm of object oriented programming (OOP). Most modern development environments and languages implement OOP. Put simply, OOP forms the basis of everything you develop today.

You may be asking yourself why we waited until Chapter 5 to present OOP using Objective-C if it is the primary development style of today. The simple answer is that it is not an easy concept for new developers. We will spend this chapter going into detail about the different aspects of OOP and how this will affect your development.

Implementing OOP into your applications correctly will take some front-end planning but you will save yourself a lot of time throughout the life of your projects. OOP has changed the way development is done. In this chapter, we will look at what OOP is. OOP was initially discussed in the first chapter of this book, but we will go into more detail here. We will revisit what objects are and how they relate to physical objects we find in our world. We will also look into what classes are and how they relate to objects. We will also discuss steps you will need to take when planning your classes and some visual tools you can use to accomplish this. When you have read this chapter and have worked through the exercises, you will have a better understanding of what OOP is and why it is necessary for you as a developer.

At first, objects and object-oriented programming may seem difficult to understand, but the hope is that as we progress through this chapter, it will begin to make sense.

The Object

As was discussed in Chapter 1, OOP is based on objects. Some of our discussion about objects will be a review, but we will also go into more depth. An object is anything that can be acted upon. In order to better explain what a programming object is, we will first look at some items in the physical world around us. A physical object can be anything around you that you can touch or feel. Take, for example, a television. Some characteristics of a television include type (plasma, LCD, or CRT), size (40 inches), brand (Sony, Vizio), weight, and cost. Televisions also have functions. They can be turned on or off. You can change the channel, adjust the volume, and change brightness.

Some of these characteristics and functions are unique to televisions and some are not. For example, a couch in your house would probably not have the same characteristics as a television. You would want different information about a couch, such as material type, seating capability, and color. A couch might have only a few functions, such as converting to a bed.

Now let's talk specifically about objects as they relate to programming. An object is a specific item. It can describe something physical like a book, or it could be something such as a window for your application. Objects have properties and methods. Properties describe certain things about an object such as location, color, or name. Conversely, methods describe actions the object can perform such as close or recalculate. In our example, a TV object would have type, size, and brand properties, while a Couch object would have properties such as color, material, and comfort level. In programming terms, a property is a variable that is part of an object. For example, a TV would use a string variable to store the brand and an integer to store the height.

Objects also have commands the programmer can use to control them. The commands are called methods. Methods are the way that other objects interact with a certain object. For example, with the television, a method would be any of the buttons on the remote control. Each of those buttons represents a way you can interact with your television. Methods can and often are used to change the values of properties, but methods do not store any values themselves.

As we described in Chapter 1, objects have a state, which is basically a snapshot of an object at any given point in time. A state would be the values of all of the properties at a specific time.

In previous chapters, we have used the example of the bookstore. A bookstore contains many different objects. It contains book objects that have properties such as title, author, page count, and publisher. It also contains magazines with properties such as title, issue, genre, and publisher. A bookstore also has some non-tangible objects such as a sale. A sale object would contain information about the books purchased, the customer, the amount paid, and the payment type. A sale object might also have some methods that calculate tax, print the receipt, or void the sale. A sale object does not represent a tangible object, but it is still an object and is necessary for creating an effective bookstore.

Because the object is the basis of OOP, it is important to understand objects and how to interact with them. We will spend the rest of the chapter describing objects and some of their characteristics.

What Is a Class?

We cannot discuss OOP without discussing what a class is. A class defines which properties and methods an object will have. A class is basically a cookie cutter that can be used to create objects that have similar characteristics. All objects of a certain class will have the same properties and the same methods. The values of those properties will change from object to object.

A class is similar to a species in the animal world. A species is not an individual animal, but it does describe many similar characteristics of the animal. In order to understand classes more, let's look at an example of classes in nature. The Dog class has many properties that all dogs have in common. For example, a dog may have a name, an age, an owner, and a favorite activity. An object that is of a certain class is called an instance of that class. If we look at Figure 5–1, you can see the difference between the class and the actual objects that are instances of the class. For example, Lassie is an instance of the dog class. In the diagram below, you can see we have a Dog class that has four properties (Breed, Age, Owner, Favorite Activity). In real life, a dog will have many more properties, but we decided to use four for this demonstration.

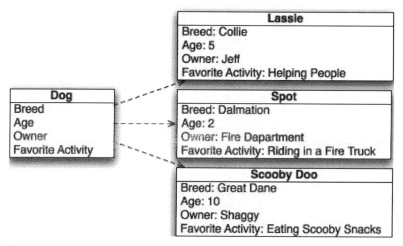

Figure 5–1. *An example of a class and individual objects*

Planning Classes

Planning your classes is one of the most important steps in your development process. While it is possible to go back and add properties and methods after the fact (and you will definitely need to do this), it is important that you know which classes are going to be used in your application and which basic properties and methods they will have. Spending time planning your different classes is very important at the beginning of the process.

Planning Properties

Let's look at the bookstore example and some of the classes we need to create. First, it is important to create a Bookstore class. A Bookstore class contains the blueprint of the information each Bookstore object stores, such as the bookstore name, address, phone number, and logo (see Figure 5–2). Placing this information in a class rather than hard coding it in your application will allow you to easily make changes to this information in the future. We will discuss the reasons for using OOP methodologies later in this chapter. Also, if your bookstore becomes a huge success and you decide to open up another one, you will be prepared because you can create another object of class Bookstore.

Bookstore
Name
Address1
Address2
City
State
Zip
Phone Number
Logo

Figure 5–2. *The bookstore class*

Let's also plan out a Customer class (see Figure 5–3). Notice how the name has been broken into First Name and Last Name. This is very important to do. There will be times in your project when you may want to use only the first name of a customer, and it would be hard to separate the first name from the last if you didn't plan ahead. Let's say you want to send a letter to a customer letting them know about an upcoming sale. You do not want your greeting to say, "Dear John Doe." It would look much more personal to say, "Dear John."

Customer
First Name
Last Name
Address Line 1
Address Line 2
City
State
Zip
Phone Number
Email Address
Favorite Book Genre

Figure 5–3. *The customer class*

You will also notice how we have broken out the address into its different parts instead of grouping it all together. We separated the Address Line 1, Address Line 2, City, State, and ZIP. This is very important and will be used in your application. Let's go back to the letter you want to send informing your customers of a sale in your store. You might not want to send it to all of the customers that live in different states. By separating the address, you can easily filter out those customers you do not want to include in your mailings.

We have also added the attribute of Favorite Book Genre to the Customer class. We added this to show you how you can keep many different types of information in each class. This field may come in handy if you have a new mystery title coming out and you want to send an e-mail alerting customers who are especially interested in mysteries. By storing this type of information, you will be able to specifically target different portions of your customer base.

A Book class is also necessary in order to create our bookstore (see Figure 5–3). We will store information about the book such as author, publisher, genre, page count, and edition number (in case there are multiple editions). The Book class will also have the price for the book.

Book
Author
Publisher
Genre
Year Published
Number of Pages
Edition
Price

Figure 5–4. *The book class*

We also added another class called the Sale class (see Figure 5–5). This class is more abstract than the other classes we have discussed because it does not describe a tangible object. You will notice how we have added a reference to a customer and a book to the Sale class. Because the Sale class will track sales of books, we will need to know which book was sold and to which customer.

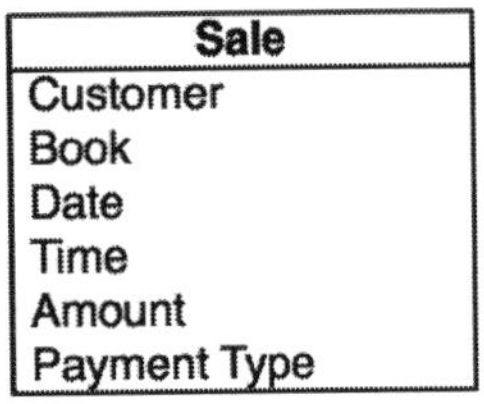

Sale
Customer
Book
Date
Time
Amount
Payment Type

Figure 5–5. *The sale class*

Now that we have planned out the properties of the classes, we will need to look at some methods that each of the classes will have.

Planning Methods

We will not add all of the methods now, but the more planning you can do at the beginning, the easier it will be for you down the line. Not all of your classes will have many methods. Some may not have any methods at all.

> **NOTE:** When planning your methods, remember to have them focus on a specific task. The more specific the method, the more likely it is that it can be reused.

For the time being, we will not add any methods to the Book class or the Bookstore class. We will focus on our other two classes.

For the Customer class, we will add methods to list the purchase history of that client. There may be other methods that you will need to add in the future but we will add just that one for now. Your completed Customer class diagram should look like Figure 5–6. You will notice the line near the bottom separates the properties from the methods.

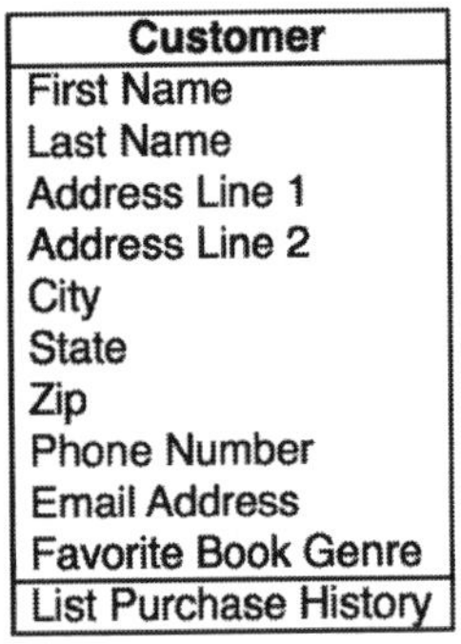

Customer
First Name
Last Name
Address Line 1
Address Line 2
City
State
Zip
Phone Number
Email Address
Favorite Book Genre
List Purchase History

Figure 5–6. *The completed customer class*

For the Sales class, we have added three methods. We added Charge Credit Card, Print Invoice, and Checkout (see Figure 5–7). For the time being, you do not need to know how to implement these methods, but you need to know that you are planning on adding them to your class.

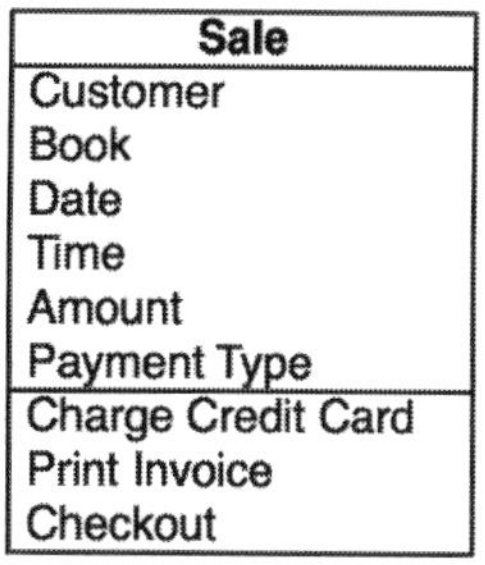

Sale
Customer
Book
Date
Time
Amount
Payment Type
Charge Credit Card
Print Invoice
Checkout

Figure 5–7. *The completed sale class*

Now that you have finished mapping out the classes and the methods you are going to add to them, you have the beginnings of a unified modeling language (UML) diagram. Basically, this is a diagram used by developers to plan out their classes, properties, and methods. Starting your development process by creating such a diagram will help you significantly in the long run. An in-depth discussion of UML diagrams is beyond the scope of this book. If you would like more information about this subject, smartdraw.com has a great in-depth overview of them.

http://www.smartdraw.com/resources/tutorials/uml-diagrams/

Figure 5–8 shows the complete diagram.

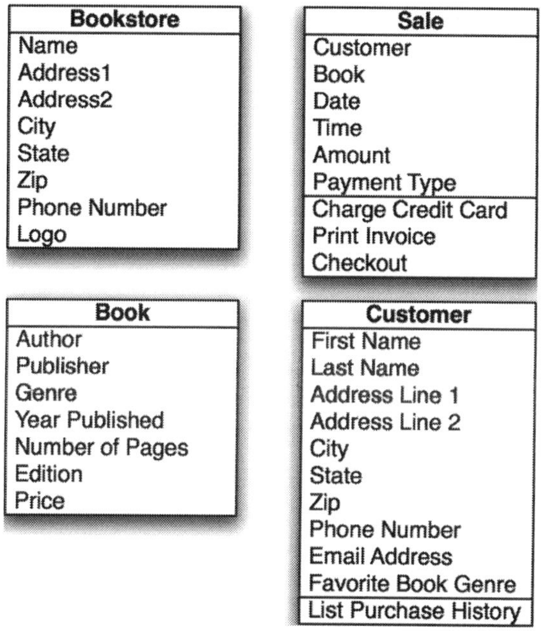

Bookstore
Name
Address1
Address2
City
State
Zip
Phone Number
Logo

Sale
Customer
Book
Date
Time
Amount
Payment Type
Charge Credit Card
Print Invoice
Checkout

Book
Author
Publisher
Genre
Year Published
Number of Pages
Edition
Price

Customer
First Name
Last Name
Address Line 1
Address Line 2
City
State
Zip
Phone Number
Email Address
Favorite Book Genre
List Purchase History

Figure 5–8. *The completed UML diagram for the bookstore*

Implementing the Classes

Now that we understand the objects we are going to be creating, we need to create our first object. In order to do so, we will start with a new project.

1. Please launch Xcode. Click on File ➤ New ➤ New Project.

2. Select iOS on the left-hand side. On the right-hand side, select **Master-Detail Application**. For what we are doing in this chapter, we could have selected any of the application types (see Figure 5–9). Click Next.

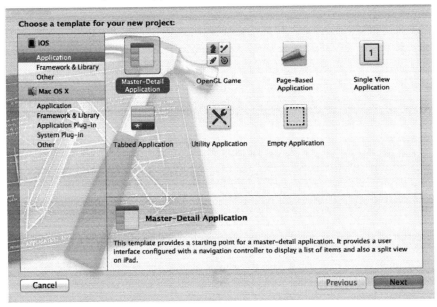

Figure 5–9. *Creating a new project*

3. You will have to enter a company name. Leave the checkboxes on this screen as they appear by default. We will not be worrying about these items right now. Select a location to save your project and then save your project. You can use the name bookstore or any other project name you want.

4. Select the **BookStore** folder on the left-hand side of the screen (see Figure 5–10). This is where the majority of your code will reside.

5. Select File ➤ New ➤ New File.

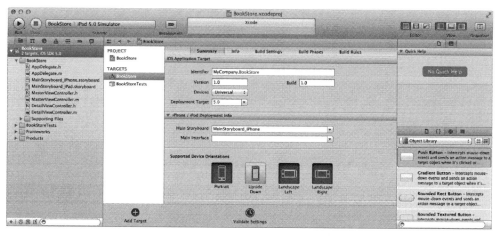

Figure 5–10. *Selecting the bookStore folder*

6. From the pop-up window, select **Cocoa Touch** under the iOS header and
    then click on **Objective-C class** on the right-hand side (see Figure 5–11).
    Then click **Next**.

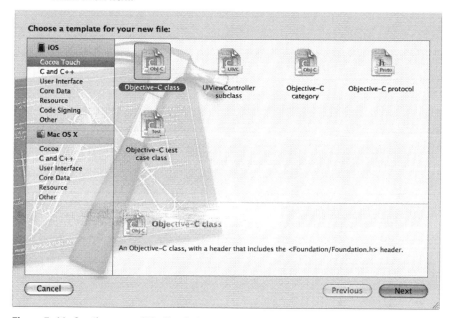

Figure 5–11. *Creating a new Objective-C class*

7. On the next screen, you will need to select the superclass for your object. This is what determines what properties and methods your object will have by default. We will select NSObject for now (see Figure 5–12). Click **Next**.

NOTE: NSObject is the base class in Objective C. It contains properties and methods required for most objects used.

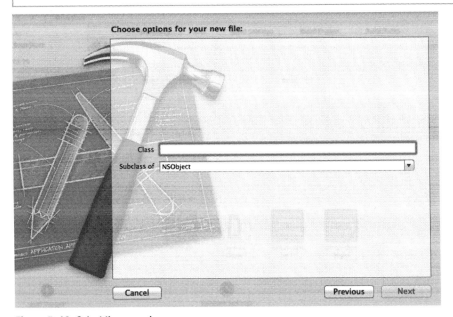

Figure 5–12. *Select the superclass*

8. You will now be given the opportunity to name your class. For this exercise, we will create the Customer class. For now, name the class Customer. Now click **Save**.

NOTE: For ease of use and for understanding your code, remember that class names should always be capitalized in Objective-C. Object names should always start lowercase. For example, Book would be an appropriate name for a class, and book would be a great name for an object based on the Book class. For a two word object, such as the book author, an appropriate name would be bookAuthor. This type of capitalization is called lower camelcase.

---

9. Now look in your main project folder; you should have two new files. One is called *Customer.h* and the other is called *Customer.m*. The *.h* file is the header file that will contain information about your class. The header file will list all of the properties and methods in your class, but it will not actually contain the code related to them. The *.m* file is the implementation file, which is where you write the code for your methods.

10. Double-click on the *Customer.h* file and you will see the window shown in Figure 5–12. You will notice it does not contain a lot of information currently. The first part, with the double slashes (//), is all comments and is not considered part of the code. Comments allow you to tell those who might read your code what each portion of code is meant to accomplish. We will not go into more detail now about the other portions of the header file, except to say that all of the properties of a class need to be inside the braces ({ }) of the @interface portion.

Figure 5–13. *Your empty customer class*

Now let's transfer the properties from our UML diagram to our actual class.

TIP: Properties should always start with a lowercase letter. There can be no spaces in an attribute name.

For the first property, First Name, we will add this line to our file.

```
NSString* firstName;
```

This creates a string object in our class called firstName. Because all of the properties for the Customer class are strings also, we will just need to repeat the same procedure for the other ones. When that is complete, your @interface portion should look like Figure 5–13.

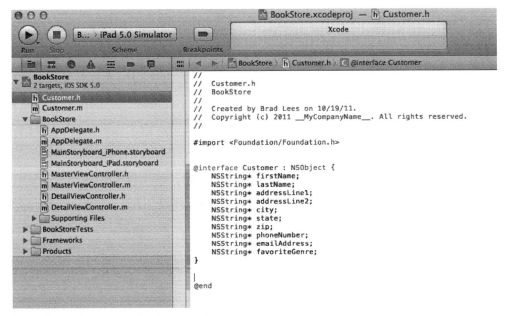

Figure 5–14. *The customer class interface with properties*

Now that the @interface portion is complete, we will need to add our method. Methods need to go outside of the @interface portion but still inside of the @interface portion of the header file. We will add a new method that returns an NSArray. This code will look as follows:

```
-(NSArray *) listPurchaseHistory;
```

> **NOTE:** NSString is a class that holds and performs actions on a string. A string is a set of characters. NSString can hold letters, numbers, and punctuation.

That is all that needs to be done in the header file to create our class. Figure 5–15 shows the final header file. In the next chapter, we will go into more detail about the implementation file.

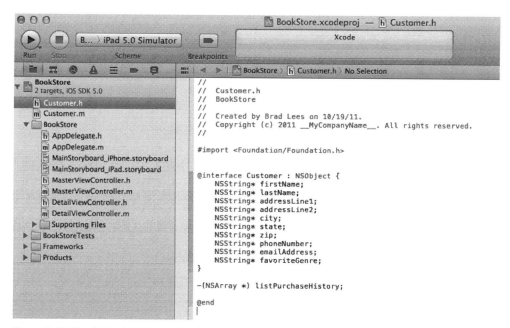

Figure 5–15. *The finished customer class header file*

Inheritance

Another major quality of OOP is inheritance. Inheritance in programming is similar to genetic inheritance. You might have inherited your eye color from your mother or hair color from your father, or vice versa. Classes can, in a similar way, inherit properties and methods from their parent classes. In OOP, a parent class is called a superclass and a child class is called a subclass.

In Objective-C, all classes created by a programmer have a superclass that is similar to a parent class. The class will inherit characteristics from that parent class. So, just as in all other OOP languages, the class is called a subclass of the parent class. In this chapter, all of our classes are subclasses of the NSObject. In Objective-C, most of the time, your classes will be subclasses of NSObject. In our previous example, the Customer class was a subclass of NSObject.

We could, for example, create a class of printed materials and use subclasses for books, magazines, and newspapers. Printed materials can have many things in common, so we could assign variables to the superclass of printed materials and not have to redundantly assign them to each individual class. By doing this, we further reduce the amount of redundant code that is necessary for you to write and debug.

In Figure 5–16, you will see a layout for the properties of a Printed Material superclass and how that will affect the subclasses of Book, Magazine, and Newspaper. The properties of the Printed Material class will be inherited by the subclasses so there is no need to define them explicitly in the class. You will notice that the Book class now has significantly fewer properties. By using a superclass, you will significantly reduce the amount of redundant code in your programs.

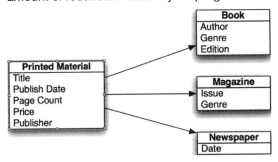

Figure 5–16. *Properties of the super- and subclasses*

Why Use OOP?

Throughout this chapter, we have discussed what OOP is and we have even discussed how to create classes and objects. However, I think it is important to discuss why you want to use OOP principles in your development.

If you take a look at the popular programming languages of the day, all of them use the OOP principles to a certain extent. Objective-C, C++, Visual Basic, C#, and Java all require the programmer to understand classes and objects to successfully develop in those languages. In order to become a developer in today's world, you will need to understand OOP. But why use it?

It is everywhere

Just about any development you chose to do today will require you to understand object-oriented principles. On Mac OS X and in iOS, everything you interact with will be an object. For example, simple windows, buttons, and text boxes are all objects and have properties and methods. If you want to be successful as a programmer, you will need to understand OOP.

Eliminate Redundant Code

By using objects, you can reduce the amount of code you have to retype. If you write code to print a receipt when a customer checks out, you will want that same code available when you need to reprint a receipt. If you placed your code to print the receipt in the Sales class, you will not have to rewrite this code again. This not only saves you time, but often will help you eliminate mistakes. If you do not use OOP and there is a change to the invoice (even something as simple as a graphic change), you have to make sure you make the change in your desktop application and the mobile application. If you miss one of them, you run the risk of having the two interfaces behave differently.

Ease of Debugging

By having all of the code relating to a book in one class, you know where to look when there is a problem with the book. This may not sound like such a big deal for a little application, but when your application gets to hundreds of thousands or even millions of lines of code, it will save you a lot of time.

Ease of Replacement

If you place all of your code in a class, then as things change in your application, you can change out classes and give your new class completely different functionality. However, it can interact with the rest of the application in the same way as your current class. This is similar to car parts. If you want to replace a muffler on a car, you do not need to get a new car. If you have code related to your invoice scattered all over the place, it makes it much more difficult to change items about a class.

Advanced Topics

We have discussed the basics of OOP throughout this chapter, but there are some other topics that are very important to your understanding.

Interface

As we have discussed in this chapter, the way the other objects interact through each other is with methods. We discussed the header files created when you create a class. This is often called the interface because it tells other objects how they can interact with your objects. Implementing a standard interface throughout your application will allow your code to interact with different objects in similar ways. This will significantly reduce the amount of object specific code you need to write.

Polymorphism

Polymorphism is the ability of an object of one class to appear and be used as an object of another class. This is usually done by creating methods and properties that are similar to those of another class. A great example of polymorphism that we have been using is the bookstore. In the bookstore, we have three similar classes: `Book`, `Magazine`, and `Newspaper`. If we wanted to have a big sale for our entire inventory, we could go through all of the books and mark them down. Then we could go through all of the magazines and mark them down, and then go through all of the newspapers and mark them down. That would be more work than we would need to do. It would be better to make sure all of the classes have a markdown method. Then we could call that on all of the objects without needing to know which class they were as long as they were subclasses of a class that contained the methods needed. This would save a bunch of time and coding.

As you are planning out your classes, look for similarities and methods that might apply to more than one type of class. This will save you time and speed up your application in the long run.

Summary

We've finally reached the end of the chapter! Here is a summary of the things that were covered.

- Object-oriented programming (OOP)
    - We discussed the importance of OOP and the reasons why all modern code should use this methodology.
- Object
    - You learned about objects and how they correspond to real-world objects. We learned that many programming objects relate directly to real-world objects. You also learned about abstract objects that do not correspond to real world objects.
- Class
    - You learned that a class determines the types of data (properties) and the methods that each object will have. Every object needs to have a class. It is the blueprint for the object.
- Creating a class
    - You learned how to map out the properties and methods of our classes.
    - We used Xcode to create a class file.
    - We edited the class header file to add our properties and methods.

Exercises

- Try creating the class files for the rest of the classes we mapped out.
- Map out an Author class. Choose the kind of information you would need to store about an author.

For the daring and advanced:

- Try creating a superclass called PrintedMaterials. Map out the properties that a class might have.
- Create classes for the other types of printed materials a store might carry.

Chapter 6

Learning Objective-C and Xcode

For the most part, all computer languages perform the typical tasks any computer needs to do—store information, compare information, make decisions about that information, and perform some action based on those decisions. Objective-C is a language that makes these tasks easier to understand and accomplish. The real trick with Objective-C (actually, the trick with any C language) is to understand the symbols and keywords used to accomplish those tasks. This chapter continues our examination of Objective-C and Xcode so you can become even more familiar with them.

A Brief History of Objective-C

Objective-C is really a combination of two languages, C language and a lesser-known language called Smalltalk. Back in the 1970s, several very bright engineers from Bell Labs created a language named **C** that made it easy to port their pet project, the Unix operating system, from one machine to another. Prior to C, people had to write programs in assembly languages. The problem with assembly languages is that each is specific to its machine, so moving software from one machine to another was nearly impossible. The C language, created by Brian Kernighan and Dennis Ritchie, solved this problem by providing a language that wrote out the assembly language for whatever machine it supported, a kind of Rosetta Stone for early computer languages. Because of its portability, C quickly became the *de facto* language for many types of computers, especially early PCs.

Fast forward to the early 1980s and the C language is on its way to becoming one of the most popular languages of the decade. Around this time, an engineer from a company called Stepstone was mixing the C language with another up-and-coming language called Smalltalk. The C Language is typically referred to as a *procedural language*, that is, a language that uses procedures to divide up processing steps. Smalltalk, on the other hand, was something entirely different. It was an *object-oriented programming language*. Instead of processing things procedurally, it used programming objects to get its work done. This new superset of the C language became known as "C with Objects" or more commonly, **Objective-C**.

In 1985, Brad Cox sold the Objective-C language and trademark to NeXT Computer, Inc. NeXT was the brainchild of Steve Jobs, who had been fired from his own company, Apple Computer, that very same year. NeXT used the Objective-C language to build the NeXTSTEP operating system and its suite of development tools. In fact, the Objective-C language gave NeXT a competitive advantage with all of its software. Programmers using NeXTSTEP and Objective-C could write programs faster than those writing in the traditional C language. While the hardware part of NeXT computers never really took off, the operating system and tools did. Quite interestingly, NeXT was purchased by Apple Computer in late 1996 with the intention of replacing its aging operating system, which had been in existence since the first Macintosh was developed in 1984. Four years after the acquisition, what had been NeXTSTEP reemerged as Mac OS X—with Objective-C still at the heart of the system.

Understanding the Language Symbols

Even though Objective-C integrates a great deal of object-oriented language, at the heart of Objective-C is C. Here are some of the symbols and language constructs used in Objective-C, some of which are part of the C language and most of which we've already encountered in one way or another. It's not important to know which are pure C and which are not; just know that the old and the newer symbols/constructs together make the Objective-C language.

- { This is the *begin* brace. It's used to begin what's commonly referred to as a **block** of code. Blocks are used to define and surround a section of code and define its scope.

- } This is the *end* brace. It's used to end a block of code. Wherever there is a begin ({), there must always be an accompanying end (}).

- - (void)methodName This is how an Objective-C method is defined. The word methodName of course can represent any name. The word (void) can also change. It represents what type of information the method represents. In this example, (void) indicates there is no data type associated with this method (data types were introduced in Chapter 3 and will be covered in more depth in later chapters). (void) could be replaced with something like (NSString*). This will be discussed further later on.

- * The asterisk (referred to as 'star' or 'splat') is used to represent what is called a *pointer* (see Chapter 13). All that's really important to know for now is that when you see something like NSString*, consider it part of the name. NSString and NSString* are completely different.

- ; The semicolon character is used to end a line of code. The thing to remember about a semicolon is that they aren't used at the end of statements that control the flow of the program, that is, if, for, while, etc. You'll eventually understand the rules of where they go and don't go.

- [ ]- These are called *brackets* and are used when sending a message to an Objective-C object. Chapter 7 covers more on this topic.

- @ While many people associate this with an e-mail address, the at sign is used in Objective-C to identify an Objective-C *directive*. A directive is a special Objective-C command, such as @interface, @implementation or @property.

- # The pound sign (or octathorpe if you like trivia) is similar to the @ sign and is used to identify a C language directive, such as #import or #define. While originally part of the C language, the use of # is still found in nearly all Objective-C programs.

So, let's see an example of Objective-C code:

```
1    - (void)logMessage
2    {
3        NSString *hello = @"Hello World!";
4        NSLog(hello);
5    }
```

Line #1 represents an Objective-C method. The (void) indicates this method is not associated with a data type and, if invoked, would not send a value back to the caller.

Lines #2 and #5 are the braces that define a block of code. This block is what defines the method. Every method has at least one block.

Line #3 defines an NSString* object and assigns it the value of @"Hello World". Remember, the at sign (@) is an Objective-C directive and is a quick way of defining a constant string object (recall that we first saw strings in Chapter 3).

Line #4 is a call to the NSLog method; it's not an object, so we can't send it a message. Instead, we're passing the method the object to print the hello NSString* object.

While it does look a little cryptic to someone who is just learning Objective-C, the simple and terse syntax doesn't take too much time to learn.

Putting the "Objective" into Objective-C

The majority of what makes Objective-C, well, objective, is its basis in Smalltalk. Smalltalk is a 100 percent object-oriented language and Objective-C borrows heavily from Smalltalk concepts and syntax. Here are a few of the high-level concepts borrowed from Smalltalk. Don't worry if some of these terms seem unfamiliar; they will be discussed in later chapters (Chapters 7 and 8 cover the basics).

- Pretty much everything is an **object**.

- Objects receive **messages**. In this context, the object is sometimes known as the **receiver** since it is receiving the message.

- Objects contain **instance** variables.

- Objects and instance variables have a defined **scope**.

- Classes hide an object's **implementation**.

> **NOTE:** As we saw in Chapter 5, the term **class** is used to represent, generically, the definition or type of an object. An **object** is what is created from the class. For example, an SUV is a *class* of vehicle. A class is a blueprint of sorts. A factory builds SUVs. The results are SUV objects that people drive. You can't drive a *class*, but you can drive an *object* built from a class.

So how do these concepts translate to Objective-C? Well, for starters, an object in Objective-C is defined using two different sections, @interface and @implementation. The @interface section defines what messages the object can respond to and any instance variables the object will be using. The @implementation section contains the actual code of the various messages from the @interface section.

Why is there a split between the interface and implementation? Well, an Objective-C object is defined only once within a program. However, it might be used in many different areas of that program. Where the object is used, the program simply reads in, or **imports**, the interface; it would be inefficient if the code for that object needed to be replicated every time it was used.

> **NOTE:** It is a common convention to have an object's interface stored in an .h file and the implementation stored in an .m file. Both files are named after the object. So, if a Library object is to be defined, its interface would be in *Library.h* and its implementation would be in *Library.m* (remember that names are case-sensitive).

Let's look at a simple example of the complete definition of an Objective-C object called HelloWorld. Following is the interface file (*HelloWorld.h*).

```
1    #import <Foundation/Foundation.h>
2
3    @interface HelloWorld : NSObject
4    {
5    }
6
7    - (void)printGreeting;
8
9    @end
```

And this is the implementation file (*HelloWorld.m*):

```
10    #import "HelloWold.h"
11
12    @implementation HelloWorld
13
14    -(void)printGreeting
15    {
16        NSLog(@"Hello World!");
17    }
18
19    @end
```

In the preceding example, an object, HelloWorld, is being defined. This object only has one message defined—printGreeting. What do all these strange symbols mean? Using the line numbers as a reference, we can review this code line by line.

Line 1 contains a compiler directive, #import <Foundation/Foundation.h>. In order for this little program to know about certain other objects (for example, the NSObject on line 3), we need to have the compiler read other interface files. In this case, the *Foundation.h* file defines the objects and interfaces to the **Foundation framework**. This framework contains the definition of most non–user-interface base classes of the iOS and Mac OS X systems. What is important here is that we have a definition to the NSObject object. The actual start of our object is on line 3, as follows.

@interface HelloWorld : NSObject

HelloWorld is the object, but what does : NSObject mean? Well, the colon (:) after our object's name indicates we plan to derive additional functionality from another class. In this case, NSObject is that class. HelloWorld is now a *subclass* of NSObject.

NOTE: Why the name NSObject and not just Object? Well, do you recall that Mac OS X actually started out as a port from the NeXTSTEP system? "NS" is an abbreviation for NeXTSTEP and is used in many of the base objects in Mac OS X and iOS— NSObject, NSString, NSDictionary, etc.

Lines 4 and 5 simply contain the { and } characters. This block is used to define instance variables used by the object, but the HelloWorld class is simple enough that instance variables are not necessary. Later, in Chapter 9, there will be examples where instance variables are defined and used.

Line 7 contains a message definition for this object, as follows.

```
- (void)printGreeting;
```

When you're defining a message, that line must start with either a + or - character. In the case of the `HelloWorld` object, we are using - to indicate this message can be used *after* the object is created. A + character is used for messages that can be used *before* the object is created. The remainder of the message, `(void) printGreeting`, represents the return value of the message. In this case, the value `(void)` is followed by the actual message name, `printGreeting`.

In line 9, `@end` indicates the definition of the object's interface is complete.

That's the complete description of the interface of the `HelloWorld` object; there's not a whole lot here. More complicated objects simply just have more messages and more instance variables.

For the implementation, the source code is stored in a different file, *HelloWord.m*. For starters, line 10 starts with the statement `#import "HelloWorld.h"`. This simply allows our object to know its own interface. While the separation of the interface and implementation files might seem a little odd at first, this convention is very consistent in Objective-C programming. Whenever an object is to be used, simply include its interface. Also, the import indicates `"HelloWorld.h"` in quotation marks, not `<HelloWorld.h>` alone. What's the difference? Quite simply, doing an import of a file in quotation marks (for example, `"HelloWorld.h"`) indicates the compiler is to look in the local project to find the file, whereas the import of `<Foundation/Foundation.h>` indicates to the compiler the file is located in some global area for *all* projects. The easy way to remember is that if you created the file, use the double quotation marks. If not, use the angle brackets (< and >).

Line 12 is the start of the implementation of the object, as follows.

```
@implementation HelloWorld
```

Line 14 is the definition of the object's message, `printGreeting`. It looks identical to the message definition in the interface file. The only difference here is that code is being defined that implements the `printGreeting` message.

Lines 15–17 form the block of code that implements the message `printGreeting`. For this simple message, the function `NSLog` is called. This base-level function simply takes in a formatted `NSString` object and outputs the result to the console. The `NSString` class is an Objective-C class that implements the behavior of a string of characters. Why have a class for this? For one thing, it gives the framework a consistent object for representing a string. Plus, there is a lot of functionality in `NSString` that can be used to manipulate, compare, and convert the actual data.

The `NSString` object is specified here in a shorthand method. The `@"Hello World!"` is a way of quickly declaring an `NSString` object. The at sign (@) is the symbol used to indicate the string specified is an `NSString` object.

Line 19 indicates to the compiler the definition of the implementation section is finished.

But wait, there is more. Now that we have a new Objective-C class defined, how is it used? Following is another piece of code that uses the newly created class, the main program (*myprogram.m*).

```
20    #import "HelloWold.h"
21
22    int main(void)
23    {
24        HelloWorld* myObject = [[HelloWorld alloc] init];
25        [myObject printGreeting];
26
27        [myObject release];
28        return 0;
29    }
```

In this new file, the program first starts by including the *HelloWorld.h* file, which allows this piece of the application access to the HelloWorld object.

In line 22, we have our main function. Remember, every Objective-C program must have a main function.

Line 24 is a complicated one. It defines and **instantiates** the HelloWorld class. You first see the text HelloWorld* myObject. This defines a variable named myObject of the type HelloWorld, which is our new class. The asterisk (*) is used to represent a **pointer to** the object. This notation basically means we don't want the object here; we just want a way to get to it or a pointer to where it is. Think of this like a person who gives you a business card. You have the card, not the actual person. But the business card is a way of getting in touch with the person.

> **NOTE:** Instantiation makes a class a real object in the computer's memory. A class by itself is not really usable until there is an instance of it. Using the SUV example, an SUV means nothing until a factory builds one (instantiates the class). Only then can the SUV be used.

The next part of the line is [[HelloWorld alloc] init]. This is a **nested** call. The innermost bracketed instructions are executed first, so [HelloWorld alloc] is the first message sent. Wait a second; we never defined the message alloc, so how is this going to work? Well, when HelloWorld was defined, it was defined as a subclass of NSObject. Another way to explain this relationship is to say that NSObject is the parent class of HelloWorld. When we send the alloc message to the HelloWorld object, the system knows that HelloWorld doesn't know that particular message, so it automatically passes the message to the parent class; in our case, this is the NSObject class.

Once [HelloWorld alloc] is called, the return value is a pointer to the newly allocated HelloWorld object (**allocation** means we use part of the computer's memory to store something). But we're not done yet. The remaining part of the nested statement, the init message, gets executed next: [[HelloWorld alloc] init]. So now the init message is sent to the new HelloWorld object created by [HelloWorld alloc]. Now, init simply does some base-level initialization of the object. The final return from all this is a pointer to the new object, which is the HelloWorld object.

> **NOTE:** In Objective-C, whenever objects are sent messages, the code must be within square brackets, [and].

Now that we've created a new object, it can be used. Line 25, [myObject printGreeting], puts our object to use. In this piece of code, we use our newly instantiated object by sending it a message, printGreeting. The program will output the text HelloWorld!

Line 27 sends another message to our object, the release message. This message tells the system this program is finished using the object and to release any system resources associated with it.

Line 28 returns the value 0 to the caller of our main function. This indicates a successful execution.

Line 29 ends the code block and the program.

> **NOTE:** Messages can also accept multiple arguments. Consider, for example, [myCarObject switchRadioBandTo:FM andTuneToFrequncy:104.7];. The message here would be switchRadioBandTo:andTuneToFrequency:. After each colon, the argument values are placed when a message is actually sent. You might also notice these messages are named in such a way as to make interpreting what they actually do easy to understand. Using helpful message names is an ideal convention to follow when developing classes because it makes using the classes much more intuitive. Being consistent in naming messages is also critical.

Writing Another Program in Xcode

When you first open Xcode, you'll see the screen shown in Figure 6–1.

Figure 6–1. *Xcode opening screen*

Figure 6–1 shows a great screen to always keep visible at the launch of Xcode. Until you are more comfortable with Xcode, keep the **Show this window when Xcode launches** check box checked. This window allows you to select the most recently created projects, access the developer documentation (that's the **Getting started with Xcode** icon), and quickly link to Apple's developer web site. Regardless of which document set is chosen, all have a wealth of information for both beginning and advanced users.

Creating the Project

We are going to start a new project, so click the **Create a new Xcode project** icon. Whenever you want to start a new iOS or Mac OS X application, library, or anything else, use this icon. Once a project has been started and saved, the project will appear in the Recents list on the right-hand portion of the display.

For this Xcode project, we're going to choose something very simple. Make sure iOS Application is chosen. Then select **Single View Application**, as shown in Figure 6–2. Then simply click on the **Next** button.

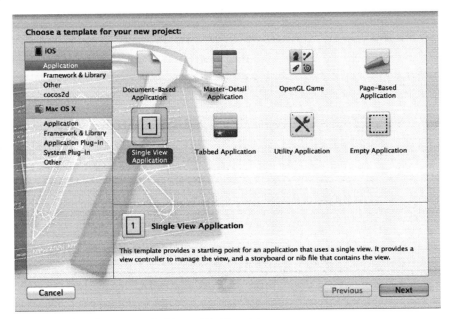

Figure 6–2. *Choosing a new project from a list of templates*

There are several different types of templates. These templates make it easier to start a project from scratch in that they provide a starting point by automatically creating simple source files.

Once the template has been chosen and the **Next** button pressed, Xcode presents us with a dialog box asking for the project's name and some other information, as shown in Figure 6–3. Type the Product Name of **MyFirstApp**. The Company Identifier needs to have some value, so just enter **MyCompany**. Also make sure the **Device Family** selection is set to **iPhone**.

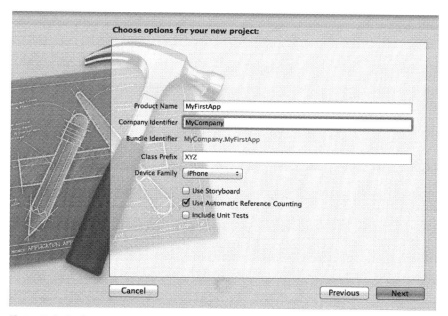

Figure 6–3. *Setting up the product name, company, and type*

The **Include Unit Tests** checkbox can be left as default. In our example, we don't have it checked. For this example, it doesn't matter if it's checked or not. Once all the information has been supplied, click on the **Next** button. Xcode will ask you where to save the project. You can save it any place, but the desktop is a good choice because it's always visible. Also, by default, the **Use Automated Reference Counting** is checked, which is preferable.[1]

---

[1] Chapter 13 covers more about Automated Reference Counting or ARC.

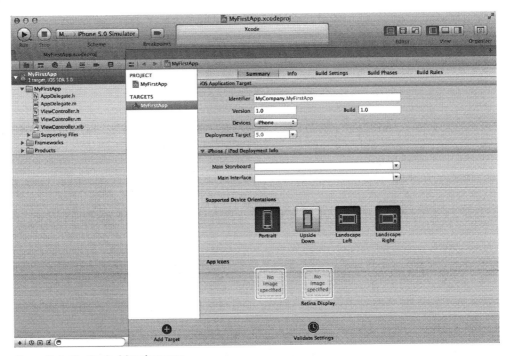

Figure 6–4. *The Xcode 4.0 main screen*

Once the project save location is chosen, the main Xcode screen will be shown. On the leftmost pane is the list of source files. The right-hand two thirds of the screen is dedicated to the context-sensitive editor. Click on a source file and the editor will show the source code. Clicking on a *.xib* (pronounced zib) will show the screen-interface editor.

> **NOTE:** Xcode 4 introduces a completely new environment in a single screen called the *Workspace Window*. For example, In Xcode 3 and earlier, Interface Builder—the system to build an interface—was a stand-alone program. Now, with Xcode 4, simply clicking on an interface file will show the interface within Xcode 4.

Our very first app is going to be very simple. This iPhone app will simply contain a pushbutton. When the button is pushed, your name will appear on the screen. So, let's start by first looking more closely at some of the stub source code that Xcode built for us. The nice thing with Xcode is that it will create a stub application that will execute without any modification. Before we start adding some code, let's look at the main toolbar of Xcode, as shown in Figure 6–5.

Figure 6–5. *The Xcode 4 toolbar*

At first glance, there are three distinct areas of the toolbar. The left area is used to run/debug the application. The middle window displays status as a summary of compiler errors and/or warnings. The far right area contains a series of buttons that customize the editing view.

Figure 6–6. *Close-up of the left portion of the Xcode toolbar*

As shown in Figure 6–6, the left portion of the toolbar contains a *Play* button (similar to iTunes) that will compile and run the application. If the application is running, the *Stop* button will not be grayed out. Since it's grayed out, we know the application is not running. The *Scheme* and *Breakpoints* can be left alone for now. They will be discussed in more detail in Chapter 14.

Figure 6–7. *Close-up of the left portion of the Xcode toolbar*

The right side of the Xcode toolbar contains buttons that change the editor. The three buttons represent the *Standard Editor* (selected), the *Assistant Editor*, and the *Version Editor*. For now, just choose the *Standard Editor*, as shown in Figure 6–7.

Next to the Editor choices are a set of View buttons. These buttons can be toggled on and off. For example, the one chosen in Figure 6–7 represents the current view as shown in Figure 6–4—a list of the program files on the left third of the screen and the main editor on the remaining two thirds. Any combination, or none, can be chosen to help customize the main workspace window. The last button is used to bring up the *Organizer* window. We'll discuss this button more in Chapter 14. For now, let's get back to our first iPhone app.

Figure 6–8. *Looking at the source code in the Xcode editor*

Click once on the *ViewController.h* file, as shown in Figure 6–8. The editor shows some Objective-C code called an *Interface* file. You can tell it's an interface file because of the @interface Objective-C directive on line #11. We'll discuss the importance of the interface file in the next chapter.

NOTE: For now, we're simply going to add a few lines of code and see what they do. It's not expected that you understand what this code means right now. What's important is simply going through the motions to become more familiar with Xcode. Chapter 7 goes into more depth about what makes up an Objective-C program and Chapter 10 goes into more depth about building an iPhone interface.

Next, we're going to add two lines of code into this file, as shown in Figure 6–9. Line #12 defines an iPhone label on the screen where we can put some text. Line #15 tells the compiler this Object can be sent a message called showName:. We'll be calling this method in order to populate the iPhone label. A label is nothing more than an area on the screen where we can put some text information.

CAUTION: Type the code **EXACTLY** as shown in the example. For instance, UILabel can't be uilabel or UILABEL. Objective-C is a case-sensitive language, so UILabel is completely different from uilabel.

```
1  //
2  //  MyFirstAppViewController.h
3  //  MyFirstApp
4  //
5  //  Created by Strider on 9/5/11.
6  //  Copyright (c)
7  //
8
9  #import <UIKit/UIKit.h>
10
11 @interface MyFirstAppViewController : UIViewController {
12     IBOutlet UILabel *nameLabel;
13 }
14
15 -(IBAction)showName:(id)sender;
16
17 @end
18
```

Figure 6–9. *Code added to the ViewController.h interface file*

Next, we're going to add the code to make the message showName: do something. First, click once on the *ViewController.m* file on the left. This file is an *implementation* file. You can tell it's an implementation file because of the @implementation Objective-C directive on line #11, as shown in Figure 6-10.

```
1  //
2  //  MyFirstAppViewController.m
3  //  MyFirstApp
4  //
5  //  Created by Strider on 9/5/11.
6  //  Copyright (c)
7  //
8
9  #import "MyFirstAppViewController.h"
10
11 @implementation MyFirstAppViewController          ⚠ Incomplete implementation
12
13 - (void)didReceiveMemoryWarning
14 {
15     [super didReceiveMemoryWarning];
16     // Release any cached data, images, etc that aren't in use.
17 }
18
```

Figure 6–10. *The ViewController.m implementation file*

Notice there is a warning symbol on line #11. Clicking on the warning will show the warning, Incomplete Implementation, which basically means we've mentioned a new message in the interface file, but it's not to be added to the implementation file. Figure 6-11 is the updated implementation file.

```
1  //
2  //  MyFirstAppViewController.m
3  //  MyFirstApp
4  //
5  //  Created by M.R. Fisher on 4/15/11.
6  //  Copyright 2011 www.committed-code.com. All rights reserved.
7  //
8
9  #import "MyFirstAppViewController.h"
10
11 @implementation MyFirstAppViewController
12
13 - (IBAction)showName:(id)sender {
14     [nameLabel setText:@"My Name is Mitch!"];
15 }
16
17 - (void)dealloc
18 {
19     [super dealloc];
20 }
```

Figure 6–11. *Code added to the ViewController.m implementation file*

Once lines #19–22, as shown in Figure 6-11, have been added, the warning message will disappear. The nice thing with Xcode 4 is that it will report any warnings or errors with the code typed in without first having to try to compile and run the program. This immediate feedback can sometimes be a pain, but it does save time.
We now have the necessary code in place, but we don't yet have an interface on the iPhone. Next, we're going to edit the interface and add two interface objects to our app.

In order to edit the iPhone's interface, we need to click once on the *ViewController.xib* file. The *.xib* file contains all the information about a single window or view. Apps that have multiple views will have multiple *.xib* files. We will use Xcode's interface editor to *connect* a UI object, such as a label, to the code we just created. Connecting is as easy as clicking and dragging.

We're not going to modify the *MainWindow.xib* file. In our example, the *MainWindow.xib* file simply holds our view, the *ViewController.xib* file.

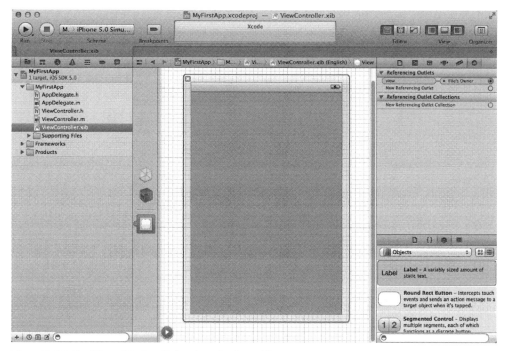

Figure 6–12. *The iPhone interface that we're going to modify*

Note that we've clicked on the last **view button** in the upper right part of the screen, as shown in Figure 6–12. This opens up the utilities view for the interface. Among other things, this utilities view shows us the various interface objects we can use in our App. We're only going to be concerned with the first two: **Round Rect Button** and Label.

The first step is to click once on the **Round Rect Button** from the utilities window. Next, drag the object and drop it on the iPhone view, as shown in Figure 6–13. Don't worry; dragging the object doesn't remove it from the list of objects in the utilities view. Dragging it out will create a new copy of that object on our iPhone interface.

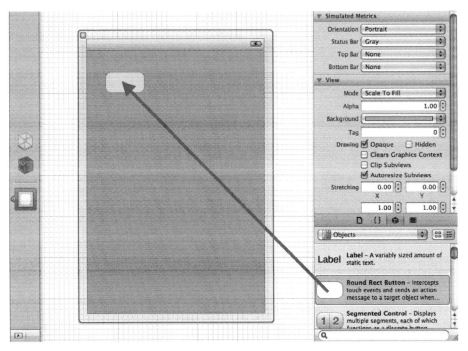

Figure 6–13. *Moving a button object onto the iPhone view*

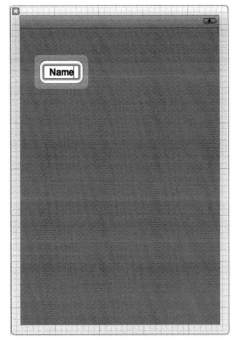

Next, double-click on the Round Rect Button that was just added to the iPhone interface. This allows the title of the button to be changed from nothing to "Name", as shown in Figure 6–14. Many different interface objects work just like this. Simply double-click and the title of the object can be changed. This can also be done in the actual code, but it's much simpler doing it in the interface editor.

Once the title has been changed, drag and drop a Label object and place it right below the button, as shown in Figure 6–15.

Figure 6–14. *Modifying the button's title*

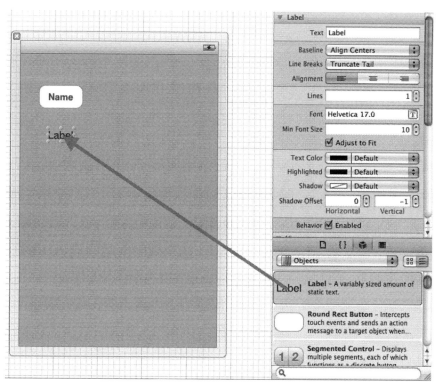

Figure 6–15. *Adding a Label object to our iPhone interface*

For now, we can leave the label's text as "Label" since it makes it easy to find on the interface. If we clear the label's text, the object will still be there, but there is nothing visible to click on in order to select the label. Expand the size of the label by dragging the center blue ball to the right, as shown in Figure 6–16.

Figure 6–16. *Expanding the label's size*

Now that we have both the button and the label, we can actually connect these visual objects to our program. We start by right-mouse clicking on the button control. This brings up a connection menu, as shown in Figure 6–17.

Figure 6–17. *Connection menu for the button object*

Next, we click and drag from the **Touch Up Inside** connection circle to the **File's Owner** icon, as shown in Figure 6–18. **Touch Up Inside** means the user clicked on the *inside* of the button. Dragging the connection to the file's owner (which is the ViewController object) connects the Touch Up Inside event to the ViewController object. What this does is cause our object to be notified whenever the button is pressed.

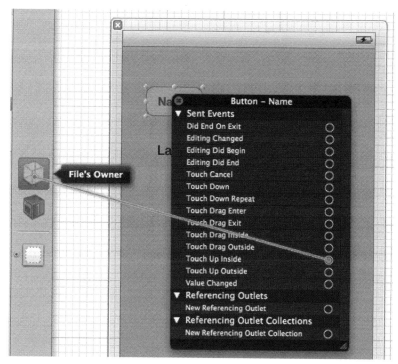

Figure 6–18. *Connecting the Touch Up Inside event to our object*

Once the connection is dropped, a list of methods that can be used in our connection is displayed, as shown in Figure 6–19. In our example, there is only one method and that is the showName: method. Selecting the showName: method connects the Touch Up Inside event to our object.

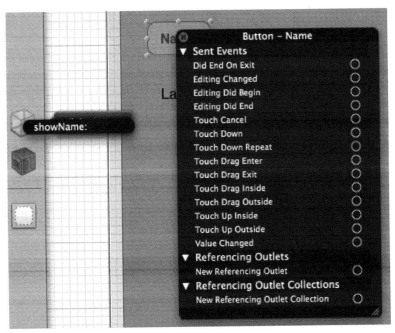

Figure 6–19. *Selecting the method to handle the Touch Up Inside event*

Once the connection has been made, the details are shown on the button's connection menu, as shown in Figure 6–20.

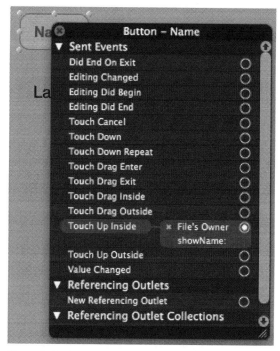

Figure 6–20. *The connection is now complete*

Next, we create a connection for the label object. In this case, we don't care about the label events; instead, we want to connect our `ViewController`'s `nameLabel` outlet to the object on the iPhone interface. This connection basically tells our object that the label we want to set text on is on the iPhone interface.

Start by right-clicking on the label object on the iPhone interface. This brings up the connection menu for the label, as shown in Figure 6–21. There are not as many options for a label object as there were for the button object.

Figure 6–21. *Connection menu for the label object*

As mentioned above, we are not here to connect an event. Instead, we connect what's referred to as a *Referencing Outlet*. This connection connects a screen object to a variable in our `ViewController` object. Just like the button, drag and drop the connection to the File's Owner icon, as shown in Figure 6–22.

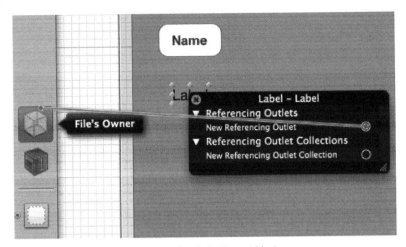

Figure 6–22. *Connecting the Referencing Outlet to our object*

Once the connection is dropped on the file's owner, a list of outlets in our ViewController object will be displayed, as shown in Figure 6–23. Of the two choices, we want to choose nameLabel. This is the name of our variable in our ViewController object we are using.

Figure 6–23. *Selecting our object's variable to complete the connection*

Once nameLabel is chosen, we're ready to run our program. Click on the Run button at the top left corner of the Xcode window (see Figure 6–6). This will automatically save your files and start the application in the iPhone emulator, as shown in Figure 6–24. By

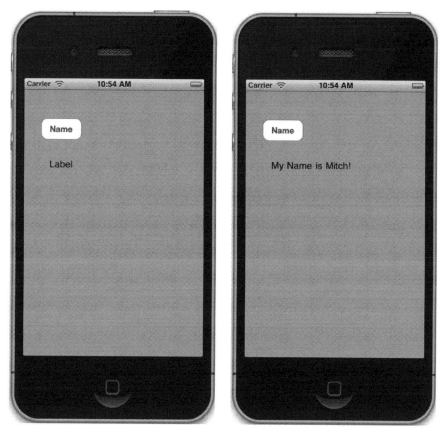

Figure 6–24. *Our app running, before and after the button is pressed*

clicking on the **Name** button, the label's text will change from its default value of "Label" to "My Name is Mitch!" or whatever value you put in. If you want to, go back into the interface and clear the default label text.

Summary

The examples in this chapter were very simple, but hopefully they've whetted your appetite for more complex applications using Objective-C and Xcode. In later chapters, you can expect to learn more about object-oriented programming and more about what Objective-C can do. Pat yourself on the back because you've learned a lot already. Here is a summary of the topics discussed in this chapter:

- the origins and brief history of the Objective-C language,
- some common language symbols used in Objective-C,
- an Objective-C class example,

▧ the @interface and @implementation sections of a program,

▧ using Xcode a bit more, including entering and compiling the *HelloWorld.m* source file, and

▧ connecting visual interface objects with methods and variables in our application object.

Exercises

▧ Clear the default text of "Label" in our program and re-run the example.

▧ Change the size of the label object on the interface to be smaller in width. How does that affect our text message?

▧ Delete the Referencing Outlet connection of the label and re-run the project. What happens?

▧ If you feel you have the hang of this, add a new button and label both to the ViewController object and to the interface. Change it from displaying your name to displaying something else.

Chapter 7

Objective-C Classes, Objects, and Methods

If you haven't already read Chapter 6, please do so before reading this one, because it provides a great introduction to some of the basics of Objective-C. This chapter builds on that foundation a bit more. By the end of this chapter, you can expect to have a greater understanding of the Objective-C language and how to use the basics to write simple programs. For Mitch personally, the best way to learn is to take small programs and write (or rewrite) them in Objective-C just to see how the language works.

This chapter will cover what composes an Objective-C class and how to interact with Objective-C objects via methods. We will use a simple radio station class as an example of how an Objective-C class is written. This will hopefully impart an understanding of how an Objective-C class can be used. This chapter will teach you how to formulate a design for objects that are needed to solve a problem. We'll touch on how to create custom objects, as well as how to use existing objects provided in the Foundation classes.

If you're coming from a C-like language, you'll find that Objective-C shares several similarities. As described in Chapter 6, Objective-C's roots are firmly planted in the C language. This chapter will expand on Chapter 6's topics and incorporate some of the concepts described in Chapter 8.

Creating an Objective-C Class

Chapter 6 introduced some of the common elements of the Objective-C language, so let's quickly review them.

- An Objective-C class is divided into two parts: a class interface and class Implementation.

- @interface: This keyword is used to define an interface to a new Objective-C class. This is written in an .h or header file.

■ **Methods**: These are the blocks of code defined in the @interface
section of a class and implemented in the @implementation section in
an .m file.

■ @implementation: This keyword is used to define the actual code that
implements the methods defined in the interface. This is written in an
.m, or Objective-C class file.

As explained in Chapter 6, an Objective-C class consists of an interface and a
corresponding implementation. For now, let's concentrate on the interface. At the most
basic level, the interface of a class tells you the name of the class, what class it's
derived from, and what **messages** the class understands. Notice that the word
message is used here. To communicate with an Objective-C object, a program will send
the object messages. These messages translate directly to code in the implementation
file—this implementation code is referred to as a method.

Here is a sample of the first line from a class's interface:

@interface RadioStation : NSObject

Here, the class name is RadioStation. The colon (:) after the class name indicates that
the class is derived from another class; that is, the RadioStation object **inherits**
functionality from the NSObject class. Put another way, in our example shown in
Listing 7–1, the RadioStation class is derived from the NSObject class.

> **TIP:** If your object is not inheriting from any other foundation class, *always* inherit from
> NSObject; without it, your class will be worthless. NSObject provides the base functions that
> make new objects behave correctly. NSObject is the base class for all foundation classes. So,
> inheriting from any foundation class is also fine.

Once the class name is defined, the rest of the interface file contains the main
components of the class (see Listing 7–1).

Listing 7–1. *An Interface File:* `RadioStation.h`

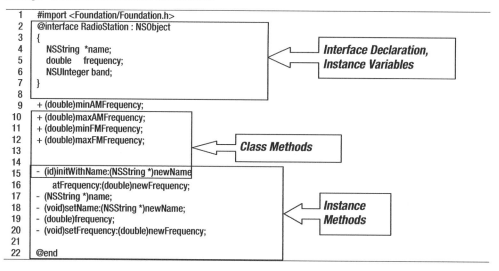

```
1    #import <Foundation/Foundation.h>
2    @interface RadioStation : NSObject
3    {
4        NSString *name;
5        double    frequency;
6        NSUInteger band;
7    }
8
9    + (double)minAMFrequency;
10   + (double)maxAMFrequency;
11   + (double)minFMFrequency;
12   + (double)maxFMFrequency;
13
14
15   - (id)initWithName:(NSString *)newName
16         atFrequency:(double)newFrequency;
17   - (NSString *)name;
18   - (void)setName:(NSString *)newName;
19   - (double)frequency;
20   - (void)setFrequency:(double)newFrequency;
21
22   @end
```

Interface Declaration, Instance Variables

Class Methods

Instance Methods

Declaring Interfaces and Instance Variables

An Objective-C class is defined by its **interface**. Since objects, for the most part, are communicated with using messages, the interface of an object defines what messages the object will respond to. Line #1 imports the Foundation class definitions (more on that in a bit). Lines 2–7 start the definition of the class's interface by defining its name (sometimes called the **type**) and the inherited class. Next, there is a block, defined within the braces ({ }). This block is used to define variables that are used by the *instance* of this class. These are called **instance variables**.

Whenever the RadioStation class is instantiated, the resulting RadioStation object has access to these variables, which are only for specific instances. If there are ten RadioStation objects, each object has its own variables independent of the other objects. This is also referred to as **scope**, in that the object's variables are within the scope of each object.

Sending Messages (Methods)

Every object has methods. In Objective-C, the common concept to interact with an object is sending an object a message:

```
[myStation frequency];
```

The preceding line will send a message to an instance of the RadioStation class named myStation. In our example, myStation is referred to as the **receiver**, since it receives the message. The message (frequency in our preceding example) is used to select which method will be called within the object. These method names that appear in a message, like the preceding one, are called **selectors**. Since a message selects the method based on the name, for all practical purposes, a message and a method name are synonymous.

If a class does not understand a message, that message is passed to the parent object; in this case, NSObject. If that parent object doesn't understand the message, the message is passed to its parent, and so on, until the message is either found or not. This behavior is called **dynamic binding**, which means the method is found at runtime instead of compile time. Dynamic binding allows an Objective-C program to react to changes while the program is running—this is one of the huge advantages Objective-C has over other languages.

Messages can also have parameters passed along with them. Why pass parameters? Parameters are passed for several reasons. First (and most common), the range of possibilities is too large to write as separate methods. Second, the data you need to store in your object is variable—like a radio station's name. In the following example, you will see that it won't be practical to write a method for each and every possible radio frequency; so instead, the frequency is passed as a parameter. The same applies to the station name.

```
[myStation setFrequency: 104.7];
```

The message is setFrequency:. The colon indicates that the message needs a parameter. Messages can have several parameters, as the following example illustrates:

```
myStation = [[RationStation alloc] initWithName:@"KZZP" atFrequency: 104.7];
```

The message we're interested in is

```
initWithName:atFrequency:
```

It's important to understand the message and how it's structured, especially once you actually implement the code. In your code, you'll need to make sure you implement the initWithName:atFrequency: method; otherwise, the program won't work.

In the preceding example, the message consists of two parameters: the station name and its frequency. What's interesting about Objective-C relative to other languages is that the methods are essentially named parameters. If this were a C++ or Java program, the call would be

```
myObject = New RadioStation("KZZP", 104.7);
```

While a RadioStation object's parameters might seem obvious, having named parameters can be a bonus, because they more or less state what the parameters are used for or what they do. Here are some examples:

```
[NSDictionary dictionaryWithContentsOfFile: filename];
[myString characterAtIndex: 1];
[myViewController willRotateToInterfaceOrientation: portrait duration: 60];
```

Using Class Methods

A class doesn't have to be instantiated to be used. In some cases, classes have methods that can actually perform some simple operations and return values. These methods are called **class methods**. In Listing 7–1, the method names that start with a plus sign (+) are class methods—all class methods must start with a + sign.

Class methods have limitations. One of their biggest limitations is that none of the instance variables can be used. Well, technically, Xcode allows instance variables to be coded in a class method. The code will compile with a warning, but accessing or using the instance variable does nothing—just don't do it. Being unable to use instance variables makes sense since we haven't instantiated anything. A class method can have its own local variables within the method itself, but can't use any of the variables defined as instance variables.

A call to a class method would look like this:

```
[RadioStation minAMFrequency];
```

Notice that the call is very similar to how a message is passed to an instantiated object. The big difference is that instead of an instance variable, the *class name* itself is used. Class methods are used quite extensively in the Mac OS X and iOS frameworks. They are used mostly for returning some fixed or well-known type of value, or to return a new instance of an object. These types of class methods are sometimes referred to as **factory methods**, since, like factories, they create something new; in this case, a new instance of a class. Here's a factory method example:

```
1.  [NSDate timeIntervalSinceReferenceDate]; // Returns a number
2.  [NSString stringWithFormat:@"%d", 1000]; // Returns a new NSString object
3.  [NSDictionary alloc];              // Returns a new uninitialized NSDictionary
    object.
```

All of the preceding messages are class methods being called.

Line 1 simply returns a value that represents the number of seconds since January 1, 2001, which is the reference date.

Line 2 returns a new NSString object that has been formatted and has a value of 1000.

Line 3 is a form that is very commonly used because it actually allocates a new object. Typically, the line is not used by itself, but in a line, like this:

```
myDict = [[NSDictionary alloc] init];
```

The preceding call is a **compound call**. The [NSDictionary alloc] class method returns a new NSDictionary object. The init message is then sent to the NSDictionary Object, which is used within a class to initialize itself (e.g., setting up instance variables). The init function then returns the new object back to the caller.

So when would you use a class method? As a general rule, if the method returns information that is NOT specific to any particular instance of the class, make the method a class method. For example, the minAMFrequency in the preceding example would be the same for ALL instances of any RadioStation object—this is a great candidate for a class method. However, the station's name or its assigned frequency would be different for each instance of the class. These should not (and indeed could not) be class methods. The reason for this is that class methods cannot use any of the instance variables defined by the class.

Using Instance Methods

Instance methods (lines 15–20 in Listing 7–1) are methods that are only available once a class has been instantiated; for example:

```
1   RadioStation *myStation;                // This declares a variable to hold the RadioStation Object.
2   myStation = [[RadioStation alloc] init]; // This creates a new object and puts it in my variable.
3   [myStation setFrequency: 104.7];         // This sets the frequency of the myStation object.
4   double f = [myStation frequency]         // This instance method returns the current frequency.
```

Lines 3 and 4 send a message to the RadioStation object; line 3 calls the method to set the frequency and line 4 retrieves it. The frequency is stored with the object in the frequency instance variable. Furthermore, instance methods have access to the instance variables defined in the **interface declaration** section of the class. All instance methods must start with a hyphen (-); this easily distinguishes them from class methods, which use a plus (+) sign.

Working with the Implementation File

Now that you've seen what an interface file looks like, let's take a look at the **implementation file**. First, the interface file had an .h extension; RadioStation.h, for example. The implementation file has an .m extension—like RadioStation.m—as shown in Listing 7–2.

Another important thing to note is that the interface and implementation files have the same name (excluding the extension). This convention is used universally: while there is nothing preventing an interface and an implementation file from having different names, having different names can cause much confusion, and tools like Xcode won't work as well. For example, the Xcode key sequence Control + Command + up-arrow (^ + ⌘ + ⬆) moves between implementation and interface files, and it will not work if the two file names are not the same.

Listing 7–2. *Part of Your Implementation File*

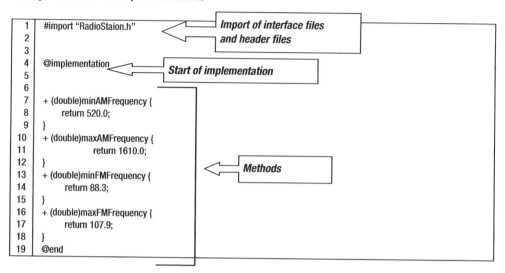

When Xcode creates a class, it creates a very rudimentary stub of an implementation file. Listing 7–2 starts with the #import statement to your interface file. The #import statement reads in your interface file for the class. As the compiler goes through your implementation (.m) file, it needs to know what class it's implementing, and the interface file provides all the information that it needs.

An #import statement tells the compiler to read in the specified file, because the compiler needs to know about certain predefined things. For example, in your interface file, the RadioStation class is a subclass of NSObject. The NSObject class needs to be defined for the program to compile successfully. All of these objects are part of the iOS Framework and are included via line #1 in the interface file from Listing 7–1.

```
#import <Foundation/Foundation.h>
```

> **NOTE:** Look at the #import statements: one uses angle brackets ($<$ $>$) and the other uses plain double quotation marks (" "). The difference is that a file in the angle brackets indicates a system-level file, which is located using a predefined path that Xcode automatically sets up for your project. Any file that has double quotation marks is searched for in the current project. In our example, the RadioStation.h interface file is part of our project, so we use double quotation marks, whereas the Cocoa.h file is a system file and uses the angle brackets.

Coding Your Methods

Listing 7–2 is a very simple example, but it demonstrates what many methods look like in a class. First of all, if you look at the implementation and interface files for one of the class methods, you can see the similarities. The following line is from the interface file:

```
+ (double)minAMFrequency;
```

As you can see, it's a class method because it starts with a (+). The next item (`double`) is the type of value the method will return; in this case, a double. The next part in the interface file is simply the name of the method, `minAMFrequency`.

The following line is from the implementation file:

```
+ (double)minAMFrequency {
        return 520.0;
}
```

This line represents an implementation of the method defined in the interface. The word "implementation" indicates that the function is coded here. It looks almost identical to the interface file, but now contains a block with some code, rather than simply ending with a semicolon.

In the preceding example, the implementation of the `minAMFrequency` class method simply performs a return of a numeric value (a double) of 520.0.

Generally, a class has a definition of a method in an interface file and the actual code of the method in an implementation file.

Now, we will look at the implementation of an **instance method** (see Listing 7–3). There are some significant differences between an instance and a class method; for one, instance methods have the option to use the instance variables defined in the interface file. Also, instance methods are only available once the class has been instantiated.

Listing 7–3. *The Implementation of an Instance Method*

```
1   - (id)initWithName:(NSString *)newName atFrequency:(double)newFrequency {
2       self = [super init];
3       if (self != nil) {
4           name = newName;
5           frequency = newFrequency;
6       }
7
8       return self;
9   }
```

Listing 7–3 illustrates the implementation of one of the instance methods of your radio station class. An initialization method accepts a new station name and frequency. Many OS X and iOS classes have similar initialization instance methods. Instead of simply initializing the class and then individually setting various values, many class initialization methods allow special initialization methods, or, in this case, multiple values to be passed on initialization.

In the preceding example, line 1 is the interface of your method, and it contains two parameters: newName and newFrequency. To use this method, the caller would simply do the following:

```
RadioStation myStation = [[RadioStation alloc] initWithName:@"WOW FM"
                                            atFrequency: 102.5];
```

This method is also defined to return an id value. An id is a generic object, and all Objective-C objects are of the type 'id', just like the class RadioStation is an object. Now, let's look at the rest of the implementation.

Line 2 references two special variables that you don't have to define anywhere. The keyword self is used to mean "this instance of this class," so line 2 is assigning "this instance of this class"—the value returned from the use of the second special variable: super init. The keyword super is short for "superclass," which can be thought of as "the parent of this class." Any initialization type of method will typically start with something that looks similar to line 2.

Why is line 2 even necessary? Well, if you have an object that is derived from another object (remember, the class is expressed as RadioStation : NSObject), you must tell the parent object to initialize itself. The parent will do the same by telling its parent to initialize itself, and so on, until the topmost object is reached. If another class used yours as a parent, your code would also have to eventually get an init call so RadioStation could be initialized. This is standard issue in the real world of Objective-C. A class needs to tell its parent to initialize when the class is created, and it needs to tell its parent to de-allocate itself whenever the class is going away.

Line 3 checks to see whether the [super init] call worked. If it worked, the value of self would be something other than nil, which is a value that effectively means "not initialized."

Lines 4 and 5 set up the instance variables of this class to the values passed into this method.

Line 8 returns `self` to the caller. Just like the call to [`super init`], your initialization function needs to return the new object back to the caller.

Using Your New Class

You've created a simple `RadioStation` class, but by itself, it doesn't accomplish a whole lot. In this section, you will create the `Radio` class and have it maintain a list of `RadioStation` classes.

Creating Your Project

Let's start up Xcode (see Figure 7–1) and create a new project named RadioStations.

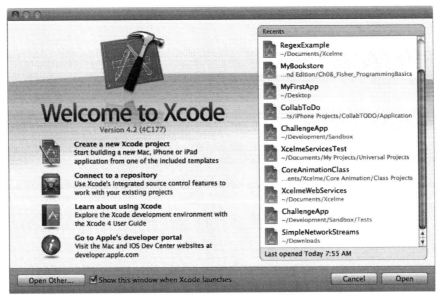

Figure 7–1. *Open Xcode so you can create a new project.*

1. Make sure you choose an iOS application and select the **Single View Application** template, as shown in Figure 7–2.

2. Once you've selected the template, click the **Next** button.

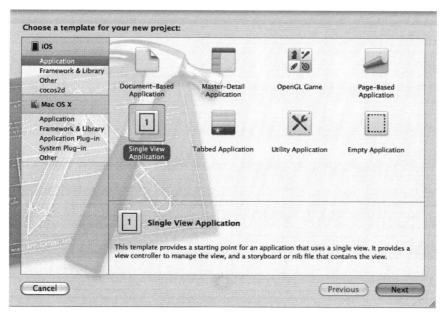

Choose a template for your new project:

iOS
Application
Framework & Library
Other
cocos2d

Mac OS X
Application
Framework & Library
Application Plug-in
System Plug-in
Other

Document-Based Application   Master-Detail Application   OpenGL Game   Page-Based Application

Single View Application   Tabbed Application   Utility Application   Empty Application

1   Single View Application

This template provides a starting point for an application that uses a single view. It provides a view controller to manage the view, and a storyboard or nib file that contains the view.

Cancel   Previous   Next

Figure 7–2. *Selecting a template in the new project window*

3. Next, set the Product Name (Application name) to RadioStations.

4. Set the Company Identifier (a pretend company will do) and set the Device Family to iPhone (as shown in Figure 7–3). Also, make sure that "Use Automatic Reference Counting" is checked.

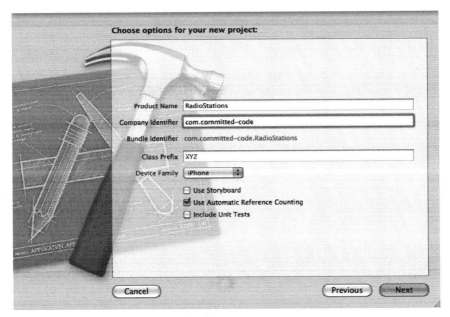

Figure 7–3. *Naming the new iPhone application*

5. Click the **Next button** and Xcode will ask you where you want to save your new project. You can save the project on your Desktop or anywhere in your Home folder. I like the Desktop because it's easy to spot. Once you've made your choice, simply click the **Create** button.

6. Once the **Create** button has been clicked, the Xcode Workspace Window should be visible, as shown in Figure 7–4.

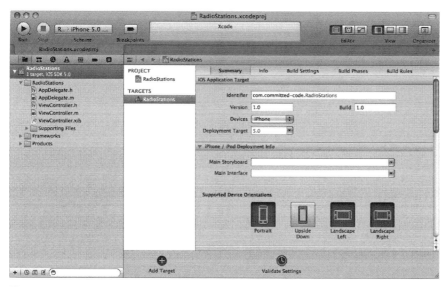

Figure 7–4. *The Workspace Window in Xcode*

Adding Objects

Now, you can add your new objects.

1. First, create your RadioStation object. Right-click the **RadioStations** group folder and select **New File...** (as shown in Figure 7–5).

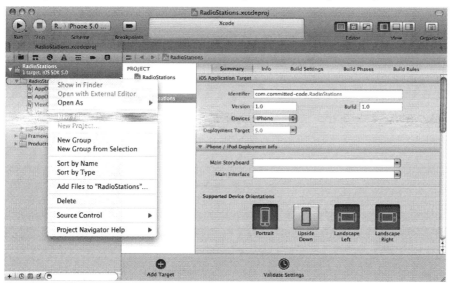

Figure 7–5. *Adding a new file*

2. The next screen, shown in Figure 7–6, asks for the new file type. Simply choose **Objective-C class** from the Cocoa Touch group, and then click **Next**.

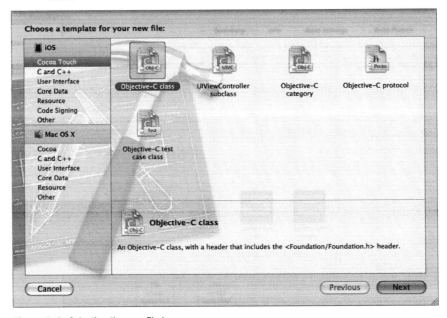

Figure 7–6. *Selecting the new file type*

3. On the next screen, enter "RadioStation" as the class and select **NSObject** as the "Subclass Of." This means that your new class will be a subclass of NSObject, as shown in Figure 7–7.

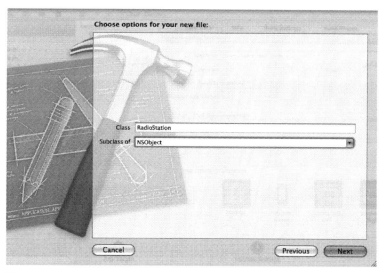

Figure 7–7. *Choosing your new object's subclass*

4. The next screen asks you where to create the files. Simply click the
    Create button, since the location in which Xcode chooses to save the
    files is within the current project, as shown in Figure 7–8.

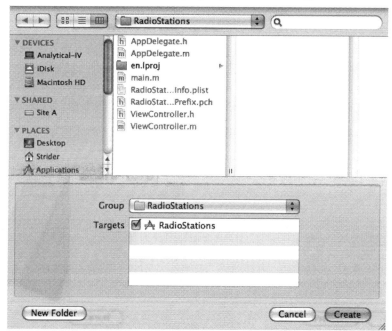

Figure 7–8. *Choosing where to create your new files*

5.   Your project window should now look like Figure 7–9. Click the
     RadioStation.h file. Notice that the stub of your new RadioStation
     class is already present. Now, fill in the empty class so it looks like
     Listing 7–1, your RadioStation interface file.

Figure 7–9. *Your newly created file in the workspace window*

Writing the Implementation File

The RadioStation.h file now defines the instance variables, class methods, and instance
methods of your new class. Let's move on to the implementation file.

1.   The implementation file you'll use here has been simplified a bit from our
     example several pages ago, but will work perfectly for our radio station
     simulation. Click the RadioStation.m file, and put code to your class, as
     shown in Listing 7–4.

Listing 7–4. *The RadioStation Implementation File*

```
1   #import "RadioStation.h"
2
3   @implementation RadioStation
4
5   + (double)minAMFrequency {
6       return 520.0;
7   }
8   + (double)maxAMFrequency {
9       return 1610.0;
10  }
11  + (double)minFMFrequency {
12      return 88.3;
13  }
14  + (double)maxFMFrequency {
15      return 107.9;
16  }
17
18  - (id)initWithName:(NSString *)newName atFrequency:(double)newFrequency {
19      self = [super init];
20      if (self != nil) {
21          name = newName;
22          frequency = newFrequency;
23      }
24
25      return self;
26  }
27
28  - (NSString *)name {
29      return name;
30  }
31
32  - (void)setName:(NSString *)newName {
33      name = newName;
34  }
35
36  - (double)frequency {
37      return frequency;
38  }
39
40  - (void)setFrequency:(double)newFrequency {
41      frequency = newFrequency;
42  }
43
44  @end
```

2. We will come back to a few items in Listing 7–4 and explain them further
    in a moment; however, with the RadioStation class defined, you can
    now write the code that will actually use it.

3. First, click on the ViewController.h file. You'll need to define a few
    instance variables for this class to use, as shown in Listing 7–5.

Listing 7–5. *The Updated ViewController.h Interface File*

```
1   #import <UIKit/UIKit.h>
2
3   @class RadioStation;
4
5   @interface ViewController : UIViewController
6   {
7       RadioStation *myStation;
8       IBOutlet UILabel* stationName;
9       IBOutlet UILabel* stationFrequency;
10      IBOutlet UILabel* stationBand;
11  }
12
13  @end
```

On Line #3, you'll add what's called a *forward declaration*. This basically tells the compiler that you'll be using a class that you've not defined yet, called RadioStation. You'll be importing your header file eventually, but not here—that's why you need this forward declaration now.

Lines #6–8 define some new instance variables. Line #8 is your RadioStation object. Lines #9–11 are going to be used by your iOS interface to show some values on the screen (more on these later). Also, don't forget to include the curly braces ({ … }). Since the original AppDelegate didn't have any instance variables declared, there was no need for the braces.

4. Next, from the main project window, click the ViewController.m file. Listing 7–5 shows the top portion of the ViewController.m file. The following method is called whenever the view is loaded into memory:

    viewDidLoad

    You'll start by putting some of your initialization code here.

Listing 7–5. *Allocating Your RadioStation Object*

```
1   #import "ViewController.h"
2   #import "RadioStation.h"
3
4   @implementation ViewController
5
6   - (void)didReceiveMemoryWarning
7   {
8       [super didReceiveMemoryWarning];
9       // Release any cached data, images, etc. that aren't in use.
10  }
11
12  #pragma mark - View lifecycle
13
14  - (void)viewDidLoad
15  {
16      [super viewDidLoad];
17          // Do any additional setup after loading the view, typically from a nib.
18      myStation = [[RadioStation alloc] initWithName:@"STAR 94"
19                                                          atFrequency:94.1];
20
21  }
```

Line #2 is the import statement that imports your RadioStation Object.

Lines #18 and 19 allocate a new RadioStation object and store it into your new instance variable, myStation.

Creating the User Interface

Next, the main window has to be set up in order to display your station information.

1. To start off, click the *ViewController.xib* file, as shown in Figure 7–10. This file is the main iPhone screen.

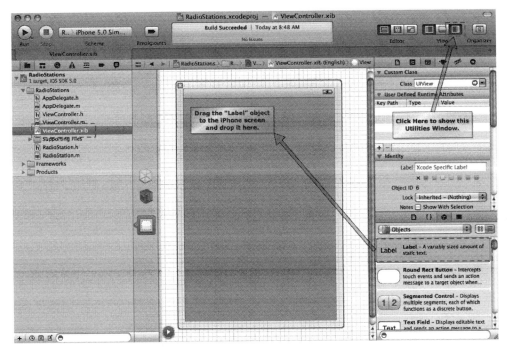

Figure 7–10. *Adding a Label object to your iPhone screen*

2. Drag and drop three Label objects onto the screen, as shown in Figure 7–11. The labels can be aligned in any manner, or as shown in Figure 7–11.

3. You're going to need space, however. Once the Label objects are on the iPhone screen, double-click the Label object in order to change its text so that the iPhone screen looks something like Figure 7–11.

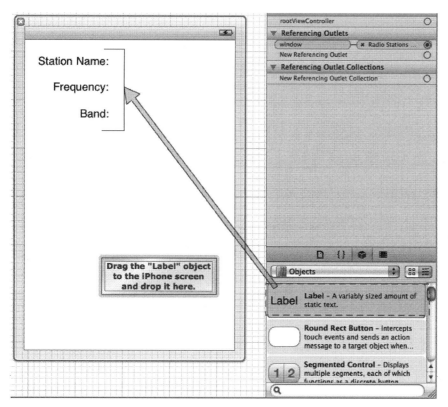

Figure 7–11. *All three labels on the iPhone screen*

4. Next, add a Round Rect Button object to the screen, as show in Figure 7–12. This button, when pressed, will cause the screen to be updated with your radio station information.

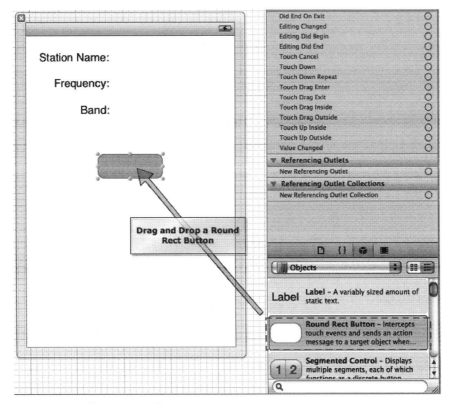

Figure 7–12. *Adding a button to the screen*

5. Just like the Label object, simply double-click the Round Rect Button object in order change its Title to **My Station**.

6. Next, you need to add the Label fields that will hold the Radio Station information. These fields are situated just after the existing labels, as shown in Figure 7–13. Once the label is placed, it needs to be re-sized so that it extends to the edge of the iPhone screen.

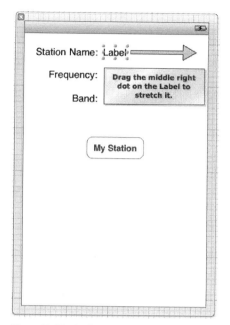

Figure 7–13. *Adding another Label object*

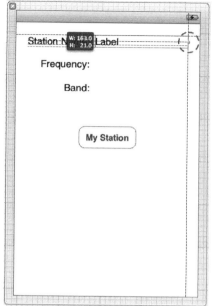

Figure 7–14. *Stretching the Label object*

NOTE: Stretching the Label object allows the Label's text to contain a reasonably long string. If you **didn't** have a sized label, the text would either be cut off (since it wouldn't fit), or the font size would get smaller[1].

7. Repeat adding and sizing a Label object next to the existing Frequency and Band Labels, as shown in Figure 7–15. It's OK to leave the default text of the Label set to *"Label"* for now.

---

[1] By using either code or the Interface Builder, you can customize how the Label object reacts to text that is too large to fit. The behavior described is based upon typical defaults for the Label object.

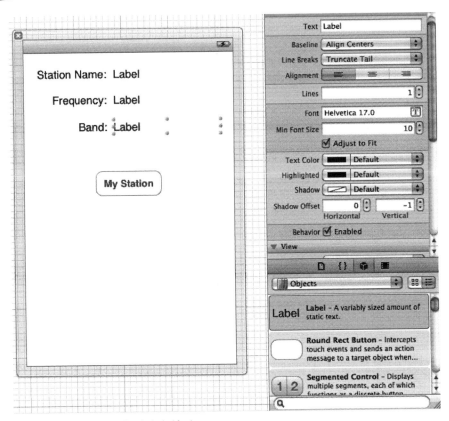

Figure 7–15. *Adding another Label object*

Hooking Up the Code

Now that all the user interface objects are in place, you can begin to hook up these interface elements to the variables in your program. As you saw in Chapter 6, you do this by *connecting* the user interface objects with the objects in your program.

1. Start by connecting the label by Station Name to your variable, as shown in Figure 7–16. Right-click the Label object *next* to the "Station Name:" label to bring up the Connection Window.

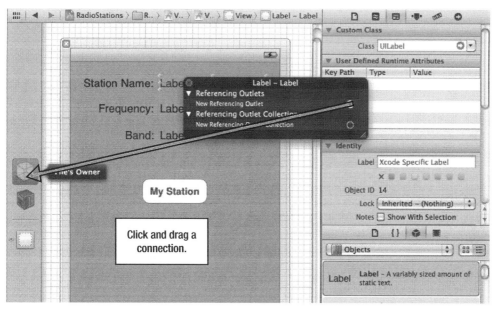

Figure 7–16. *Creating a connection*

2. When the connection is dropped on the "File's Owner" icon, another small menu will be shown. Click the instance variable name that you want to display in this label—in this case, you want the `stationName` instance variable, as shown in Figure 7–17.

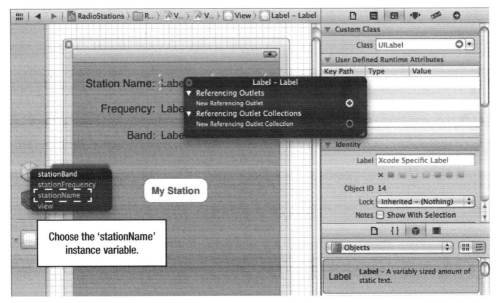

Figure 7–17. *Connecting the interface Label to your stationName instance variable*

3. Now, the interface Label object is *connected* to the `stationName` instance variable. Whenever you set the instance variable's value, the screen will also be updated. **Repeat the above connection steps for the Frequency and Band labels.**

Next, you need to connect the button to your code; but, before you can do that, you need to add some code to handle the actual button-click, as shown in Listing 7–7. Add this code to the bottom of the ViewController.m file.

Listing 7–7. *Creating the buttonClick Function*

```
1   - (IBAction)buttonClick:(id)sender {
2       [stationName setText:[myStation name]];
3       [stationFrequency setText:[NSString stringWithFormat:@"%.1f",
4                                          [myStation frequency]]];
5
6       if (([myStation frequency] >= [RadioStation minFMFrequency]) &&
7           ([myStation frequency] <= [RadioStation maxFMFrequency])) {
8           [stationBand setText:@"FM"];
9       } else {
10          [stationBand setText:@"AM"];
11      }
12  }
```

Listing 7–7 is a method that you will set up to be called whenever the button on the iPhone screen is pressed. First, on line #1, you'll notice the `IBAction` type. This lets Xcode know that this method can be called as a result of an action. So, when you go to connect an action to your application, you will see this method.

Line #2 and Line #3 both set the text fields to the values found in your RadioStation class.

```
[stationName setText:[myStation name]]
```

The stationName variable is what you just connected to the user interface Label object, and [myStation name] is used to return the name of the station.

Line #3 effectively does the same thing as line #2, but you have to first convert the double value (the station's frequency) to an NSString. The "@"%.1f" means that you convert a floating point value and should only see one digit after the decimal point.

Lines #6–11 make use of both your instance variables and your class methods of the RadioStation class. Here, you simply check to see if the frequency of the radio station is between minFMFrequency and maxFMFrequency. If so, the station is an FM station; otherwise, assume it's the AM band. Lines #8 and #10 will show the band value on the screen.

You also need to make sure that your interface file contains the new method that you just coded. As shown in Listing 7–8, simply add the following line **before** the @end in the ViewController.h file:

Listing 7–7.

```
1   - (IBAction)buttonClick:(id)sender;
2   @end
3
```

Now you can connect your Button on the iPhone screen to the newly created method, as shown in Figure 7–18.

1. Right-click the Button to bring up the connection window.

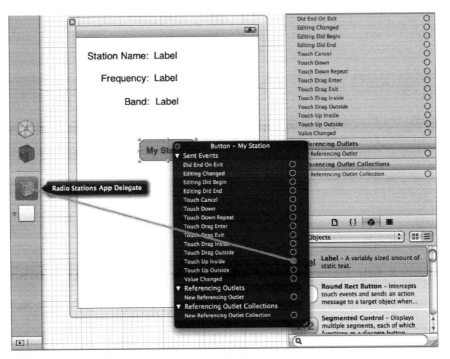

Figure 7–18. *Connecting an event to your new method*

2. As you did for the Label objects, drag a connection from the ***Touch Up Inside*** event and drop it on the Radio Station App Delegate. This will bring up the IBAction method you just created in Listing 7–7.

3. Simply choose **buttonClick:** (as shown in Figure 7–19). This will connect the Touch Up Inside event to your action, which will then set the Label text values to your Radio Station.

> **TIP:** The "Round Rect Button" sends the Touch Up Inside event whenever a user touches the *inside* of the button and then releases—not until the user lifts his or her finger does the event actually get sent.

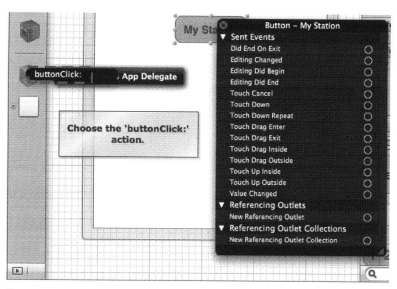

Figure 7–19. *Choosing an action to connect to the Touch Up Inside event*

Running the Program

Once the connection has been made, you're ready to run and test your program! To do this, simply click the **Run** button at the top-left of the Xcode window, as shown in Figure 7–20.

Figure 7–20. *Running your program*

If there are no compile errors, the iPhone emulator should come up and you should see your application. Simply click the "My Station" button and the radio station information will be displayed, as shown in Figure 7–21.

Figure 7–21. *Showing your Radio Station information*

If things don't quite look or work right, retrace your steps and make sure all the code and connections are in place as described above.

Taking Class Methods to the Next Level

In your program, you've not taken advantage of all the class methods for RadioStation, but this chapter does describe what a class method is and how it is used. Use that knowledge to try a few of the exercises mentioned at the end of this chapter. Just play around with this simple working program by adding or changing class or instance methods to get an idea of how they work.

Accessing the Xcode Documentation

We cannot emphasize enough the wealth of information provided in the Xcode **Developer Documentation** dialog. When Xcode is opened, the **Help** menu will appear in the main menu (see Figure 7–10). This is where the Developer Documentation window can be opened.

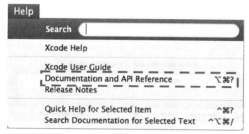

Figure 7–22. *The Xcode help menu*

Once opened, the search window can be used to look up any of the classes we've used in this chapter, including the NSString class documentation, as shown in Figure 7–23.

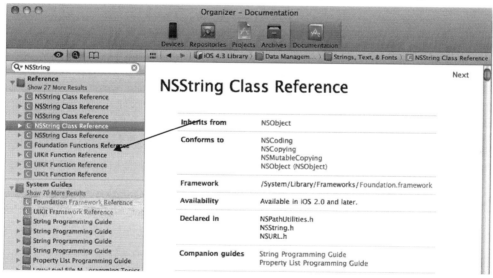

Figure 7–23. *The developer documentation window*

There are several different things to discover about the NSString class shown in Figure 7–23. Go through the documentation and the various companion guides that Apple provides. This will give you a more thorough understanding of the various classes and the various methods supported by them.

Summary

Here we are at the end of another chapter. Once again, congratulate yourself for being able to single-handedly stuff your brain with a lot of information! Here is a summary of what was covered in this chapter:

- Objective-C classes review
- Interface files
  - Instance variables
  - Class methods
  - Instance methods
- Implementation files
  - Defining the method's interface in the interface file and putting code to that interface in the implementation file
  - Limitations of using class methods vs. instance methods
  - Initializing the class and making use of the instance variables
- Making use of your new RadioStation object
  - Building an iPhone App that uses your new object
  - Connecting interface classes to instance variables
  - Connecting user interface events to methods in your class.

Exercises

- Change the code that creates your RadioStation class and make the station's name much longer than what can appear on the screen. What happens?
- Modify the RadioStation class using the instance variable that will indicate whether the station is AM or FM (hint: you'll need to change the initWithName:Frequency: method to accept a new parameter for the radio band).
- Change the current button and add a new button. Label the buttons FM and AM. If the user clicks on the FM button, show an FM station. If the user clicks on the AM button, display an AM station (hint: you'll need to add a second RadioStation object to the RadioStationsAppDelegate.h interface file).
- Clean up the interface a little by making sure that the user doesn't see the text "Label" when the iPhone application first starts.

▨ Fix the issue by using the interface tool.

▨ How could you fix this by adding code to the application instead?

▨ Add more validation to the `(IBAction)buttonClick:(id)sender` method. Right now, it validates FM ranges but not AM ranges. Fix the code so that it also validates an AM range.

▨ If the Radio Station frequency is out of bounds, use the existing labels to display some type of error message.

Chapter 8

Programming Basics in Objective-C

Objective-C is a very elegant language. It mixes the efficiency of the C language with the object-oriented goodness of Smalltalk. This combination was introduced in the mid-1980s and is still powering the fantastic applications behind the iPhone, iPad, and Mac OS X. How does a language that is over 20 years old stay relevant and useful after all of that time? Well, some of its success has to do with the fact that the two languages that make up Objective-C are very well tested and very well designed. Another reason is less obvious; the various frameworks available for the iPhone and Mac OS X make developing full-featured applications much easier. These frameworks benefit from the fact that they have been around awhile, which equates to stability and high functionality. Lastly, Objective-C is highly dynamic. While we won't be focusing on that particular feature in this chapter, the dynamic nature of Objective-C provides a flexibility not found in many compiled languages. With all of these great features, Objective-C and the corresponding frameworks provide an excellent palette from which to create a masterpiece!

This chapter will introduce some of the more common concepts of Objective-C, such as properties and collection classes. This chapter will also show how properties and instance variables are used from within Xcode when dealing with user-interface elements. This sounds like a lot to accomplish, but Objective-C, the Foundation framework, and the Xcode tool provide a wealth of objects and methods and a way to build applications with ease.

Collections

Understanding collections is a fundamental part of learning Objective-C. In fact, collection objects are fundamental constructs of nearly every modern object–oriented language library—sometimes they are referred to as **containers**. Simply put, a collection is a type of class that can hold and manage other objects. The whole purpose of a collection is that it provides a common way to store and retrieve objects efficiently.

There are several different types of collections. While they all fulfill the same purpose of being able to hold other objects, they differ mostly in the way objects are retrieved. Here is a list of the most common collections used in Objective-C:

- NSSet
- NSArray
- NSDictionary
- NSMutableSet
- NSMutableArray
- NSMutableDictionary

Notice that, among the three collection classes listed, there is one that contains the word `Mutable`. A mutable (vs. non-mutable) class is one that can have items added and removed from it after the collection has been created. Mutable means that it can be modified. Non-mutable collections must be initialized with all of their values when they are first created and, thereafter, cannot be modified.

Using NSSet

The `NSSet` class is used to store an unordered list of objects. *Unordered* means exactly that—the objects are stored in the set without regard to order. The advantage of the `NSSet` is performance—it's the fastest collection class available. Use `NSSet` when it is necessary to store a collection of objects and the order in which they are stored or retrieved is not crucial.

Here is a typical NSSet initialization method:

```
NSSet *mySet = [NSSet setWithObjects:@"String 1", @"String 2", @"Whatever", nil];
```

As you can see, the set is initialized with a list of objects, in this case a list of strings. The last object must be `nil` to indicate the end of the list of objects. Also, the example uses strings, but an `NSSet` can be comprised of any object or even different types of objects, including objects from other collections!

> **TIP:** All collection classes have the ability to store and manage any type of object at once. However, in typical cases, most programmers tend to store a single type of object in any one particular collection class to make the code less complicated.

In order to go after data in the `NSSet`, a few typical methods of accessing the elements within an `NSSet` are used.One method, as shown in Listing 8–1, is to use what is referred to as a *fast enumerator* and retrieve each object one by one. Note that the fast enumeration below (lines #3–5) works on all collection classes.

Listing 8–1. *Iterating through an NSSet via an enumerator.*

```
1   NSSet *mySet = [NSSet setWithObjects:@"One", @"Two", @"Three", nil];
2
3   for (id value in mySet) {
4       NSLog(@"%@", value);
5   }
```

> **NOTE:** On line #3, the class of the value is id. Recall that an id is a generic type that represents any Objective-C class. The reason that id is used is that the value that we store in the NSSet can be of any type. For example, if the NSSet were to contain a class called Animal and another class called Zoo, the code would fail because we don't have a class that is both a Zoo and an Animal type. On the other hand, if the NSSet always had the same class, we could substitute that class for the id on line 3.

Another common method of accessing an NSSet, especially when programming for an iOS device capturing touches, is to use the following:

Listing 8–2. *Selecting any of the objects in the NSSet collection.*

```
1   NSSet *mySet = [NSSet setWithObjects:@"One", @"Two", @"Three", nil];
2
3   NSString *value = [mySet anyObject];
```

Line #3 calls the method anyObject. This does exactly as it says; it returns any object from the set. The object returned is determined at the set's convenience so there can be no guarantee that the first item will be returned. Of course, using the anyObject method assumes that any object will do. As previously mentioned, when dealing with touches on an iOS device, sometimes all that's necessary is to know that at least one finger has touched the screen. Each touch to the screen is stored as an entry in the NSSet, one for each finger. Using anyObject will return any one of the touches.

There are many other ways to actually get objects from an NSSet—far too many to cover in this chapter.[1] However, there is one particular method that involves the next collection—the NSArray class.

Using NSArray

The NSArray class is like any other collection, in that it allows the programmer to manage a group of objects. The NSArray differs from the NSSet in that the NSArray allows an object to be retrieved by its *index* into the array. An index is the numeric position that an object would occupy in the NSArray. For example, if there are three elements in the

---

[1]http://developer.apple.com/library/mac/#documentation/Cocoa/Reference/Foundation/Classes/NSSet_Class/Reference/Reference.html

NSArray, the objects can be referenced by an index from 0 to 2. As with most things in the C and Objective-C languages, an index starts at 0.

Listing 8–3. *Accessing objects within an NSArray.*

```
1  NSArray *myArray = [NSArray arrayWithObjects: @"One", @"Two", @"Three", nil];
2
3  NSLog (@"%@", [myArray objectAtIndex:0]);
4  NSLog (@"%@", [myArray objectAtIndex:1]);
5  NSLog (@"%@", [myArray objectAtIndex:2]);
```

As can be seen, objects within the NSArray can be retrieved via the *index*. The index starts at 0 and can't exceed the size of the array−1. The size of the array can be easily calculated by sending a count message to the NSArray object:

```
        int entries = [myArray count];
```

In fact, every collection type, NSSet, NSArray, NSDictionary (and their mutable counterparts) all respond to the count message.

> **NOTE:** You may have noticed that the NSLog command passes a string like :@"%@". The %@ is a format that can be used with any Objective-C object. It simply tells the object to describe itself. In the case of NSString, the description is the string itself. Different types of objects have different descriptions. In Listing 8–3 the [myArray objectAtIndex:0] returns an NSString object. If the argument is NOT an Objective-C class, your program will crash!

As mentioned earlier, there is a method to get at an NSSet using an NSArray.

Listing 8–4. *Creating an NSArray from an existing NSSet.*

```
1  NSSet *mySet = [NSSet setWithObjects:@"One", @"Two", @"Three", nil];
2  NSArray *myArray = [NSSet allObjects];
3
4  NSLog(@"%@", [myArray objectAtIndex:1);
```

Aside from *fast enumeration*, using the allObjects method will create an NSArray from the NSSet. Generally, one wouldn't create a set and then copy it into an array— why not just create the array in the first place? Well, sometimes a list of objects is given only in an NSSet (touchesBegan: withEvent: method when dealing with touches on an iOS device is a perfect example).

NSDictionary

The NSDictionary class is also a very useful type of collection class. It allows the storage of objects, just like the NSSet and NSArray, but the NSDictionary is different in that it allows a *key* to be associated with the entry. For example, an NSDictionary could be created that stores a list of Animal objects. Instead of accessing the Animal objects by an index like an NSArray, the NSDictionary could use an NSString like "monkey".

However, all keys must be unique—that is, "monkey" cannot exist more than once. Depending on your program, finding unique names is normally not a problem.

Using the "monkey" example above—if there are 5 different monkeys, the NSDictionary would contain one entry for "monkey". However, that entry could be in another NSDictionary that contains five unique monkey names:

```
"monkey" -> NSDictionary object
```

The NSDictionary object contains:

```
"Spider" -> Animal Object
"Capuchin" -> Animal Object
"Tamarin" -> Animal Object
"Mandril" -> Animal Object
"Orangutan" -> Animal Object
```

Of course, an NSDictionary could be organized in many different ways, depending on how the keys are defined. In most cases, there aren't NSDictionary entries of NSDictionaries—the above example was just provided to show how flexible the NSDictionary, or collections in general, can be.

Let's see how the above example would look in code. For example, assume that a list of Animal objects already exists and we're just assigning it to the dictionary:

Listing 8–5. *Creating an NSDictionary with another NSDictionary.*

```
1   NSDictionary *zoo = [NSDictionary dictionaryWithObjectsAndKeys:
2                       @"elephant", myElephantObject,
3                       @"giraffe", myGiraffeObject,
4                       @"monkey", [NSDictionary dictionaryWithObjectsAndKeys:
5                                   @"Spider", mySpiderMonkey,
6                                   @"Capuchin", myCapuchinMonkey,
7                                   @"Tamarin", myTamarinMonkey,
8                                   @"Mandril", myMandrilMonkey,
9                                   @"Orangutan", myOrangutanMonkey, nil]
10                      @"zebra", myZebraObject, nil];
```

Now that the main NSDictionary is set up, how do we know when we get an Animal object and when we get an NSDictionary object? (Hint: read the next section title.)

Determining Class Type in a Collection

When iterating through a collection, we generally use the **id** class type to indicate that we don't know what class is in the collection. Each Objective-C object has two nifty methods to help us out. Let's take a look at them now.

Using the code in Listing 8–3 as an example, consider the following code fragment:

Listing 8–6. *Handling different classes within a collection.*

```
11  for (id element in [zoo allValues]) {
12      if ([element isKindOfClass:[Animal class]]) {
13          NSLog(@"%@", id);
```

```
14        }
15        if ([element isKindOfClass:[NSDictionary class]]) {
16            ... // Process the monkey dictionary above.
17        }
18    }
```

In Listing 8–6, we use fast enumeration to go through our zoo NSDictionary. Since there are only two possibilities: an Animal class or an NSDictionary of animals, the code needs to check for two different class types. As previously mentioned, each Objective-C object has two handy methods.

- The first is the isKindOfClass: method. This method returns a Boolean value if the current class, our element variable, is a type of class.
- The second handy method is the class method. This method simply returns the class of the object; line #12 is the Animal class. Line #15 is the NSDictionary class.

Using a combination of the isKindOfClass: and the class methods makes it fairly simple to process different types of classes within a collection.

Using the Mutable Classes

Up to this point, we've only discussed collection objects that are initialized once and can never change. While there are definitely places this is useful, what's even more useful is a collection class that can be modified. Each of the collection classes has a **mutable** version—we've only talked about the **non-mutable** classes. The classes are fundamentally the same except that elements can be added and removed from the mutable versions.

NSMutableSet

This can be initialized the same as the NSSet or can be initialized without any values and then values added. Consider the code in Listing 8–7:

Listing 8–7. *Adding objects to an NSMutableSet.*

```
1    NSMutableSet *mySet = [[NSMutableSet alloc] init];
2
3    [mySet addObject:@"One"];
4    [mySet addObject:@"Two"];
5    [mySet addObject:@"Three"];
6
7    for (id val in mySet) {
8        NSLog(@"%@", val);
9    }
```

The nice thing about any of the mutable classes is that elements can be added and removed programmatically instead of having to declare the class with all the values at once. All objects in a set can be removed with the following line:

```
[mySet removeAllObjects];
```

A specific object can also be removed as long as we have a reference to that object:

Listing 8–8. *Removing a specific object in an NSMutableSet.*

```
10   NSString *testString = @"Zero";
11
12   [mySet addObject: testString];
13   [mySet addObject: testString];  // Just a test
14
15   for (id val in mySet) {
16       NSLog(@"%@", val);
17   }
18
19   [mySet removeObject:testString];
20
21   for (id val in mySet) {
22       NSLog(@"%@", val);
23   }
```

In Listing 8–8, line #19 will remove the string "Zero". We can only do this because we have a reference to the object already in the `testString` variable. This brings up another good point: the `NSSet` and `NSMutableSet` will only store *unique* objects. Two objects that are exactly the same (i.e., identical) cannot be added more than once. For example, line #13 effectively replaces the first `testString` added on line #12.

> **HINT:** Adding the exact same object means that the pointer to that object is the same. There is no comparison to see if the value of the object being added is identical to what's already in the set—it's the pointers that are checked. Pointers are discussed in depth in Chapter 11.

NSMutableArray

As with the `NSMutableSet`, the `NSMutableArray` is similar to its parent, the `NSArray`. In fact, an object can be added to the `NSMutableArray` object exactly as it's done in the `NSMutableSet` and that is by using the `addObject:` method. However, unlike the `NSMutableSet`, the `NSMutableArray` can also insert elements into the array—the `NSMutableSet` can only add objects to the set. Take a look at Listing 8–9.

Listing 8–9. *Adding and inserting values into an NSMutableArray.*

```
1    NSMutableArray *myArray = [[NSMutableArray alloc] init];
2
3    [myArray addObject:@"One"];
4    [myArray addObject:@"Two"];
5    [myArray addObject:@"Three"];
6
7    for (id val in myArray) {
8        NSLog(@"%@", val);
9    }
10
11   [myArray insertObject:@"One and a Half" atIndex:1];
12
13   for (id val in myArray) {
```

```
14      NSLog(@"%@", val);
15  }
```

In Listing 8–9 a new array is created similarly to the NSMutableSet. However, on line #11 a new element is being inserted into the array at position 1. Remember, position 0 is the first element of the array. The contents of the array after the insert would look like:

Index	Value
0	One
1	One and a Half
2	Two
3	Three

Line #11 inserted a new element—the remaining elements were moved up in the array to make room. This is critical to know, especially if there is a code assumption that a particular index into an array will have a specific value.

With the NSMutableArray, there are several ways to remove an object. Following are a few of the more commonly used methods:

- removeAllObjects – This method does exactly as advertised. It removes all objects from a given NSMutableArray.

- removeLastObject – This method removes the last object at the end of the array. The array size is reduced by one.

- removeObjectAtIndex:(NSUInteger index) – This methods removes an object at a given index. The value is from 0 to the length of the array—1.

NSMutableDictionary

By this point, it must be pretty obvious to you how the mutable versions of the collection classes work—the NSMutableDictionary is no different. The NSMutableDictionary provides all the capabilities of NSDictionary but, of course, elements can be added and removed, as shown in Listing 8–10:

Listing 8–10. *Adding objects to an NSMutableDictionary.*

```
1
2   NSMutableDictionary *myDict = [[NSMutableDictionary alloc] init];
3
4   [myDict setObject:@"Number One" forKey:@"1"];
5   [myDict setObject:@"Number Two" forKey:@"2"];
6   [myDict setObject:@"Number Three" forKey:@"3"];
7
8   for (id val in myDict) {
9       NSLog(@"%@", val);
```

```
10  }
11
12  [myDict setObject:@"One and a Half" forKey:@"1.5"];
13
14  for (id val in myArray) {
15      NSLog(@"%@", val);
    }
```

In the example above, the object @"One and a Half" is being added to the dictionary. It's different than an array since an object can't be inserted into the dictionary at a specific position, as can be done with an NSMutableArray.

Creating the BookStore Application

First things first. Let's start by creating the base application project. We start by opening Xcode and creating a new Master-Detail Application project. In this project, we will create a few simple objects for what is to become our bookstore application: a Book object and the Bookstore object itself. We'll visit instance variables again and see how to get and set the value of one during this project. Lastly, we'll put our bookstore objects to use, and you'll learn how to make use of objects once we've created them.

Fire up Xcode, and start by creating a new project, as shown in Figure 8–1.

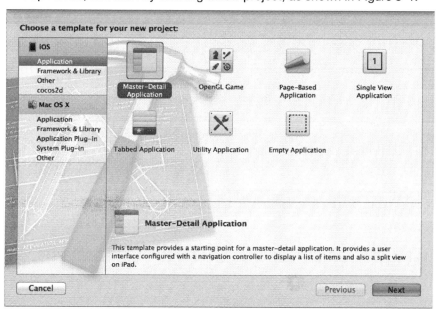

Figure 8–1. *Creating the initial project as a Master-Detail application.*

1. Click the **Next** button, and name the project MyBookstore, as shown in Figure 8–2. The company name is required—any company name, real or otherwise, can be used. The example uses "com.mycompany" which is perfectly fine. Make sure the device family is iPhone and that the option "Use Automatic Reference Counting" is checked.

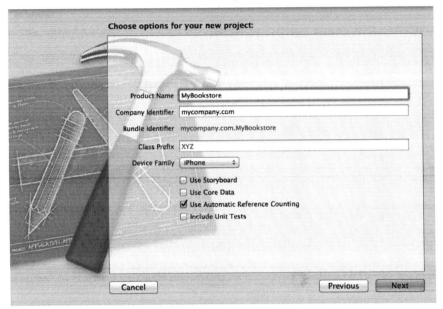

Figure 8–2. *Selecting the product (application) name and options.*

2. Once everything is filled out, press the **Next** button. Xcode will prompt you to specify a place to save the project. Anywhere you can remember is fine—the Desktop is a good place too.

3. Once you decide on a location, click on the **Create** button to create the new project. This will create the boilerplate Bookstore project, as shown in Figure 8–3.

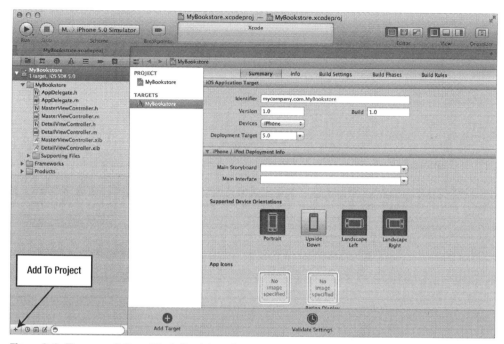

Figure 8–3. *The source listing of the boilerplate project.*

4. Click on the plus (**+**) sign at the lower left of the screen in the Navigation Area to add a new object to the project. Choose **Cocoa Touch** under the iOS section on the left and then choose the **Objective-C Class** on the right, as shown in Figure 8–4. It's also possible to right-click over the navigation area and then select the "New File…" menu option. There is no difference between this approach and clicking on the plus sign—do whatever feels more natural.

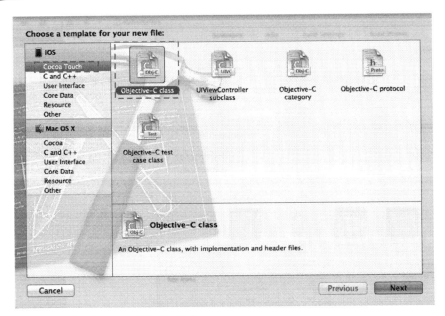

Figure 8–4. *Creating a new Objective-C class.*

5. We're choosing a plain Objective-C class, which will create a new empty
    Objective-C object that we're going to use for our Book class. After
    selecting this, click on the **Next** button.

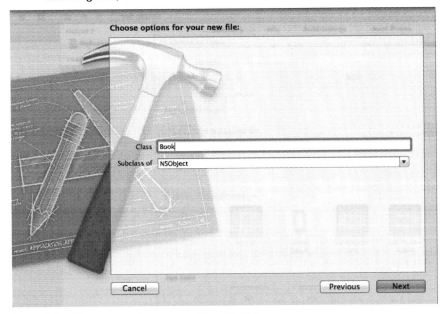

Figure 8–5. *Giving our new class a name and parent class.*

6. Xcode will now prompt for the object name and which main object we're going to be a subclass of. Choose the name "Book" and make book a subclass of NSObject, as shown in Figure 8–5, and then click the **Next** button.

7. Finally, Xcode will ask to which folder it should save the new class files. To keep things simple, choose the "MyBookstore" folder in our project, as shown in Figure 8–6. This is where all the other class files for our project are stored.

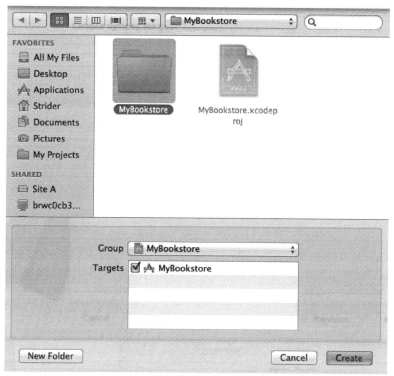

Figure 8–6. *Choosing the place to save our new class files.*

Double-click on the "MyBookstore" folder and then click on the **Create** button. You'll see the main edit window for Xcode and our new class files, Book.m and Book.h, in the Navigation window, as shown in Figure 8–7.

8. Repeat the above steps and create a second object called Bookstore. This will create a Bookstore.m and a Bookstore.h file. We'll be using this class later in this chapter. For now, we'll concentrate on the Book object.

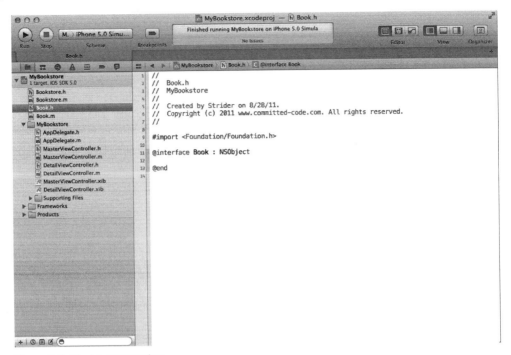

Figure 8–7. *Viewing our new class.*

   9. Click on the Book.h file and let's start defining our new class!

Introducing Instance Variables

Our object is simply called Book and is a subclass of NSObject. True, we have an object, but it doesn't *store* anything at this point. In order for this class to be useful, it needs to be able to hold some information, which is done with instance variables. When an object is used, it has to be instantiated. Once the object is instantiated, it has access to its instance variables. These variables are available to the object as long as the object stays in scope. As we know from Chapter 7, scope defines the context in which an object exists. In some cases, an object's scope may be the life of the program. In other cases, the scope might be just a function or method. It all depends on where the object is declared and how it's used. Scope will be discussed more later. For now, let's add some instance variables to our Book class to make it more useful.

Listing 8–11. *Adding instance variables to the Book.h file.*

```
1  //
2  //  Book.h
3  //  MyBookstore
4  //
5  //  Created by Mitch Fisher on 8/28/11.
6  //  Copyright 2011 www.committed-code.com. All rights reserved.
7  //
```

```
 8
 9   #import <Foundation/Foundation.h>
10
11   @interface Book : NSObject {
12           NSString *title;
13           NSString *author;
14           NSString *description;
15   }
16
17   @end
```

This is the same Book object from before, but now, there are three new instance variables placed inside the brackets, lines 12–14. These are all NSString objects, which means that they can hold text information for our Book object. So, the Book object now has a place to store title, author, and description information.

Accessing Instance Variables

Now that we have some instance variables, how can we use them? How are they accessed? As you learned in previous chapters, Objective-C objects respond to messages. Unfortunately, simply declaring an instance variable doesn't necessarily give us access to it. There are two ways to access these variables.

- One way is, of course, within our Book object.

- The second way is from outside of the object—that is, another part of the program that uses the Book object.

If we are writing the code for a method within our Book object, accessing an instance variable is quite simple. For example, you could simply write the following:

```
title = @"Test Title";
```

The preceding line is written within the Book class. Outside of the object, the title instance variable is not visible at all. Of course, outside objects need to be able to access these instance variables as well. To accomplish this, you need to create two types of methods: a getter and a setter.

- A **getter** is a method that returns the value of something in the object, typically an instance variable like the author variable from the Book object.

- A **setter** is a method that updates or sets that instance variable.

Let's take a look at the traditional getter and setter methods that were common before the introduction of Objective-C 2.0 back in 2007.

> **TIP:** Sometimes instance variables are referred to as ivars. Ivar is just the short form of instance variable.

Using Getter and Setter Methods

Here is the Book object's header (.h) file, which contains the Book's interface definition.

Listing 8-12. *Defining a getter and setter for the Book object.*

```
1    #import <Foundation/Foundation.h>
2
3    @interface Book : NSObject {
4            NSString *title;
5            NSString *author;
6            NSString *description;
7    }
8
9    - (NSString *)title;
10   - (void)setTitle:(NSString *)newString;
11
12   @end
```

The two methods declared on lines 9 and 10 are the getter and setter methods, respectively. Conventionally, the getter method is named the same as the instance variable. In our example, we are fetching the title of a book object so our getter method is simply title. It is defined to return an NSString object to the caller.

The setter object is named by convention to set*InstanceVariableName*. So for our example, the setter method is named setTitle. Notice that the instance variable name's first character uses an uppercase letter; this is also part of the standard convention.

> **NOTE:** A naming convention called camel case (or CamelCase) uses an uppercase letter to distinguish different words in a method, variable, or class name. The text is suggestive of a camel, since the uppercase letters tend to form humps. It makes the label easier to read. For example, stringWithContentsOfURL is much easier to read than stringwithcontentsofurl.

Now, the word "convention" has been mentioned several times. Objective-C does not require that a method be named anything specific. However, since most applications follow the guidelines we discussed, the convention becomes the *de facto* standard. Knowing this becomes very important when the topic of properties is discussed later. For now, however, we are going to manually write a getter and a setter method so that they can be better understood.

First, the getter—this is the simplest of the methods to implement:

```
- (NSString *)title
{
    return title;
}
```

In the preceding example, the method title simply returns the local instance variable called title. To access the method, the syntax [object title] is used.

It might seem that the instance variable and the method name might somehow get confused. Because an instance variable is accessed completely differently from a method name, the Objective-C runtime environment doesn't have a problem with instance variable and method names that are the same.

Now, here is the setter:

```
- (void)setTitle:(NSString *)newTitle
{
    if ([newTitle length] > 0) {
        title = newTitle;
    }
}
```

This example is a little more complicated than our getter method, although it doesn't have to be. In our setter example, there is a check to see if the newTitle has a length greater than 0 before assigning the string (The NSString class' length method returns the number of characters in the string). Clearly, our setter code doesn't want the current title to be blank.

Using the getter/setter methods above, they would be used as shown in the following snippet of code:

```
1  Book *myBook = [Book alloc] init];
2
3  [myBook setTitle:@"My Great Book"];  // Call the setter
4
5  NSString *title = [myBook title];  // Call the getter and put it into the 'title'
   NSString object.
```

The benefit of a setter method is that the object can perform some validation logic on the parameters before accepting the value. If the object were to allow direct access to the instance variable, either this type of validation would have to be everywhere or there would be no validation at all and the object's title could potentially be set to something invalid (like a blank title).

Now, it is not necessary to *always* create a getter and/or a setter for every instance variable. A good example of this might simply be an object that represents today's date. There is no need to set it, just retrieve it, so there would only be a getter method.

The needs of the object and variables will dictate how the getter and setter methods are built. If a getter gets the value and the setter sets the value, it's going to take a lot of coding to simply write all the getters and setters in an object, especially if there are many instance variables. Fortunately, Objective-C 2.0 introduced a way to reduce this burden with minimal effort on the programmer's part. These features in Objective-C 2.0 are called properties.

> **NOTE:** Objective-C 2.0 was introduced in 2006 with Xcode 3.4 and is included in Xcode 4 and later.

Introducing Properties

When we created instance variables for the Book object, we manually created the methods that could be used to access these variables. Now that you know how to do this manually, let's look at how to take advantage of something called properties. A **property** is a short way of having the compiler create functions to get and/or set the value of an instance variable. As you learned earlier, instance variables are generally not accessible from outside of the object itself, so having methods to get and set these variables becomes essential.

The following is the **interface** (header) file to the Book object that we created earlier. Let's see what it takes to have the Objective-C compiler create our getters and setters for us.

Listing 8–13. *Adding properties to the Book object.*

```
1   //
2   //   Book.h
3   //   MyBookstore
4   //
5   //   Created by M.R. Fisher on 8/28/11.
6   //   Copyright (c) 2011 www.committed-code.com. All rights reserved.
7   //
8
9   #import <Foundation/Foundation.h>
10
11  @interface Book : NSObject {
12  }
13
14  @property(nonatomic,strong) NSString *title;
15  @property(nonatomic,strong) NSString *author;
16  @property(nonatomic,strong) NSString *description;
17
18  @end
```

Lines 14–16 show the property declarations for the instance variables. Properties are not required for all instance variables, just the ones we want to expose to the world. In the example, however, we are creating properties for all of our instance variables. Notice that the actual instance variable declarations that used to be between the { ... } brackets are now gone. When using properties with Xcode 4 and over, it is no longer necessary to declare the instance variables **and** the properties. The compiler is now smart enough to do this for you.

A property starts with a @property directive. This tells the Objective-C compiler to build us the automatic getter and/or setter. Whether it is a getter and/or setter is included in the declaration. Let's dissect this code:

@property[1] (nonatomic,strong)[2] NSString* title[3];

1. This is the property directive.

2. The parentheses and the comma-separated keywords contained therein are sometimes optional. In our particular case, we are specifying nonatomic and strong. The nonatomic keyword tells the compiler not to generate special code for use in threading—we're not using threads, so using nonatomic is fine. The second, strong, is used to indicate that this is a strongly typed variable—this will be discussed further in Chapter 13 when we discuss memory management. Many other options can be included here; one is readonly, which tells the compiler to only create a getter, not a setter, and thereby prevents the ability for the instance variable from being set external to the object.

3. Last, NSString* title, is the instance variable declaration. It must include the type and, of course, the instance variable name.

This defines half of the property. What's that you say, "Only half? What else is missing?" Well, the second half of the @property is declared in the implementation (.m) file.

Listing 8–14. *Defining a getter and setter for the Book object.*

```
1   //
2   //  Book.m
3   //  MyBookstore
4   //
5   //  Created by M.R. Fisher on 8/28/11.
6   //  Copyright (c) 2011 www.committed-code.com. All rights reserved.
7   //
8
9   #import "Book.h"
10
11  @implementation Book
12  @synthesize title, author, description;
13
14  @end
```

This is the implementation file to the Book object. Line 12 is significant, because it is the second half of what is required to complete our property. This part is much simpler than the interface file. All that is necessary is to use the @synthesize keyword and provide a list of one or more property names. There can be many property names specified on a @synthesis statement, and there can be many @synthesize lines, too. It's all a matter of personal preference.

Now that we've created three different properties, how are the properties used?

Using Properties

Once a property has been specified in both the interface and implementation files, using the properties is very straightforward and simple. First, the syntax changes a bit. Let's look at a traditional setter:

```
[myBookObject setTitle:newTitle]; // Traditional setter
```

Here is an example of sending a set message to set the title to our book object—like we said, pretty straightforward. However, when using properties, things change:

```
myBookObject.title = newTitle; // Setter example
```

Some things are very important to note. For starters, the object access is not within brackets ([…]). Second, we use the property called title, not the setTitle method. Internally, there is still a setTitle method; it's just hidden. Why is this important? Well, if we create our own explicit setTitle method, our new method will be called rather than the compiler-created one. This may or may not be the behavior we specifically want.

For the getter, things look remarkably familiar:

```
NSString* title = myBookObject.title;  // Getter example
```

The property that gets the information is also called title. The significance here is that how the object's property is accessed determines whether the getter or setter is called. If we are trying to set the variable, the setter is called. If we are trying to get the value of the variable, the getter is called

One last big difference is that the syntax to access a property now uses a period (.) between the object and the method. This is necessary because the brackets are gone, so the period distinguishes between using a property and sending a message to an object.

Understanding the Importance of Conventions

As mentioned earlier, there is a convention to naming a getter and a setter. While these naming guidelines are not strictly enforced, the value of understanding the convention comes in handy when using properties. Here is our previous example:

```
- (void)setTitle:(NSString *) newTitle
{
    if ([newTitle length] > 0) {
        title = newTitle;
    }
}
```

If we create a property like @property title and pair that with the @synthesize keyword, the compiler will generate two methods—one named title as the getter and one called setTitle as the setter. However, if we provide our own setter and name it according to the convention (like the preceding code), the compiler won't generate its own.

```
        myBookObject.title = newTitle; // Call the custom setter
```

The preceding code will call our own custom setter instead of the standard one. The same would be true had we written our own getter method. Now, let's continue with the Bookstore application.

Finishing the MyBookstore Program

With the understanding of instance variables and properties, we are going to now venture forth to create the actual bookstore program. The idea is simple enough—create a class called Bookstore that will be stocked with a few Book objects.

Creating the View

Let's start by first getting our view ready. If you need a refresher on how to build an interface in Xcode, please refer to Chapter 6.

1. Click on the DetailViewController.xib file in the Navigation Window. This will display Xcode's interface builder, as shown in Figure 8–8.

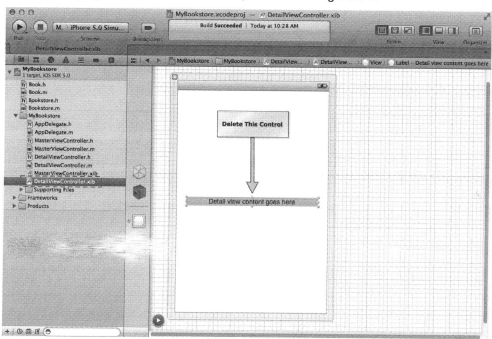

Figure 8–8. *Preparing the MyBookstore detail view.*

2. Simply delete the existing control that is just a placeholder for the detail view. We're going to add some new fields to display some details about a selected book. Since we deleted this control, we also need to remove the code that references it.

   a. In the DetailViewController.h file, remove the following line:

```
@property (strong, nonatomic) IBOutlet UILabel *detailDescriptionLabel;
```

   b. In the DetailViewController.m file, remove the following line near the top of the file:

```
@synthesize detailDescriptionLabel = _detailDescriptionLabel;
```

   c. In the DetailViewController.m file, in the method named configureView, remove the following line:

```
self.detailDescriptionLabel.text = [self.detailItem description];
```

3. Next, click on the Utilities icon for the view, as shown in Figure 8–9. This will bring up the view of controls that we can place onto the view.

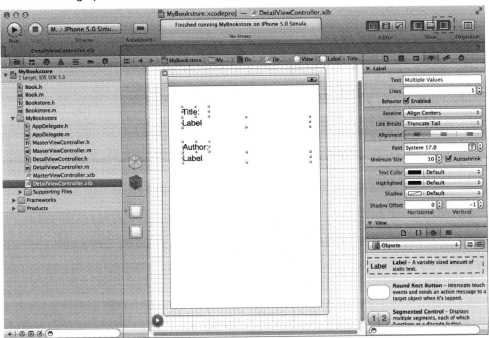

Figure 8–9. *Selecting the Utilities Window and adding some Labels.*

4. Drag and drop some Label objects from the Object Library onto the detail view, as shown in Figure 8–9. Make sure that the bottom Label controls are set to the width of the view. This is so that they can hold a fairly long amount of text. The two Label objects with the text "Label" in them are the ones we're going to hook up to hold two of the values from our Book object: the Title and Author(s).

Adding Instance Variables

Next, we're going to add some instance variables to the DetailViewController class. These instance variables will correspond to the detail view's labels.

1. First, open up the DetailViewController.h file and delete the detailDescriptionLabel property—we've deleted it from the interface and we don't need it anymore.

2. Next, we'll add two fields that will represent the labels on the detail view that we want to store our book data into, as shown in Listing 8–14

Listing 8–14. *Modifying the DetailViewController.h file to include the new Labels.*

```
1   #import <UIKit/UIKit.h>
2
3   @interface DetailViewController : UIViewController
4
5   @property (strong, nonatomic) id detailItem;
6
7   @property (strong, nonatomic) IBOutlet UILabel *titleLabel;
8   @property (strong, nonatomic) IBOutlet UILabel *authorLabel;
9
10  @end
```

3. If you recall from Chapter 7, the IBOutlet identifiers included in the properties let Xcode know that these instance variables (titleLabel and authorLabel) are controls that appear in a view. Next, right-click on the label right below the "Title" and drag a New Referencing Outlet to the topmost object called the "File's Owner", as shown in Figure 8–10.

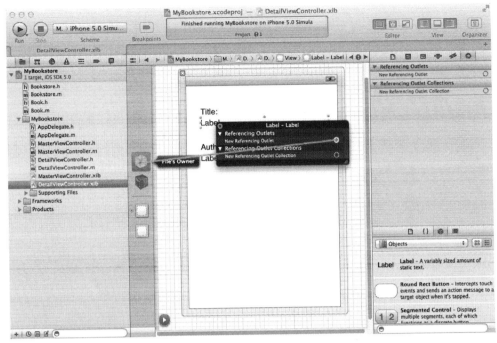

Figure 8–10. *Defining a new referencing outlet for a Label object.*

4. When dropped on the File's Owner, a secondary menu will pop up asking which variable the new outlet should be connected to. We will connect this Label to the `titleLabel` outlet, as shown in Figure 8–11 and Figure 8–12.

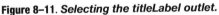

Figure 8–11. *Selecting the titleLabel outlet.*

Figure 8–12. *Connection is complete.*

5. Repeat this step for the Label object under the "Author:" Label, except connect the Label to the `authorLabel` outlet.

Adding a Description

Now, we need to add the description to the view. The description is a little different in that it can span multiple lines. For this, we're going to use the Text View object.

1. Start by adding a "Description:" label to the view, as shown in Figure 8–13.

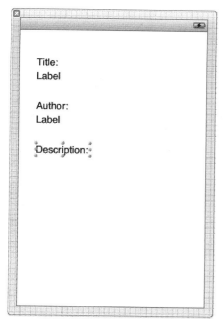

Figure 8–13. *Adding a new Label object for the Description.*

2. Next, add the Text View object to the detail view, as shown in Figure 8–14. The advantage the text view has is that it's easy to display multiple lines of text. While the Label can display multiple lines, it's not as clean as the Text View object.

> **NOTE:** By default, the Text View control is filled with all kinds of seemingly random text. This text is called Lorem Ipsum text. If you ever need to load up a page with text, you can find any number of Lorem Ipsum generators on the web. As for our Text View, the text can stay as it is since we'll remove it during runtime. Plus, if it's cleared, it becomes a little more difficult spotting exactly where the Text View is on the screen—it's white on white!

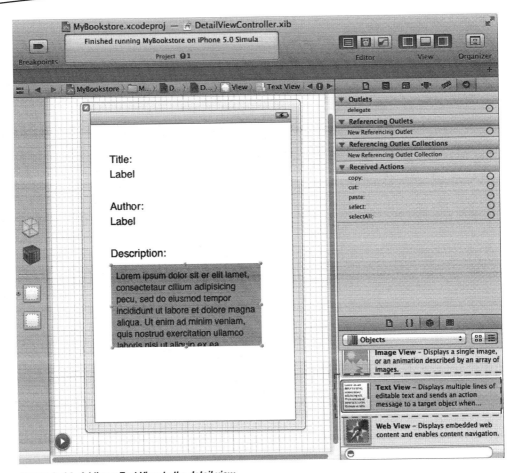

Figure 8–14. *Adding a Text View to the detail view.*

   3. In order for the program to take advantage of the Text View, we'll need to create an outlet for it, just as we did for the title and description. Simply add a new property to the DetailViewController.h file, as shown on line #9 in Listing 8–15.

Listing 8–15. *Adding an outlet for the Text View to hold a description.*

```
1   #import <UIKit/UIKit.h>
2
3   @interface DetailViewController : UIViewController
4
5   @property (strong, nonatomic) id detailItem;
6
7   @property (strong, nonatomic) IBOutlet UILabel *titleLabel;
8   @property (strong, nonatomic) IBOutlet UILabel *authorLabel;
9   @property (strong, nonatomic) IBOutlet UITextView *descriptionTextView;
10
    @end
```

4. Notice that the type is `UITextView` instead of `UILabel`—this is very important. Also, don't forget to add the `descriptionTextView` to the `@synthesize` statement in the `DetailViewController.m` file, as shown below:

```
@synthesize titleLabel, authorLabel, descriptionTextView;
```

5. Next, right-click on the Text View of the DetailViewController.xib and connect it to the `descriptionTextView` outlet. The process is the same as shown in Figure 8–10, 8–11, and 8–12, except that we're connected to the `descriptionTextView` outlet.

CAUTION: As mentioned above, it's important to make the `descriptionTextView` property a `UITextView` type. If, for example, it was accidentally made a UILabel object, when trying to connect the Text View from the screen to the outlet, Xcode won't be able to find the `descriptionTextView` outlet. Why? Because Xcode knows that the control is a `UITextView` and is looking for an outlet that is of type `UITextView`.

Creating a Simple Data Model Class

In order for our application to work, it needs to have some data to display. To do this, we're going to use the `Bookstore` object we created earlier as our data model class. There's nothing different about a data model class except that its whole purpose is to allow an application to access data via an object.

Modify the Bookstore.h file to look like Listing 8–16.

Listing 8–16. *Modifying the Bookstore.h class to include an NSMutableArray.*

```
   //
2  //  Bookstore.h
3  //  MyBookstore
4  //
5  //  Created by M.R. Fisher on 8/28/11.
6  //  Copyright (c) 2011 www.committed-code.com. All rights reserved.
7  //
8
9  #import <Foundation/Foundation.h>
10 #import "Book.h"
11
12 @interface Bookstore : NSObject
13
14 @property(strong, nonatomic) NSMutableArray *theBookStore;
15
16 - (NSUInteger)count;
17 - (Book *)bookAtIndex:(NSUInteger)index;
18
19 @end
```

In Listing 8–16, we add an #import "Book.h" on line #10. This lets our Bookstore object know about the Book object. Next, on line #14, we add a property that will hold our list of books; the property is simply named theBookStore. Note that theBookStore is an NSMUtableArray, which will allow us to add a series of objects—in this case, a set of Book objects. Lastly, we add two new methods to our class on lines #16 and #17. The first method, count, will simply return how many books are in our bookstore. The second method, bookAtIndex, will return a Book object, given a specific index into theBookStore array.

Next, let's add the code to the implementation file, Bookstore.m.

Listing 8–17. *Implementing the Bookstore data object.*

```
1   //  Bookstore.m
2   //  MyBookstore
3   //
4   //  Created by M.R. Fisher on 8/28/11.
5   //  Copyright (c) 2011 www.committed-code.com. All rights reserved.
6   //
7
8   #import "Bookstore.h"
9
10  @implementation Bookstore
11  @synthesize theBookStore;
12
13  - (id)init
14  {
15      self = [super init];
16      if (self) {
17          self.theBookStore = [[NSMutableArray alloc] init];
18          Book *newBook = [[Book alloc] init];
19          newBook.title = @"Objective-C for Absolute Beginners";
20          newBook.author = @"Bennett, Fisher and Lees";
21          newBook.description = @"iOS Programming made easy.";
22          [self.theBookStore addObject:newBook];
23
24          newBook = [[Book alloc] init];
25          newBook.title = @"A Farewell To Arms";
26          newBook.author = @"Ernest Hemingway";
27          newBook.description = @"The story of an affair between an English "
28                                "nurse and an American soldier "
29                                "on the Italian front "
30                                "during World War I.";
31          [self.theBookStore addObject:newBook];
32      }
33
34      return self;
35  }
36
37  - (NSUInteger)count
38  {
39      return theBookStore.count;
40  }
41
42  - (Book *)bookAtIndex:(NSUInteger)index
43  {
```

```
44      return [theBookStore objectAtIndex:index];
45  }
46  @end
```

In Listing 8–7, lines #13–35 define the init method of the object, which is called whenever the object is first initialized. In this method, we initialize the two books we plan to add to our bookstore. Line #17 initializes our theBookStore array—this is the NSMutableArray object where the books will be stored. Line #18 is where the first Book object is allocated and initialized. Lines #19–21 add a title, author, and description to our first book. Finally, line #22 adds the new Book object to our theBookStore array. The important thing to note here is that once the object is added to the array, our code can forget about it; the array now owns that object. Because of this, line #24 is not a problem.

Line #24 allocates a new Book object overwriting the old value. This tells the compiler that we're no longer interested in using the old value—plus, as mentioned above, the NSMutableArray object, theBookStore, now owns the old Book object anyhow.

Lines #25–31 simply add the second book to the array.

Lines #37–40 define a method called count. This method simply returns the number of elements in our bookstore array. The method to get the number of elements in an array is also called count.

Lines #42–45 define a method called bookAtIndex:. Notice that it returns a Book object and takes in an NSUInteger value. This method simply calls the NSMutableArray method, objectAtIndex:, and returns the object at that specific index. We'll use this method to get at the Book objects in our Bookstore.

That's it! That's all we need to define a simple data model class. Next, we need to allow main program access to this class so that it can start displaying some data.

Modifying the MasterViewController

Our simple application has two view controllers, the main view controller, which is called the MasterViewController, and a secondary one called the DetailViewController. View controllers are objects that simply control the behavior of a view. In order for our application to start displaying data from our data model, we need to first modify the MasterViewController—this is where the navigation of our application begins. The following code is already in place in the template that Xcode has provided. We're just going to modify it to add in our data model.

First, we'll need to modify the MasterViewController.h file. We need to add in an instance variable to hold the Bookstore object. Listing 8–18 shows that the instance variable is added in as a property on line #17. Also note that there is what's called a *forward reference* on line #12. This doesn't define the Bookstore class, it just tells the compiler that there will be a Bookstore object defined at some point. This prevents line #17 from generating an error because the compiler doesn't know about the Bookstore object.

Listing 8–18. *Adding in our Bookstore object.*

```
1   //
2   //  MasterViewController.h
3   //  MyBookstore
4   //
5   //  Created by M.R. Fisher on 8/28/11.
6   //  Copyright (c) 2011 www.committed-code.com. All rights reserved.
7   //
8
9   #import <UIKit/UIKit.h>
10
11  @class DetailViewController;
12  @class Bookstore;
13
14  @interface MasterViewController : UITableViewController
15
16  @property (strong, nonatomic) DetailViewController *detailViewController;
17  @property (strong, nonatomic) Bookstore *myBookStore;
18
19  @end
```

Next, we need to modify the MasterViewController.m implementation file to actually make use of the object. First, we need to let the `MasterViewController` know about our `Bookstore` class. We do this by importing the header file on line #13, as shown in Listing 8–19.

Line #18 is the @synthesize of our `myBookStore` property we declared earlier. Line #25 allocates a new `Bookstore` object and assigns it to our property. The best place to put one-time initializations like our books store is in the `initWithNibName:bundle:` method. This method is only called once when this class is loaded.

Listing 8–19. *Allocating our Bookstore object.*

```
1   //
2   //  MasterViewController.m
3   //  MyBookstore
4   //
5   //  Created by M.R. Fisher on 8/28/11.
6   //  Copyright (c) 2011 www.committed-code.com. All rights reserved.
7   //
8
9   #import "MasterViewController.h"
10
11  #import "DetailViewController.h"
12  #import "Book.h"
13  #import "Bookstore.h"
14
15  @implementation MasterViewController
16
17  @synthesize detailViewController = _detailViewController;
18  @synthesize myBookStore;
19
20  - (id)initWithNibName:(NSString *)nibNameOrNil bundle:(NSBundle *)nibBundleOrNil
21  {
22      self = [super initWithNibName:nibNameOrNil bundle:nibBundleOrNil];
```

```
23          if (self) {
24              self.title = NSLocalizedString(@"Master", @"Master");
25              self.myBookStore = [[Bookstore alloc] init];
26          }
27          return self;
28      }
```

OK, now that our Bookstore object is initialized, we need to tell the MasterViewController how to display our list of books—not the detail, just the book titles. To do this, we'll need to modify a few methods. Fortunately, Xcode has provided a nice template so our modifications are small.

Our MasterViewController is a subclass of what's called a UITableViewController. This class controls the displaying of rows of data to the screen. In our case, these are rows of book titles (well, just two for our simple program, but a list nonetheless).

There are three main methods that control what and how data is displayed in a UITableViewController.

▣ The first is numberOfSectionsInTableView:. Since our application only has one list, or section, this method returns 1.

▣ The second is tableView:numberOfRowsInSection:. In our program, we return the number of books in our bookstore array. Since this is the only section, the code is very straightforward.

▣ The third method is tableView:cellForRowAtIndexPath:. This method is called for each row that is to be displayed on the screen, and it's called one row at a time.

Listing 8–20 details the changes we need to make in order to get our list of books displaying on the view. The changes start at line 83 in the source file.

Listing 8–20. *Setting up the view to display our books.*

```
83   - (NSInteger)tableView:(UITableView *)tableView
84    numberOfRowsInSection:(NSInteger)section
85   {
86        return self.myBookStore.count;
87   }
88
89   // Customize the appearance of table view cells.
90   - (UITableViewCell *)tableView:(UITableView *)tableView
91            cellForRowAtIndexPath:(NSIndexPath *)indexPath
92   {
93        static NSString *CellIdentifier = @"Cell";
94
95        UITableViewCell *cell =
96            [tableView dequeueReusableCellWithIdentifier:CellIdentifier];
97        if (cell == nil) {
98            cell = [[UITableViewCell alloc] initWithStyle:UITableViewCellStyleDefault
99                                          reuseIdentifier:CellIdentifier];
100           cell.accessoryType = UITableViewCellAccessoryDisclosureIndicator;
101       }
102
```

```
103        // Configure the cell.
104        cell.textLabel.text = [self.myBookStore bookAtIndex:indexPath.row].title;
105        return cell;
106    }
```

Out of all of this code, we only need to modify two lines. Everything else can stay the way it is. This is one of the advantages of using the Xcode templates. Line #86 used to simply return 1; we need to change it so that it now returns the count of items in our Bookstore class.

Line #104 looks a little more complicated. Basically, each line of the UITableView is what is called a cell (a UITableViewCell to be specific). Line #104 sets the text of the cell to the title of a book. Let's look at that code a little more specifically:

```
[self.myBookStore bookAtIndex:indexPath.row].title;
```

First, self.myBookStore is our Bookstore object, which is pretty clear. We're calling one of its methods called bookAtIndex:. The value indexPath.row specifies which row we're interested in—the indexPath.row will always be one less than the total count (returned on Line #86). So, calling [self.myBookStore bookAtIndex:indexPath.row] returns a Book object. The last part, .title, accesses the title property from the returned Book object. The code below is equivalent to what we just did in one line:

```
1    Book *book;
2    book = [self.myBookStore bookAtIndex:indexPath.row];
3    cell,textLabel.text = book.title;
```

Now, you should be able to build and run the application and see the two books we created in our data model, as shown in Figure 8–15.

But, we're not done yet. We need to make the application display our book when we click on one of them. In order to make this happen, we need to make one last modification to the MasterViewController.

The method tableView:didSelectRowAtIndexPath: is called whenever a row is touched on the screen. The method is already there as part of our template, but it doesn't do anything with our book. Listing 8–21 shows what small changes we need to make in order to hook up the detail view with our book data.

Figure 8–15. *Running the application for the first time.*

Listing 8–21. *Selecting the book when touched.*

```
146   - (void)tableView:(UITableView *)tableView didSelectRowAtIndexPath:(NSIndexPath *)indexPath
147   {
148       Book *selectedBook = [self.myBookStore bookAtIndex:indexPath.row];
149
150       if (!self.detailViewController) {
151           self.detailViewController = [[DetailViewController alloc]
152                                       initWithNibName:@"DetailViewController"
153                                       bundle:nil];
154       }
155       self.detailViewController.detailItem = selectedBook;
156       [self.navigationController pushViewController:self.detailViewController
157                                       animated:YES];
158   }
```

If Line #148 looks very similar to Line #104 in Listing 8–20 that's because it's basically the same thing. Based upon the indexPath.row, we select the specific book from our Bookstore object and we save it in a variable called selectedBook.

On Line #155, we take the selectedBook and store it into a property called detailItem that is already part of the existing DetailViewController class. That's all we need to do in the MasterViewController. We've basically passed off the book to the DetailViewController. We're almost done. Now we need to make a few small modifications to the DetailViewController so that it displays the Book object properly.

Modifying the DetailViewController

Earlier in this chapter, we modified the DetailViewController so that it would display some detail information about a book. In the code we just finished, we modified the MasterViewController so that it passes the selected book to the DetailViewController. Now all that remains is to simply move the information from the Book object in the DetailViewController to the appropriate fields on the screen. All of this is done in one method—configureView.

Listing 8–22. *Moving the Book object data to our detail view.*

```
33   - (void)configureView
34   {
35       // Update the user interface for the detail item.
36
37       if (self.detailItem) {
38           Book *theBook = (Book *)self.detailItem;
39           self.titleLabel.text = theBook.title;
40           self.authorLabel.text = theBook.author;
41           self.descriptionTextView.text = theBook.description;
42       }
43   }
```

The configureView method is one of many convenience methods included in the Xcode template and is called whenever the DetailViewController is being initialized. This is where we will move our selected Book object's information to the fields in the view.

Lines #38–41 in the DetailViewController.m file is where we move the information from the Book object to the view. If you recall, Line #155 in Listing 8–21 set the selected book into a property on the DetailViewController called detailItem. Line #38 pulls that item out into a Book object called theBook.

Lines #39–41 simply move each of the Book object's properties to the view controls we built earlier in the chapter. That's all we need to in this class. If you build and run the project and click on one of the books, you should see something like Figure 8–16.

Don't forget to add an import of the "Book.h" file, as shown in Listing 8–23, line #10.

Listing 8–23. *Importing the Book.h header file.*

```
1   //
2   // DetailViewController.m
3   // MyBookstore
4   //
5   // Created by M.R. Fisher on 8/28/11.
6   // Copyright (c) 2011 www.committed-code.com. All rights reserved.
7   //
```

```
8
9   #import "DetailViewController.h"
10  #import "Book.h"
```

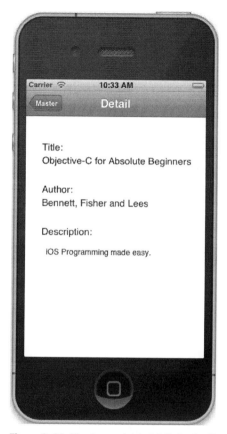

Figure 8–16. *Viewing our book details for the first time.*

Summary

We've finally reached the end of this chapter! Here is a summary of the things that we covered.

- *Understanding Collection classes:* Collection classes are a very powerful set of classes that come with the Foundation and allow us to store and retrieve information efficiently.

▓ *Using instance variables*: Instance variables are variables that are defined in the interface file of the class and are accessible once the class has been instantiated.

▓ *Working with properties*: Properties are short ways of creating getters and/or setters. Getters and setters get or set the values of an instance variable.

▓ *Looping with* `for...in`*: This* feature offers a new way to iterate through an enumerated list of items.

▓ *Building a Master-Detail application:* We used Xcode and the Master-Detail template to build a simple Bookstore program to display books and the detail of an individual book.

▓ *A simple Data Model:* Using the Collection classes we learned about, we used an NSMutableArray to construct a Bookstore Object and use it as a data source in our Bookstore program.

▓ *Connect data to the View:* We connected our Book object's data to the interface fields using Xcode.

Exercises

▓ Add more books to the bookstore using the original program as a guide.

▓ Enhance the Book class so it can store another attribute—a price or ISBN number, for example.

▓ Modify the DetailViewController so that the new fields are displayed. Remember to connect an interface control to an instance variable.

▓ Change the Bookstore object so that a separate method is called to initialize the list of Book objects (instead of putting it all in the init method).

▓ There is another attribute to a UITableViewCell called the detailTextLabel. Try to make use of this by setting its text property to something.

▓ Using Xcode to modify the interface, play with changing the background color of the DetailViewController.xib file.

For a tougher challenge:

▓ Sort the books in the Bookstore object so they appear in ascending order on the MasterDetailView.

Chapter 9

Comparing Data

In this chapter, we will discuss one of the most basic and frequent operations you will perform as you program: comparing data. In our bookstore example, you may need to compare book titles if your clients are looking for a specific book. You may also need to compare authors if your clients are interested in purchasing books by a specific author. Comparing data is a common tasks performed by developers. Many of the loops you learned about in the previous chapter will require you to compare data so that you know when your code should stop looping.

Comparing data in programming is like using a scale. You have one value on one side and another value on the other side. In the middle, you have an operator. The operator determines what kind of comparison is being done. Examples of operators are "greater than," "less than," or "equal to."

The values on either side of the scale are usually variables. We learned about the different types of variables in Chapter 3. In general, the comparison functions for different variables will be slightly different. It is imperative that you become very familiar with the functions and syntax to compare data, as this will form a basis for your development.

For the purpose of this chapter, we will use an example of a bookstore application. This application will allow users to log in to the application, search for books, and purchase them. We will try to relate the different ways of comparing data to show how they would be used in this type of application.

Revisiting Boolean Logic

In a previous chapter in this book, we introduced Boolean logic. Due to its prevalence in programming, we will revisit this subject in this chapter and go into more detail.

The most common comparison that you will program your application to perform is Boolean logic. Boolean logic usually comes in the form of `if then` statements. Boolean logic can have only one of two answers: yes or no. The following are some good examples of Boolean questions that you will use in your applications:

- Is 5 larger than 3?

- Does "now" have more than 5 letters?

- Is 6/1/2010 later than today?

Notice that there are only 2 possible correct answers to these questions: yes and no. If you are asking a question that could have more than 2 answers, that question will need to be worded differently for programming.

Each of these questions will be represented by an if then statement (for example, if 5 is greater than 3, then print a message to the user). Each if statement is required to have some sort of relational operator. A relational operator can be something like "is greater than" or "is equal to".

In order to start using these types of questions in your programs, you will first need to become familiar with the different relational operators available to you in the C and Objective-C languages. We will cover those first. After that, we will look into how different variables can behave with these operators.

Using Relational Operators

Objective-C uses 6 standard relational operators. These are the standard algebraic operators with only one real change: in the Objective-C language, as in most other programming languages, the equal to operator is made by two equal signs (==). In chapter 4, Table 4-7, we describe the different operators available to you as a developer.

> **NOTE:** A single equal sign (=) is used to assign a value to a variable. Two equal signs (==) are needed to compare two values. For example, if(x=9) will assign the value of 9 to the variable x and return "yes" if 9 is successfully assigned to x, which will be in most, if not all, of the cases. if(x==9) will actually do a comparison to see if x equals 9.

Comparing Numbers

One of the difficulties developers have had in the past was dealing with different data types in comparisons. Earlier in this book, we discussed the different types of variables. You may remember that 1 is an integer. If you wanted to compare an integer with a float such as 1.2, this could cause some issues. Thankfully, Objective-C helps us out with this. In Objective-C, you can compare any two numeric data types without having to typecast (typecasting is still sometimes needed when dealing with other data types, and we cover this later in the chapter). This allows you to write code without worrying about the data types that need to be compared.

> **NOTE:** Typecasting is the conversion of a number from one type to another.

In our application, we will need to compare numbers in many ways. For example, let's say that our bookstore offers a discount for people who spend over $30 in a single transaction. We will need to add the total amount the person is spending and then compare this to $30. If the amount spent is larger than $30, we will need to calculate the discount. See the following example.

```
float totalSpent;
int discountThreshhold;
int discountPercent;

discountThreshold=30;
discountPercent=0;
totalSpent=calculateTotalSpent();

if(totalSpent>discountThreshold) {
        discountPercent=10;
}
```

Let's walk through the code. First, we declare our variables (totalSpent, discountThreshhold, and discountPercent). As we discussed in Chapter 3, if the number can contain decimals, we should declare it as a float rather than as an int. We know that the discountThreshold and the discountPercent will not contain decimals, so we can declare these as ints. In this example, we assume that we have a function called calculateTotalSpent, which will calculate the total spent in this current order. We then simply check to see if the total spent is larger than the discount threshold; if it is, we set the discount percent. Also notice that it was not necessary to tell the code to convert the data when comparing the different numeric data types. As we mentioned earlier, this is all handled by Objective-C.

Another action that requires the comparison of numbers is looping. As discussed in Chapter 4, looping is a core action in development and many loop types require some sort of comparison to determine when to stop. Let's take a look at a for loop.

```
int numberOfBooks;
numberOfBooks=50;

for (int y = 1; y <= numberOfBooks; y++) {
    doSomething();
}
```

In this example, we iterate, or loop, through the total number of books that we have in the bookstore. The for statement is where the interesting stuff starts to happen. Let's break it down.

```
int y=1;
```

This portion of the code is declaring y as an int and then assigning it a starting value of 1.

```
y <= numberOfBooks;
```

This portion is telling the computer to check to see if our counting variable y is less than or equal to the total number of books we have in our store. If y becomes larger than the number of books, the loop will no longer run.

y++

This portion of code increases *y* by 1 every time the loop is run.

Creating an Example Xcode App

Now let's create an Xcode application so that we can start comparing numeric data.

1. Launch Xcode. From your hard drive, go to Developer ➤ Applications folder. Drag it to the Dock, as we will be using it throughout the rest of this book. See Figure 9–1.

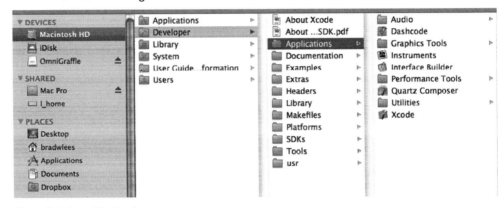

Figure 9–1. *Launching Xcode*

2. Click on Create a New Xcode Project to open a new window. On the left-hand side of that window, under iOS, select Application. Then select Single View Application on the right hand side. Click on Next.

NOTE: The Window-Based Application is the most generic and basic of the iOS application types.

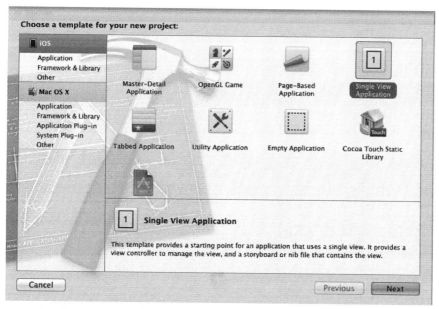

Figure 9–2. *Creating a new project*

3. On the next page, enter the name of your application. We used
Comparison as the name, but you can choose any name you like. This is
also the window where you will select which device you would like to
target. We will leave it as universal for the time being. See Figure 9–3.

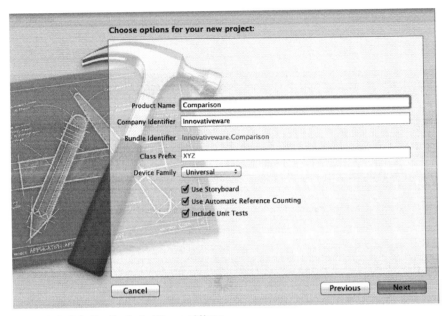

Figure 9–3. *Selecting the Project Type and Name*

> **NOTE:** Xcode projects, by default, are saved in the Documents Folder in your user home.

4. Once the new project is created, you will see the standard Xcode Window. Select the expand arrow next to the Comparison folder to expand it. You will see two files, ComparisonsAppDelegate.m and ComparisonsAppDelegate.h. The .h file is a header file and we will not be changing anything in that file at this moment. The actual names will change depending on the name you used when creating the project. For the purpose of these examples, we are only going to be focusing on the ComparisonsAppDelegate.m file.

5. Double-click on the main.c file and you will see the following code:

```
#import "ComparisonsAppDelegate.h"
@implementation TestingComparisonsAppDelegate
@synthesize window=_window;

- (BOOL)application:(UIApplication *)application
didFinishLaunchingWithOptions:(NSDictionary *)launchOptions
{
    // Override point for customization after application launch.
    [self.window makeKeyAndVisible];

}
```

6. At this point, our applications will just launch and display a window. We are going to add a little "Hello World" to our application. After the line [self.window makeKeyAndVisible], we need to add the following code:

```
NSLog(@"Hello World");
```

This line creates a new NSString with the contents "Hello World" and passes it to the NSLog function that is used for debugging.

Let's run our application to see how it works.

1. Click on the Run button in the default toolbar.

2. The iOS simulator will launch. This will just display a window. Back in Xcode, a debug window will appear at the bottom of the screen, as shown in Figure 9–4. You can always toggle this window by selecting View ➤ Show Debug Area.

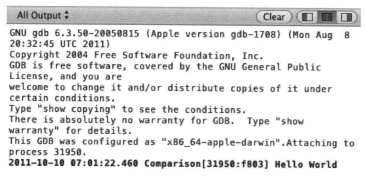

```
All Output ▼                                    Clear   ▢ ▣ ▢
GNU gdb 6.3.50-20050815 (Apple version gdb-1708) (Mon Aug  8
20:32:45 UTC 2011)
Copyright 2004 Free Software Foundation, Inc.
GDB is free software, covered by the GNU General Public
License, and you are
welcome to change it and/or distribute copies of it under
certain conditions.
Type "show copying" to see the conditions.
There is absolutely no warranty for GDB.  Type "show
warranty" for details.
This GDB was configured as "x86_64-apple-darwin".Attaching to
process 31950.
2011-10-10 07:01:22.460 Comparison[31950:f803] Hello World
```

Figure 9–4. *Debugger Window*

Most of the information in this window will mean very little to you. The most important line is the bold section that actually shows the output of your application. The first part of the line shows the date, time, and name of the application. The "Hello World" part was generated by the NSLog line that we added before.

1. Go back to the application and open the ComparisonsAppDelegate.m file.

2. Go to the beginning of the line that begins with NSLog. This is the line that is responsible for printing the "Hello World" section. We are going to comment out this line by placing two backslashes (//) in front of the line of code. Commenting out code tells Xcode to ignore it when it builds and runs the application. Code that is commented out will not run.

3. Once you comment out the line of code, you will no longer see the line in bold if you run the program, because the application is no longer outputting any line.

4. In order for the application to output the results of our comparisons, we
    will have to add one line.

```
NSLog(@"The result is %@", (6>5 ? @"True" : @"False"));
```

> **NOTE:** The above code (6>5 ? @"True" : @"False"); is called a Ternary operation. It is
> essentially just a simplified way of writing an If/Then statement.

5. Place this line into your code. This line is telling your application to print
    out "The result is." Then it will print "True" if 6 is greater than 5, or
    "False" if 5 is greater than 6.

Because 6 is greater than 5, it will print out True.

You can change this line to test any of the examples we have put together thus far in
this chapter, or any of the examples we will do further on.

Let's try another example.

```
int i=5;
int y=6;
NSLog(@"The result is %@", (y>i ? @"True" : @"False"));
```

In this example, we created an integer and assigned its value to 5. We then created
another variable and assigned the value to 6. We then changed the NSLog example to
compare the variables i and y instead of using actual numbers. When you run this
example, you will get the following result:

```
[Switching to process 24637]
Running…
2010-05-31 14:44:17.979 Comparison[24637:a0f] The result is True

Debugger stopped.
Program exited with status value:0.
```

Figure 9–4. *NSLog output*

We will now explore other kinds of comparisons, and then we will come back to our
application and test some of them.

Using Boolean Expressions

A Boolean expression is the easiest of all comparisons. Boolean expressions are used to
determine if a value is true or false. False is defined as 0 and true as non-zero. For
example:

```
int j;
j=5;
if(j) {
      some_code();
}
```

The If statement will always evaluate to true because our variable j is not equal to zero or null. Because of that, our program will run the some_code() method.

```
int j;
j=0;
if(j) {
        some_code();
}
```

If we change the value of j, the statement will evaluate to false, because j is now 0. This can be used with BOOL and number variables.

```
int j;
j=0;
if(!j) {
        some_code();
}
```

Placing an exclamation point in front of a Boolean expression will change it to the opposite value (a false becomes a true and a true becomes a false). This line now asks "if not j," which, in this case, is true because j is equal to 0. This is an example of using an integer to act as a Boolean variable, As we discussed earlier, Objective C also has variables called BOOL that have only two possible values: YES or NO.

> **NOTE:** Many programming languages use the terms TRUE and FALSE instead of YES and NO used by Objective C. When Objective C was developed, the C language did not have true Boolean variables.

Let's look at an example related to the bookstore. We have a frequent buyer's club that entitles all members to a 15% discount on all books that they purchase. This is easy to check. We simply set the variable clubMember to YES if they are a member and NO if they are not. The following code will apply the discount only to club members:

```
int discountPercent;
BOOL clubMember;

clubMember=FALSE;
discountPercent=0;
if(clubMember) {
        discountPercent=15;
}
```

Comparing Strings

Strings are a very difficult data type for most C languages. In ANSI C (or standard C), a string is just an array of characters. Objective-C has taken the development of the string even further and made it an object called the NSString. Many more properties and methods are available to us when working with an object. Fortunately for us, NSString has many methods for comparing data, which makes our job much easier.

While developing for the Mac and the iPhone, you will be able to use both NSStrings and standard C strings. For the purposes of this book, we will be focusing on comparing the NSString objects. If you have C type strings in your application, they will need to be converted to NSStrings in order to use to code included in this book. Fortunately for us, this conversion is very simple.

```
char *myCString;
NSString *myNsstring;

myCString = "testing a string";
myNsstring = [NSString stringWithUTF8String: myCString];
```

The first two lines are code you have seen before. They are your variable declarations. You are declaring a standard C string called myCString and a NSString called myNsstring. The third line is just a simple initiation of your standard C string. We are assigning a value to it.

The last line is where everything happens. You are assigning your NSString object to be equal to creating a new NSString object, with the value coming from a UTF8string and passing it to the standard C string that we created. Once you have all of your standard C strings as NSStrings, we can take advantage of the powerful comparison features provided to us by the class.

Let's look at another example. Here, we will compare passwords to see if we should allow a user to log in.

```
NSString *enteredPassword, *myPassword;

myPassword=@"duck";
enteredPassword=@"Duck";
bool continueLogin=NO;

if([enteredPassword isEqualToString:myPassword]) {
        continueLogin=YES;
}
```

The first line just declares two NSStrings. The next two lines initialize the strings. Remember, before you use any objects, they need to be initialized. In your actual code, you will need to get the enteredPassword string from the user. These lines use a shortcut. Notice the @ symbol before the C style string. The @ symbol creates a new NSString from the C style string that follows it.

The next line is the part of the code that actually does the work. We are sending a message to the enteredPassword object asking it if it is equal to the myPassword string. The method always needs to have an NSString passed to it. The example code will always be false, because of the capital on the enteredPassword versus the lowercase on the myPassword.

> **NOTE:** If you need to compare two NSStrings, regardless of case, you would simply use the caseInsensitiveCompare method instead of the isEqualToString.

There are many other different comparisons you might have to perform on strings. For example, you may want to check the length of a certain string. This is easily done.

```
NSString *enteredPassword;
NSString *myPassword;
myPassword=@"duck";
enteredPassword=@"Duck";
bool continueLogin=NO;

if([enteredPassword length] > 5) {
        continueLogin=YES;
}
```

This code checks to see if the entered password is longer than 5 characters.

There will be other times when you will have to search within a string for some data. Fortunately, Objective-C makes this very easy to do. NSString provides us with a function called rangeOfString, which allows you to search within a string for another string. The function rangeOfString only takes one argument, which is the string for which you are searching.

```
NSString *searchTitle, *bookTitle;
searchTitle=@"Sea";
bookTitle=@"2000 Leagues Under the Sea";

if([bookTitle rangeOfString:searchTitle].location !=NSNotFound) {
        addToResults();
}
```

This code is very similar to other examples we have examined. This example takes a search term and checks to see if the book title has that same search term in it. If it does, it adds the book to the results. This can be adapted to allow users to search for specific terms in book titles, authors, or even descriptions.

NOTE: All string searches are case sensitive by default. If you want to search inside of a string, regardless of the case, you can change the preceding call from:

```
[bookTitle rangeOfString: searchTitle]
```

to:

```
[bookTitle rangeOfString: searchTitle options:NSCaseInsensitiveSearch]
```

For a complete listing of the methods supported by NSString, see the Apple documentation at http://developer.apple.com/mac/library/documentation/cocoa/reference/Foundation/Classes/NSString_Class/Reference/NSString.html.

Comparing Dates

Dates are a fairly complicated variable type in any language and, unfortunately, depending on the type of application you are writing, they are very common. Objective-

C previously used the NSCalendarDate class, but recently it has been replaced with a more up-to-date NSDate. The new NSDate has a lot of nice methods that make comparing dates easy. We will focus on the compare function. The compare function returns an NSComparisonResult, which has three possible values: NSOrderedSame, NSOrderedDescending, NSOrderedAscending.

```
NSDate *today = [NSDate date];

//Sale Date as of 12/4/2011
NSDate *saleDate = [NSDate dateWithString:@"2011-12-04 04:00:00 -0700"];

NSComparisonResult result;
bool saleStarted;

result=[today compare:saleDate];

        if(result==NSOrderedAscending) {
                //Sale Date is in the future
                saleStarted=NO;
        } else if(result==NSOrderedDescending) {
                //Sale Date is in the past
                saleStarted=YES;
        } else {
                //Sale Date and Today are the same
                saleStarted=YES;
        }
```

This may seem like a lot of work just to compare some dates. Let's walk through the code and see if we can make sense of it.

```
NSDate *today = [NSDate date];
NSDate *saleDate = [NSDate dateWithString:@"2011-09-04 04:00:00 -0700"];
```

Here, we declare two different NSDate objects. The first one, named today, is initialized with the system date or your computer or iPad date. The second one, named saleDate, is initialized with a date some time in the future. We will use this date to see if this sale has begun. We will not go into detail about the initialization of NSDates, but they can be initialized using the dateWithString function similar to what we showed previously.

> **NOTE:** In most programming languages, dates are dealt with in a very specific pattern. They usually start out with the 4 digit year followed by a hyphen, then a two digit month followed by a hyphen, then a 2 digit day. If you are using a data format with a time, these data are usually presented in a similar manner. Times are usually presented with the hour, minute, and second, each separated by a colon. Objective C also has time zone support. The "-0700" tells Objective C that the time is 7 hours less than Greenwich Mean time or Mountain Standard Time.

```
NSComparisonResult result;
```

The results of using the compare function of an NSDate object is an NSComparisonResult. We have to declare an NSComparisonResult to capture the output from the compare function.

```
result=[today compare:saleDate];
```

This simple line runs the comparison of the two dates. It places the resulting
NSComparisonResult into the variable called result.

```
if(result==NSOrderedAscending) {
//Sale Date is in the future
        saleStarted=NO;
} else if(result=NSOrderedDescending) {
//Sale Date is in the past
        saleStarted=YES;
} else {
//Sale Date and Today are the same
        saleStarted=YES;
}
```

Now we need to find out what value is in the variable result. In order to accomplish this,
we perform an if statement that compares the result to the three different options for
the NSComparisonResult. The first line finds out if the sale date is greater than today's
date. This means that the sale date is in the future, and thus the sale has not started. We
then set the variable saleStarted to No. The next line finds out whether the sale date is
less than today. If it is, then the sale has started and we set the saleStarted variable to
Yes. The next line just says else. This captures all other options. We know, though, that
the only other option is NSOrderedSame. This means that the two dates are exactly the
same, and thus the sale is just beginning.

There are other methods that you can use to compare NSDate objects. Each of these
methods will be more efficient at certain tasks. We have chosen the compare method
because it will handle most of your basic date comparison needs.

> **NOTE:** Remember that an NSDate holds both a date and a time. This can affect your
> comparisons with dates as it not only compares the date but the time.

Combining Comparisons

As we discussed in Chapter 4, sometimes something more complex than a single
comparison is needed. This is where logical operators come in. Logical operators enable
you to check for more than one different requirement. For example, if we have a special
discount for people who are members of our book club and who spend over $30, we
can write one statement to check this.

```
float totalSpent;
 int discountThreshhold;
int discountPercent;
BOOL clubMember = TRUE;

discountThreshhold=30;
discountPercent=0;
totalSpent=calculateTotalSpent();

if(totalSpent > discountThreshhold && clubMember) {
```

```
        discountPercent=15;
}
```

We have combined two of the examples from above. The new comparison line reads as follows: If totalSpent is greater than discountThreshold AND clubMember is true, then we set the discountPercent to 15. In order for this to return True, both items need to be true. || can be used instead of && to signify "or." We can change the line above to this:

```
if(totalSpent> discountThreshhold|| clubMember) {
        discountPercent=15;
}
```

Now this reads: If totalSpent is greater than discountThreshold **OR** clubMember is true, then set the discount percent. This will return True if either of the options is true.

You can continue to use the logical operations to string as many comparisons together as you need. In some cases, you may need to group comparisons together using parentheses. This can be more complicated and is beyond the scope of this book.

Using the Switch Statement

Up to this point, we've had several example of comparing data by simply using the if statement and/or the if/else statements.

```
if (some_value == SOME_CONSTANT) {
    ...
} else if (some_value == SOME_OTHER_CONSTANT) {
    ...
} else if (some_value == YET_SOME_OTHER_CONSTANT) {
    ...
}
```

If you need to compare a specific ordinal type to several constant values, you can use a different method that can simplify the comparison code: the switch statement.

> **NOTE:** An ordinal type is a built-in C data type that can be ordered. Examples are int, long, char, BOOL.

The switch statement allows the comparison of one or more constant values against the ordinal data type. This is important to understand. The switch statement does not allow the comparison of the ordinal type to a variable. Here is an example of a proper switch statement:

```
char value;
value = 'd';

switch (value) {        // The switch statement followed by a begin brace
case 'a':      // Equivalent to if (value == 'a')
    ...                 // Call functions and put any other statements here after the
case.
    ...
```

```
break;              // This indicates that this is the end of the "case 'a':"
statement.
case 'b':
   ...
   ...
break;
case 'c':          // If there is a case without a break, the program continues to execute.
case 'd':              // So, in this case, if value is a 'c' or a 'd', this code will
be executed.
   ...
   ...
break;
default:              // Default is optional and is only used if there is no case
statement
   ...              // for 'value'. So, if value was equal to 'x', the default part of
the switch
   ...              // statement will be executed since there is no "case 'x':" present.
break;
}  // End of the switch statement.
```

The switch statement is very powerful, and it simplifies and streamlines comparisons of an ordinal type to several possible constants. That said, this is also the limiting factor of the switch statement. It is not possible, for example, to use the switch statement to compare an NSString variable to a series of string constants. This is because an NSString value is not an ordinal type. The switch statement also must compare an ordinal type to a constant. Therefore, it is not possible to write:

```
switch (value) {
case variable: //case must be a constant, not a variable.
   ...
break;
```

While it does seem that these are severe limitations to the switch statement, the switch statement is still a very powerful statement that can be used to simplify certain if/else statements.

Summary

We've reached the end of the chapter! Here is a summary of the things that were covered.

- Comparisons
    - Comparing data is an integral part of any application.
- Relational operators
    - You learned about the six standard relational operators and how each is used.
- Integers
    - Integers are the easiest pieces of information to compare. You learned how comparison of integers will be used in your programs and how to implement it.

■ Example

- ■ You created a sample application where you could test your comparisons and make sure that you are correct in your logic.

- ■ You learned how to change the application to add different types of comparisons.

■ Boolean

- ■ You learned how to check Boolean values.

■ Strings

- ■ You learned how strings behave differently from other pieces of information you have tested. You learned some of the pitfalls of comparing strings.

■ Objects

- ■ You learned how difficult it can be to compare objects and that care must be taken to make sure you are getting the response you desire.

Exercises

■ Modify the example application to compare some string information. This can either be in the form of a variable or a literal.

■ Create a loop in your application to display a number using the methods you learned in the Boolean portion of the chapter.

■ Write an Objective-C app that determines if the following years are leap years: 1800, 1801, 1899, 1900, 2000, 2001, 2003, and 2010. Output should be written to the console in the following format: "The year 2000 is a leap year," or "The year 2001 is not a leap year."

Chapter 10

Creating User Interfaces

Interface Builder is an application that enables iPhone/iPad and Mac developers to easily create their user interfaces using a powerful graphical user interface. It provides the ability to build user interfaces by simply dragging objects from Interface Builder's library to your app's user interface.

Interface Builder stores your user interface design in one or more resource files, called XIBs. These resource files are set to interface objects and their relationships. Changes that you make with your user interface are automatically synchronized with Xcode.

To build a user interface, simply drag objects from Interface Builder's Library Pane onto your view. Actions and Outlets are two key components of Interface Builder that help us streamline the development processes.

Actions that our objects trigged in our views are connected to our methods in the app's code. **Outlets** (pointers) declared in our object's interface file are connected to specific instance variables. See Figure 10–1.

> **NOTE:** Interface Builder was once a stand-alone application that developers used to design their user interfaces. Starting with Xcode 4.0, Apple integrated Interface Builder within Xcode.

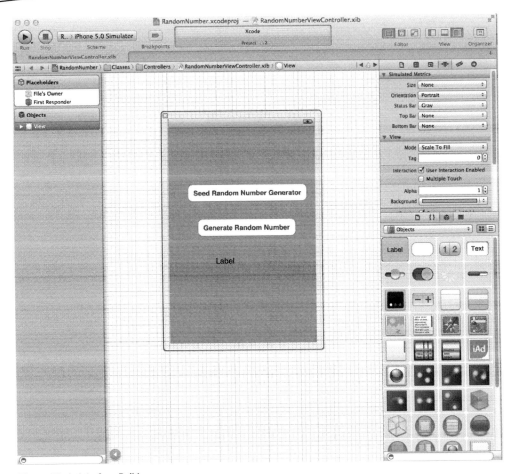

Figure 10–1. *Interface Builder*

Understanding Interface Builder

The operating system is responsible for the memory management of the objects it creates for iPhone and iPad apps. This relieves the developer of having to allocate memory if the developer used Interface Builder to create the object.

Interface Builder saves the user interface file as a bundle that contains the interface objects and relationships used in the application. These bundles had the file extension ".NIB". With version 3.0 of Interface Builder, a new XML file format was used and the file extension changed to ".XIB". However, developers still call these files "NIB" files when saying or referring to the file name.

Unlike most other graphical user interface applications, NIBs are often referred to as freeze-dried because they contain the archived objects themselves and are ready to run.

The XML file format is used to facilitate storage with source control systems like Subversion and Git.

In the next section, we'll discuss an app design pattern called Model-View-Controller. This design pattern enables developers to more easily maintain code and reuse objects over the life of an app.

The Model-View-Controller

Model-View-Controller (MVC) is the most prevalent design pattern used in iPhone/iPad development, and learning about it will make your life as a developer much easier. MVC is used in software development and is considered an **architectural pattern.**

Architectural patterns describe solutions to software design problems that developers can use in their code. The MVC pattern is not unique to Apple OOP developers; it is being adopted by many makers of IDEs, including those running on Windows and Linux platforms.

Software development is considered an expensive and risky venture for businesses. Frequently, apps take longer than expected to write, come in over budget, and don't work as promised. OOP produced a lot of hype and gave the impression that companies would realize savings if they adopted its methodology, primarily because of the reusability of objects and easier maintainability of the code. Initially, this didn't happen.

As engineers looked at why OOP wasn't living up to these expectations, they discovered a key shortcoming with how developers were designing their objects: developers were frequently mixing objects together in such a way that the code became difficult to maintain as the application matured, moved to different platforms, or hardware displays changed.

Objects were often designed so that, if any of the following changed, it was difficult to isolate the objects that were impacted:

- Business rules
- User interfaced
- Client-server or Internet-based

Objects can be broken down into three task-related categories. It is the responsibility of the developer to ensure that each of these categories keeps their objects from drifting across other categories. They are:

1. **Models:** Business objects
2. **Views:** User interface objects
3. **Controllers**: Objects that communicate with both the Models and the Views

As objects are categorized in these groups, apps can be developed and maintained more easily over time. The following are examples of objects and their associated MVC category for an iPhone banking application:

Model

- Account balances
- User encryption
- Account transfers
- Account login

View

- Account balances table cell
- Account login spinner control

Controller

- Account balance view controller
- Account transfer view controller
- Logon view controller

The easiest way to remember and classify your objects in the MVC paradigm is the following:

Model: Unique business or application rules or code that represent the real world

View: Unique user interface code

Controller: Anything that controls or communicates with the Model or View objects

Figure 10–2 represents the MVC paradigm.

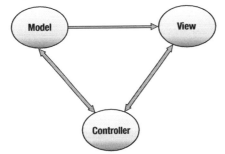

Figure 10–2. *MVC paradigm*

Neither Xcode nor Interface Builder force developers to use the MVC design pattern. It is up to the developer to organize their objects in such a way to use this design pattern.

It is worth mentioning that Apple *strongly* embraces the MVC design pattern and all of the frameworks are designed to work in an MVC world. This means that if you also embrace the MVC design pattern, working with Apple's classes will be much easier. If you don't, you'll be swimming upstream.

Human Interface Guidelines (HIGs)

Before you get too excited and begin designing dynamic user interfaces for your app, you need to learn some of the ground rules. Apple has developed one of the most advanced operating systems in the world with iOS 5. Additionally, Apple's products are known for being intuitive and user-friendly. Apple wants users to have the same experience from one app to the next.

In order to insure a consistent user experience, Apple provides developers guidelines on how their apps should look and feel. These guidelines, called the human interface guidelines (HIGs), are available for the Mac, iPhone, and iPad. You can download these docs at `http://developer.apple.com`. See Figure 10–3.

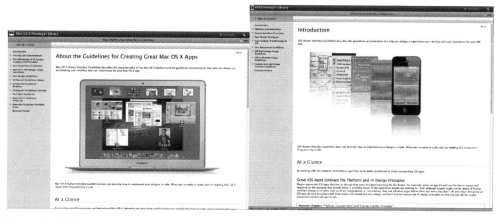

Figure 10–3. *Apple's human interface guidelines (HIGs) for iOS devices and Macs*

> **NOTE:** Apple's HIGs are more than recommendations or suggestions. Apple takes them very seriously. While the HIGs don't describe how to implement your user interface designs in code, they are great for understanding the proper way to implement your views and controls.

The following are the top reasons apps are rejected in Apple's iTunes App store:

1. The app crashes

2. **Violation of the HIGs**

3. Uses Apple Private APIs

4. Doesn't function as advertised on iTunes App Store

You can read, learn, and follow the HIGs before you develop your app, or you can read, learn, and follow the HIG after your app gets rejected by Apple and you have to rewrite part or all of it. Either way, all iOS developers will end up becoming familiar with the HIGs.

Many new iOS developers find this out the hard way, but if you the follow the HIGs from day one, your iOS development will be a far more pleasurable experience.

Creating an Example iPhone App with Interface Builder

Let's get started by building an iPhone app that generates and displays a random number. See Figure 10–4. This app will be similar to the app we created in Chapter 4, but we'll see how much more interesting the app becomes with an iOS user interface (UI).

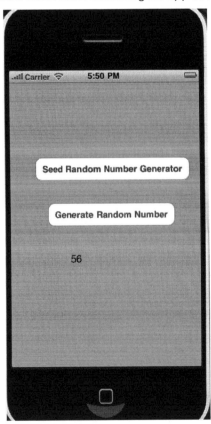

Figure 10–4. *Completed iOS random number generator app*

1. Open up Xcode and select **Create a New Project**. Make sure you select a **Single View Application** for the iPhone. See Figure 10–5.

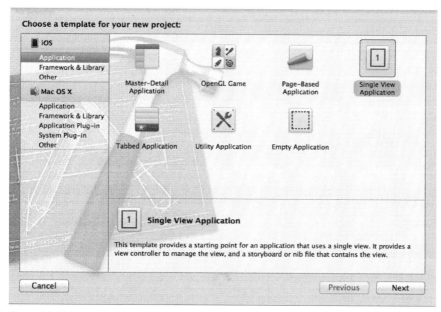

Figure 10–5. *Create an iPhone Single View Application*

2. Name your project "**RandomNumber**" and save the project. See Figure 10–6.

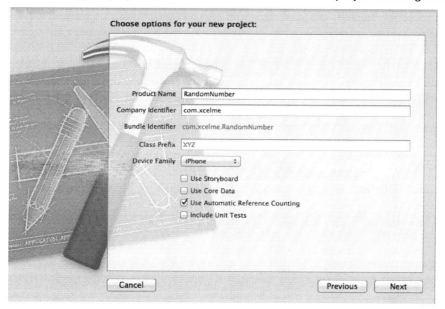

Figure 10–6. *Naming our iPhone project*

3. Your project files and settings are created and displayed. See Figure 10–7.

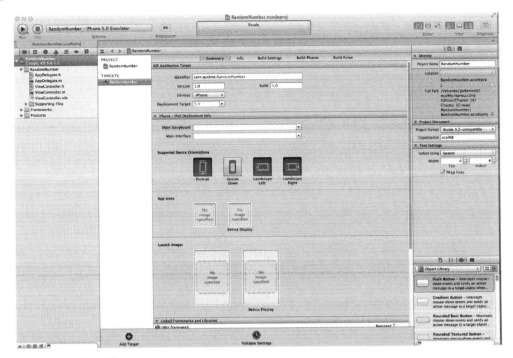

Figure 10–7. *Source files*

Although we only have one controller in this project, it's good programming practice to make your MVC groups at the beginning of your development. This helps remind developers to keep the MVC paradigm and not put all of their code unnecessarily in their controller.

4. **Right-click** the RandomNumber Project, and then select **New Group**. See Figure 10–8.

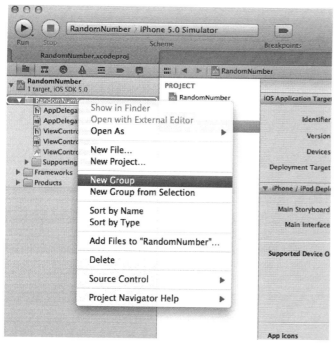

Figure 10–8. *Creating new groups*

5. Create a Models Group, Views Group, and Controllers Group.

6. Drag the ViewController.m and .h file the Controllers Group. Having these groups reminds you to follow the MVC design pattern as you develop your code and prevents you from placing all of your code in the controllers. See Figure 10–9.

Developers have found it helpful to keep their XIB files with their controllers as their projects grow. It is not uncommon to have dozens of controllers and XIB files in your project. Keeping them together helps keep everything organized.

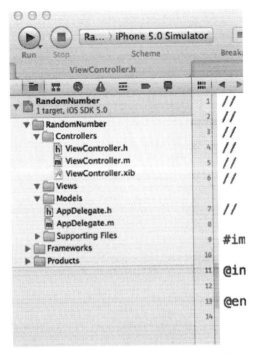

Figure 10–9. *MVC groups with Controller and XIB files organized*

    7.   Click the ViewController.xib to open Interface Builder.

Using Interface Builder

The most common way to launch Interface Builder and begin working on our view is to click the XIB file related to the view. See Figure 10–10.

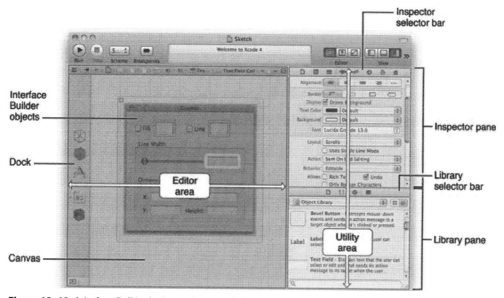

Figure 10–10. *Interface Builder in the workspace window*

When Interface Builder opens, we can see our view displayed in the canvas. We are now able to design our user interface. First we need to understand some of the sub-windows within Interface Builder.

The Dock

The Document window shows all the objects that our view contains. Some examples of these objects are:

- Buttons
- Labels
- Text fields
- Web views
- Map views
- iAd
- Picker views
- Table views

> **NOTE:** You can expand the width of the dock to see a detailed list of all your objects. See Figure 10–11. To get more real estate for the canvas, you can shrink or remove your file list window.

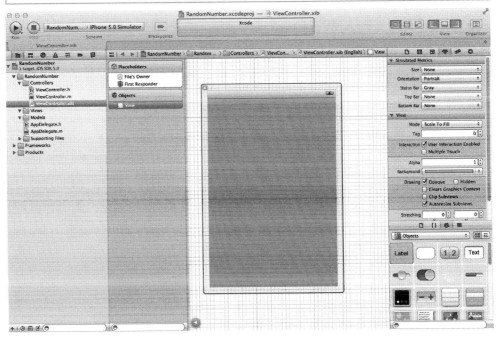

Figure 10–11. *The Doc's width is expanded to show a detailed view of all the objects in our XIB.*

The Library

The Library is where you can exploit your creativity. It's a smorgasbord of objects that you can drag and drop into the view window.

- The library window can grow and shrink by moving the window splitter. See Figure 10–12.

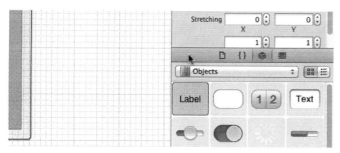

Figure 10–12. *Expand the Library Pane to see more controls. Slide the spitter to resize the window with the mouse.*

For Cocoa Touch objects, the Library pane is divided into the following five sections:

- Controls
- Data Views
- Gesture Recognizers
- Objects & Controllers
- Window & Bars

Figure 10–13. *Various Cocoa Touch Objects in the Library Pane*

Inspector Pane and Selector Bar

The Inspector pane enables you to change the properties of the controls to make your objects follow your command. The Inspector pane has six tabs across the top. See Figure 10–14.

- File Inspector
- Quick Help Inspector
- Identity Inspector
- Attributes Inspector
- Size Inspector
- Connections Inspector

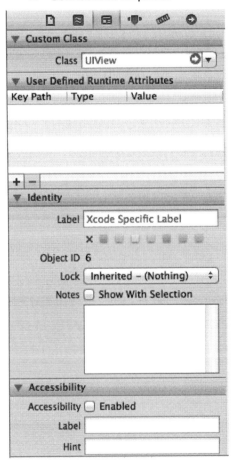

Figure 10–14. *The Identity Inspector and Selector Bar*

Creating the View

Our random number generator will have three objects in the view: one label and two buttons. One button will generate the seed, another button will generate the random number, and the label shows the random number generated by the app.

1. Drag a Label from the Library Pane Controls section to the View window.

2. Drag two rounded rect buttons from the Library window to the View Window.

3. Click the top button and label the button **Seed Random Number Generator**.

4. Click the bottom button and label it **Generate Random Number**. See Figure 10–15.

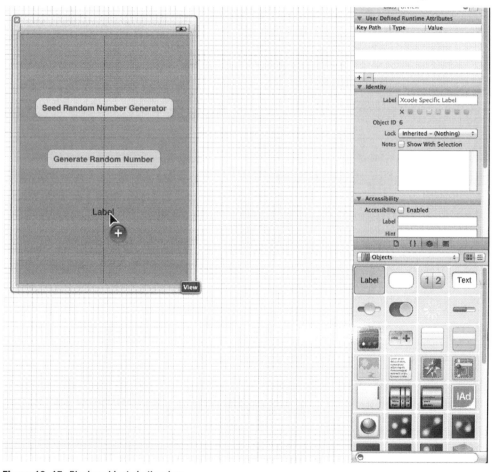

Figure 10–15. *Placing objects in the view*

Now we get to use a new feature with Xcode 4.2 and iOS 5. We now have the ability to quickly and easy connect our Outlets and Actions to our code. Xcode 4.2 actually goes one step further; it will create some of the code for us. All we have to do is drag and drop.

5. Click the Assistant Editor icon at the top right of the screen. This will display the *.h* file for the XIB file we are working on. See Figure 10–16.

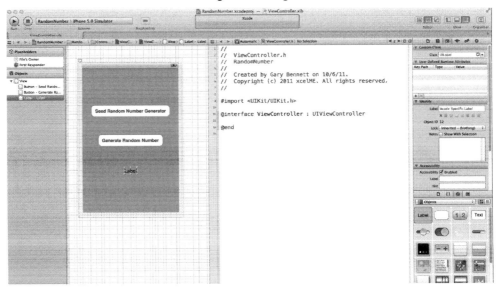

Figure 10–16. *Using the Assistant Editor to display the .h and .XIB files together*

Using Outlets

Now we can connect our label to our code by creating an outlet.

1. Insert curly brackets for your instance variables. Control-Drag from the label in the view to inside the curly brackets in the .h file and drop. See Figure 10–17.

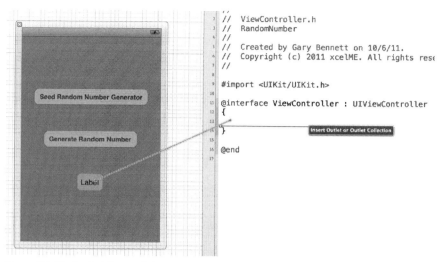

Figure 10–17. *Control-Drag and drop to create the code for randNumber outlet*

A popup window will appear. This enables us to name and specify the type of Outlet.

2. Complete the popup as in Figure 10–18 and **press the Connect button**.

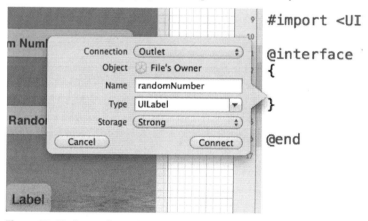

Figure 10–18. *Pop-up for randomNumber Outlet*

The code is now created for the outlet and the outlet is now connected to the Label object in our .XIB file. The shaded circle next to line number 14 indicates the outlet is connected to an object in the XIB file. See Figure 10–19.

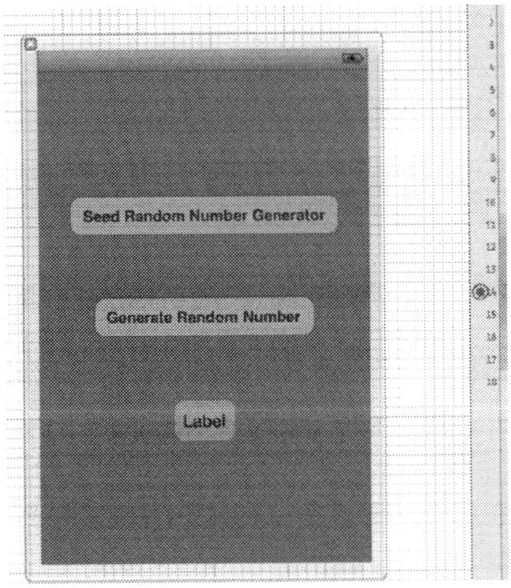

Figure 10–19. *Outlet instance variable code generated and connected to the Label Object.*

As a reminder, outlets (pointers) are declared in our object's interface file and connected to specific instance variables.

There is also a declaration that may be new to you called an IBOutlet, commonly referred to simply as an outlet. **Outlets** signal your controller that this instance variable is a pointer to another object that is set up in Interface Builder. IBOutlet will enable Interface Builder to see the outlet and enable you to connect the variable to the object in Interface Builder.

Using the analogy of an electrical wall outlet, these instance variable outlets are connected to objects. Using Interface Builder, we can connect these instance variables to the appropriate object.

Connecting Actions and Objects

User interface object events, also known as Actions, trigger methods.

Now we need to connect the object actions to the buttons.

1. Control-Drag from the "Seed Random Number Generator" button to below the last curly bracket and drop. Complete the pop-up as indicated in Figure 10–20 and **press the connect button**. Make sure you change the connection as an Action and not an Outlet.

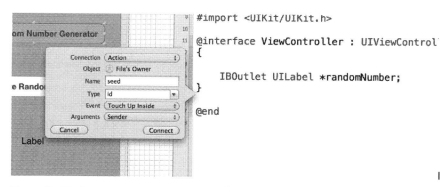

```
#import <UIKit/UIKit.h>

@interface ViewController : UIViewControl
{

    IBOutlet UILabel *randomNumber;
}

@end
```

Figure 10–20. *Complete the pop-up for the Seed method.*

2. Repeat Step 8 for the Generate Random Number button.

```
//
//  ViewController.h
//  RandomNumber
//
//  Created by Gary Bennett on 10/6/11.
//  Copyright (c) 2011 xcelME. All rights reserved.
//

#import <UIKit/UIKit.h>

@interface ViewController : UIViewController
{

    IBOutlet UILabel *randomNumber;
}
- (IBAction)seed:(id)sender;
- (IBAction)generate:(id)sender;

@end
```

Figure 10–21. *Generate and Seed actions connected to their Button Objects*

Implementation File

All that is left is to complete the code for our outlet and actions in the implementation file for the controller.

Open ViewController.m file and complete the seed: and generate: methods. See Figure 10–22.

```
- (IBAction)seed:(id)sender {
    srandom(time(NULL));
    [randomNumber setText: @"Generator seeded"];
}

- (IBAction)generate:(id)sender {
    // Generate a number between 0 and 100 inclusive
    int generated;
    generated = (random() % 101);
    [randomNumber setText:[NSString stringWithFormat:@"%i",generated]];
}
```

Figure 10–22. *The seed: and generate: methods completed.*

There is some code we should examine a bit further: [randNumber setText:. The method setText: sets the UILabel value in your view. The connections you established in Interface Builder from your outlet to the Label object do all the work for you.

That's it!

To run your iPhone app in the iPhone simulator, click the Play button and your app should launch in the simulator. See Figure 10–23.

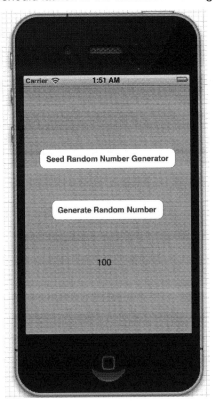

Figure 10–23. *The completed random number generator app running in the iPhone Simulator*

To seed the random function, tap Seed Random Number Generator. To generate the random number, tap Generate Random Number Generator.

Summary

Great job! Interface Builder saves you a lot of time when creating User Interfaces. You have a powerful set of objects to use in your application and are responsible for a minimal amount of coding. Interface Builder handles many of the details you would normally have to deal with.

You should be familiar with the following terms:

- XIB files
- Model-View-Controller (MVC)
- Architectural pattern
- Human interface guidelines (HIGs)
- Outlets
- Actions

Exercises

- Extend the random number generator app to show a date and time in a Label when the app starts.
- Adjust the Date and Time message for "Generator Seeded" to fit nicely in the label.
- After showing a date and time label, add a button to update the data and time label with the new time.

Chapter 11

Storing Information

As a developer, there will be many different situations in which you will need to store data. Users will expect your application (app) to remember preferences and other information each time they launch it. In previous chapters, we discussed the Book Store app. With this app, users will expect your application to remember all of the books in the bookstore and have it default to a database location. Your application will need a way to store this information, retrieve it, and possibly search and sort this data. Working with data can sometimes be difficult. Fortunately, Apple has provided methods and frameworks to make this process easier.

In this chapter, we discuss two different formats in which data will need to be stored. We will start by discussing saving preferences for the Mac and the iPhone, and then move on to using a SQLite database in our application that stores and retrieves data.

Storage Considerations

There are some major storage differences between the Mac and the iPhone, and these differences will affect how you work with data. Let's start by first discussing the Mac and how you will need to develop for it.

On the Mac, by default, applications are stored in the Applications folder. Each user has their own home folder where preferences and information related to that user are stored. Not all of the users will have access to write to the Applications folder or to the application bundle itself.

On the iPhone and iPad, developers do not need to deal with different users. Every person who uses the iPhone has the same permissions and the same folders. There are some other factors to consider with the iPhone, though. Every application on the iPhone is in its own "sand box." This means that files written by an application can only be seen and used by that individual application. This makes for a more secure environment for the iPhone, but it also presents some changes in the way we work with data storage.

Preferences

There are some things to consider when deciding where to store certain kinds of information. The easiest way to store information is within the preferences file, but this method has some downsides.

- All of the data is both read and written at the same time. If you are going to be writing often or writing large amounts of data, this could take time and slow down your application. As a general rule, your preference file should never be larger than 100K. If your preference file starts to become larger than 100k, consider using Core Data as a way to store your information.

- The Preference file does not provide many options when it comes to searching and ordering information.

The preference file is really nothing more than a standardized file with accompanying classes and methods to store application specific information. A preference would be, for example, the sorting column and direction (ascending/descending) of a list. Anything that is generally customizable within an app should be stored in a preference file.

Writing Preferences

Apple has provided developers with the NSUserDefaults class; this class makes it very easy to read and write preferences for the iPhone and Mac OS X.. The great thing is that, in this case, you can use the exact same code for the iPhone and Mac OS X. The only difference between the two implementations is the location of the preference file.

> **NOTE:** For Mac OS X, the preference file is named
> com.yourcompany.applicationname.plist and is located in the
> /Users/username/Library/Preferences folder. On the iPhone, the preference file is located in your
> application bundle in the Library/Preferences folder.

All you need to do to write preferences is to create an NSUserDefaults object. This is done with the following line:

```
NSUserDefaults *prefs = [NSUserDefaults standardUserDefaults];
```

This instantiates the object's prefs and you can now use it to set preference values. Next, you need to set the preference keys for the values that you would like to save. The previous Book Store app example will be used to demonstrate specific instructions throughout the rest of this chapter. As a bookstore, you might want to save a username or password in the preferences. You also might want to save things such as a default book category or recent searches. The preference file is a great place to store this type of information because this is the kind of information that only needs to be read when the application is launched.

Also, on the iPhone, it is often necessary to save your current state. If a person is using your application and then gets a phone call, you want to be able to bring them back to the exact place they were on your application when they are done their phone call. This is less necessary now with iOS 4 and 5 and the implementation of multitasking, but your users will still appreciate it if your application remembers what they were doing the next time it is launched.

Once you have instantiated the object, you can just call `setObjectforKey` to set an object. If we wanted to save the username of sherlock.holmes, we would just call the following line of code:

```
[prefs setObject:@"sherlock.holmes" forKey:@"username"];
```

You can use `setInteger`, `setDouble`, `setBool`, `setFloat`, and `setURL` instead of `setObject`, depending on the type of information you are storing in the preference file. Let's say you store the number of books a user wants to see in the list. Here is an example of using `setInteger` to store this preference:

```
[prefs setInteger:10 forKey:@"booksInList"];
```

After a certain period of time your app will automatically write the preference file. You can force your app to save the preferences by calling the `synchronize` function but this is not necessary in most cases. To call the synchronize function you would write the following line:

```
[prefs synchronize];
```

With just three lines of code, we are able to create a preference object, set two preference values, and write the preference file. It is a very easy and clean process. Here is all of the code together:

```
NSUserDefaults *prefs = [NSUserDefaults standardUserDefaults];
[prefs setObject:@"sherlock.holmes" forKey:@"username"];
[prefs setInteger:10 forKey:@"booksInList"];
```

Reading Preferences

Reading preferences is very similar to writing preferences, and is just as easy. Just like writing, the first step is to obtain the NSUserDefaults object. This is done in exactly the same way as it was done in the writing process:

```
NSUserDefaults *prefs = [NSUserDefaults standardUserDefaults];
```

Now that we have the object, we are able to access the preference values that are set. For writing, we use the `setObject` syntax; for reading, we use the `stringForKey` function. In the writing example, we set preferences for the username and for the number of books in the list to display. We can read those preferences out by using the following simple lines of code:

```
NSString *username = [prefs stringForKey:@"username"];
NSInteger booksInList = [prefs integerForKey:@"booksInList"];
```

Pay close attention to what is done in each of these lines. We start out by declaring the variable username, which is an NSString. This variable will be used to store the preference value of the username we stored in the preferences. Then, we just assign it to the value of the preference username. You will notice that in the read example we do not use the synchronize function. This is because we have not changed the values of the preferences; therefore, we do not need to make sure it is written to a disk.

Databases

We have discussed how to store some small pieces of information and retrieve them at a later point. What if you have more information that needs to be stored? What if you need to conduct a search within this information or put it in some sort of order? These kinds of situations call for a database.

Let's start by discussing what a database is. A database is a tool for storing a significant amount of information in a way that it can be easily searched for or retrieved. When using a database, usually small chunks of the data are retrieved at a time rather than the entire file. Many applications you use in your daily life are based on databases of some sort. Your online banking application retrieves your account activity from a database. Your supermarket uses a database to retrieve prices for different items. A simple example of a database is a spreadsheet. You may have many columns and many rows in your spreadsheet. The columns in your spreadsheet represent different pieces of information you want to store. In a database, these are considered attributes. The rows in your spreadsheet would be considered different records in your database.

Storing Information in a Database

Databases are usually an intimidating subject for a developer; most developers associate databases with enterprise database servers such as Microsoft SQL Server or Oracle. These applications can take time to set up and require constant management. For most developers, a database system like Oracle would be too much to handle. Luckily, Apple has included a small compact database engine called SQLite in the Mac, iPhone, and iPad. This allows you to gain many of the features of the complex database servers without the overhead.

SQLite will provide you with a lot of flexibility in storing information for your application. It stores the entire database in a single file. It is fast, reliable, and easy to implement in your application. The best thing about the SQLite database is that there is no need to perform any installation of software; Apple has taken care of that for you.

However, SQLitedoes have some limitations that, as a developer, you should be aware of:

- SQLite was designed to be used as a single user database. You will not want to use SQLite in an environment where more than one person will be accessing the same database. This could lead to data loss or corruption.

■ In the business world, databases can grow to become very large. It is not surprising for a database manager to handle databases as large as 500GB, and in some cases databases can become much larger than that. SQLite should be able to handle smaller databases without any issues, but you will begin to see performance issues if your database starts to get too large.

■ SQLite lacks some of the backup and data restore features of the enterprise database solutions.

For the purposes of this chapter, we will focus on using SQLite as our database engine. If any of the mentioned limitations are present in the application you are developing, you may need to look into an enterprise database solution, which is beyond the scope of this book.

> **NOTE:** SQLite gets its name from structured query language or SQL. SQL is the language used to enter, search, and retrieve data from a database.

Apple has worked hard to iron out a lot of the challenges of database development. As a developer, you will not need to become familiar with SQL, as Apple has taken care of the direct database interaction for you. Apple has created a framework called Core Data that makes interacting with the database much easier. Core Data has been adapted by Apple from a NeXT product called Enterprise Object Framework and it will handle all of the database interaction for you. Working with Core Data is a lot easier than interfacing directly with the SQLite database. Directly accessing a database via SQL is beyond the scope of this book.

Getting Started with Core Data

Let's start by creating a new Core Data project.

1. Open Xcode and select File ➤ New Project. To create a Mac OS X Core Data project, select Application from the left-hand menu. It is located underneath the Mac OS X header. See Figure 11–1.

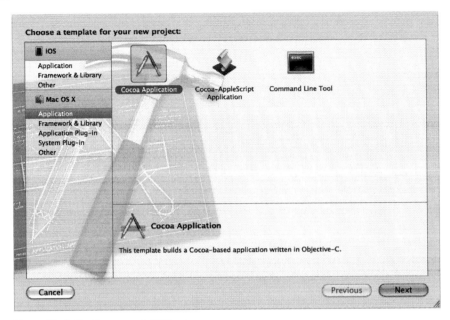

Figure 11–1. *Creating a new project.*

2. Click on the Next button when done. The next screen will allow you to decide where to save your project and the name you want to use. For the purposes of this chapter, we will use the name BookStoreCoreData.

3. Near the bottom, you will see three checkboxes. The first check box is labeled Use Core Data. Make sure this is checked and then click on Next.

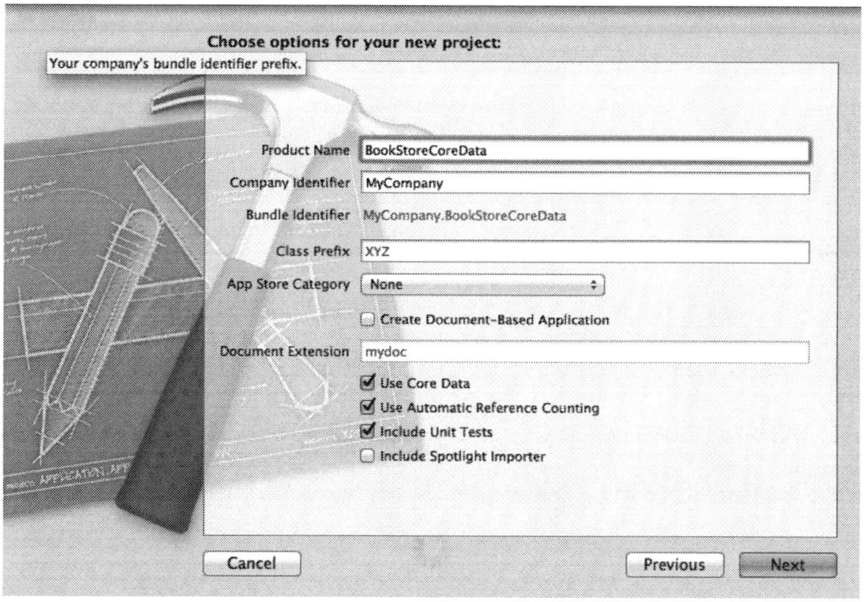

Figure 11–2. *Using Core Data.*

Once you are done with that, your new project will open. It will look similar to a standard application, except, now you will have a BookStoreCoreData.xcdatamodel. This file is called a data model and will contain the information about the data that you will be storing in Core Data.

The Model

If you click on the triangle next to the folder, you will see a file called BookStoreCoreData.xcdatamodel. This file will contain information about the data you want stored in the database. Click on the model file and it will open. You will see a window similar to to the one shown in Figure 11–3.

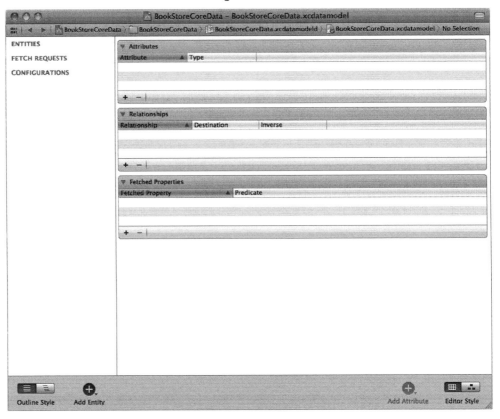

Figure 11–3. *The blank model.*

The window is divided into four sections. On the left you have your entities. In more common terms, these are the objects or items that you want to store in the database.

The right top window contains the attributes. Attributes are pieces of information about the entities. For example, a book would be an entity and the title of the book would be an attribute of that entity.

> **NOTE:** In database terms, entities are your tables and the attributes of the entities are called columns. The objects created from those entities are referred to as rows.

The right middle window will show you all the relationships of an entity. A relationship connects one entity to another. For example, we will create a Book and an Author entity. We will then relate them so that every book can have an author. The right bottom portion deals with fetched properties. Fetched properties are beyond the scope of this book, but they allow you to create filters for your data.

Let's create an entity.

1. Click on the plus sign in the bottom left corner of the window, or select Editor ➤ Add Entity from the menu. See Figure 11–4

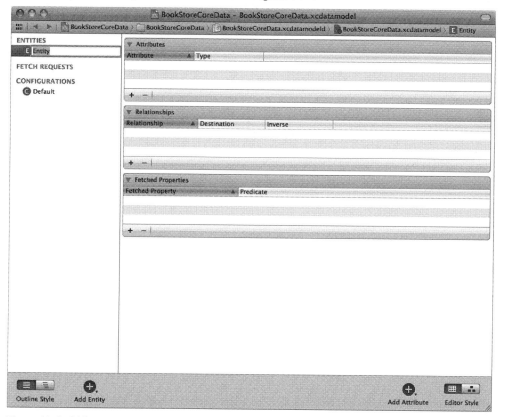

Figure 11–4. *Adding a new entity.*

2. On the left hand side, you will now have the option to name the entity. We will use the name Book for this entity.

> **NOTE** It is generally considered good practice to capitalize your entities' names.

3. Now let's add some attributes. Attributes would be considered as the details of a book, so we will store the title, author, price, and year the book was published. Obviously in your own applications, you may want to store more information, such as the publisher, page count, and genre, but we want to start out simple. Click on the plus sign at the bottom right of the window, or select **Editor ➤ Add Attribute**, as shown in Figure 11–5. If you do not see the option to add an attribute, make sure that you have selected the Book entity on the left-hand side.

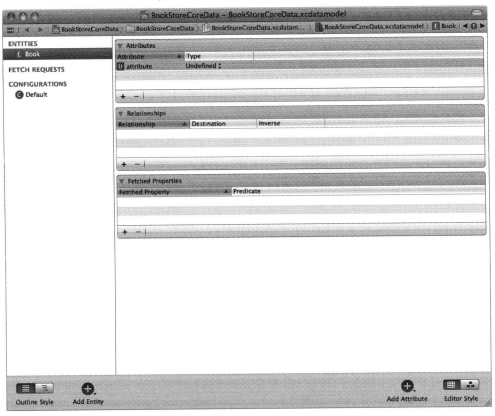

Figure 11–5. *Adding a new attribute.*

4. You will only be given two options for your attribute, the name and the data type. Let's call this attribute `title`.. Unlike entities, attribute names should be lowercased.

5. Now, we will need to select a data type. Selecting the correct data type is very important. It will affect how your data is stored and retrieved from the database. The list has 12 items in it and can be very daunting. We will discuss the most common options and, as you become more familiar with Core Data, you can experiment with the other options. The most common options are String, Integer 32, Float, and Date. For the title of the book, select String.

> **String**: This is the type of attribute used to store text. This should be used to store any kind of information that is not a number or a date. In this example, the book title and author will be strings.

> **Integer 32**: There are actually three different integer values possible for the attribute. Each of the integer types only differ in the minimum and maximum values possible. Integer 32 should cover most of your needs when storing an integer. An integer is a number without a decimal. If you try to save a decimal in an integer attribute, the decimal portion will be truncated. In this example, the year published will be an integer.

> **Float**: A float is a type of attribute that can store numbers with decimals. A float is similar to a double attribute, but they differ in their minimum and maximum values. A float should be able to handle any values. In this example, we will use a float to store the price of the book.

> **Date**: A date attribute is exactly what it sounds like. It allows you to store a date and time, and then performs searches and lookups based on these values. We will not use this type in this example.

6. Let's create the rest of the attributes for the book. Now, add `price`. It should be a float. Add the year the book was published. For two-word attributes, it is standard to make the first word lowercase and the second word initial capped. For example, an ideal name for the year the book was published attribute would be something like, `yearPublished`. Select integer 32 as the attribute type. Once you have added all of your attributes, your screen should look like Figure 11–6.

NOTE: Attributes' names cannot contain spaces.

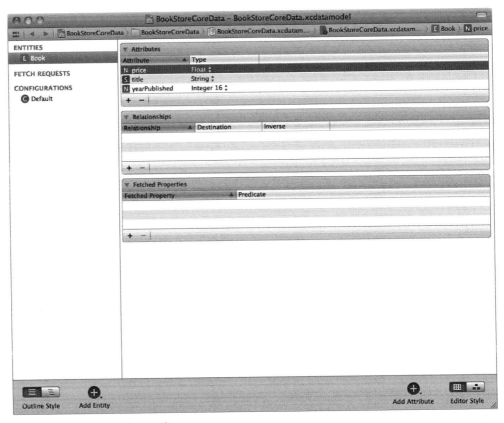

Figure 11–6. *The finished book entity.*

> **NOTE:** If you are used to working with databases, you will notice that we did not add a primary key. A primary key is a field (usually a number) that is used to uniquely identify each record in a database. In Core Data databases, there is no need to create primary keys. The framework will manage all of that for you.

Now that we have finished the Book entity, let's add an Author entity.

1. Add a new entity and call it Author.

2. To this entity, add lastName and firstName, both of which are considered strings.

Once this is done, you should have two entities in your relationship window. Now we need to add the relationships.

1. Click on the Book entity, then click and hold on the plus sign that is located on the bottom right of the screen. Select Add Relationship, as seen in Figure 11–7.

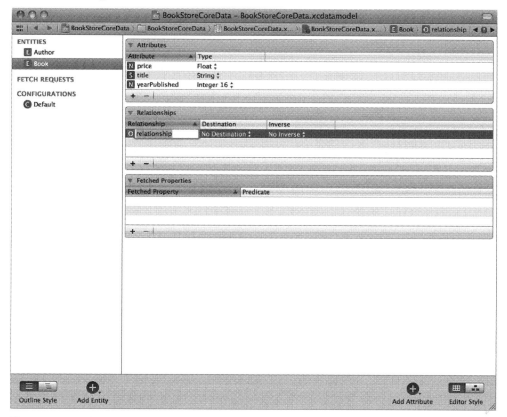

Figure 11–7. *Adding a new relationship.*

2. You will now be given the opportunity to name your relationship. We usually give a relationship the same name as the entity to which it derived from. Type in "author" as the name, or select Author from the drop-down menu.

3. Now, we have created one half of our relationship. To create the other half, click on the Author entity. Now, click the plus sign located at the bottom of the screen and select Add Relationship. We will use the entity name that we are connecting to as the name of this relationship, so we will call it books. We will add an "s" to the entity name because an author can have many books. Under Destination, select Book, and under Inverse, select the relationship you made in the previous step. Your model should now look like Figure 11–8.

NOTE: Sometimes in Xcode, when working with models, it is necessary to hit the tab key for the names of entities, attributes, and relationships to update. This little quirk can be traced all the way back to WebObjects tools.

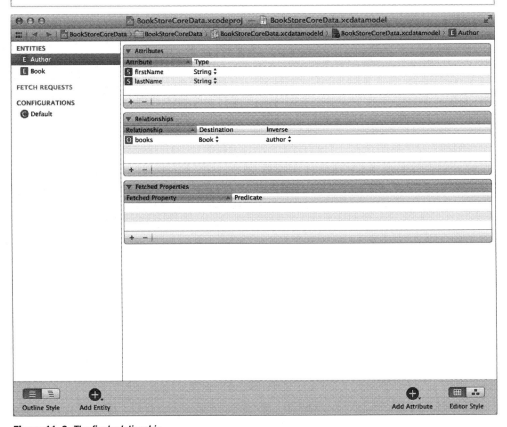

Figure 11–8. *The final relationship.*

Now we need to tell our code about our new entity. To do this, select the Book entity and the Author entity and then select **Editor ▸ Create NSManagedObject Subclass**. Your screen should look like Figure 11–9.

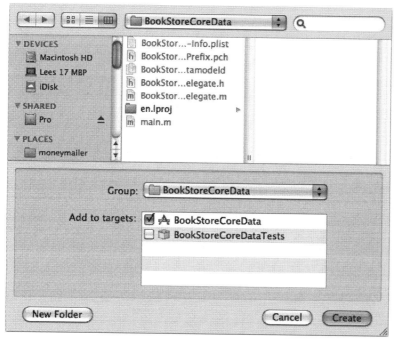

Figure 11–9. *Adding the managed objects to your project.*

Select the storage location and add it to your project. You should not need to change any of the defaults on this page. Then click Create. You will notice that four files have been added to your project. Book.h and Author.h contain the header information about your book, and Book.m and Author.m contain the actual implementation. These files are fairly simple, as Core Data will do most of the work with them. You should also notice that, if you go back to your model and click on Book, it will have a new class. Instead of an NSManagedObject, it will have a Book class.

Let's look at the contents of some of Author.h:

```
#import <Foundation/Foundation.h>
#import <CoreData/CoreData.h>

@class Book;

@interface Author : NSManagedObject {
@private
}
@property (nonatomic, retain) NSString * lastName;
@property (nonatomic, retain) NSString * firstName;
@property (nonatomic, retain) Book * book;

@end
```

You will see that the file starts out including the Core Data framework. This allows Core Data to manage your information. Further down, you will see the three attributes you created.

Managed Object Context

We have created a managed object called Book. The nice thing with Xcode is that it will generate the necessary code to manage these new data objects. In Core Data, every managed object should exist within a managed object context. The context is responsible for tracking changes to objects, carrying out undo operations, and writing the data to the database. In this example, we will not have to write code to create or manage the object context, but as you explore using Core Data in your own projects, you will need to be aware of it. For now, the base functionality of what is provided for the generated classes will work fine.

Setting Up the Interface

The following steps will assist you in setting up your interface:

1. In the Resources folder in your project, you should have a MainMenu.xib. Double-click on this file and Interface Builder should open in a new window. On the left-hand side of the window, you should have a list of current objects. If you do not have this window, click on the little arrow at the bottom left-hand side of the window. Click on the Window object. Your window will be shown on the right-hand side of the screen. See Figure 11–10.

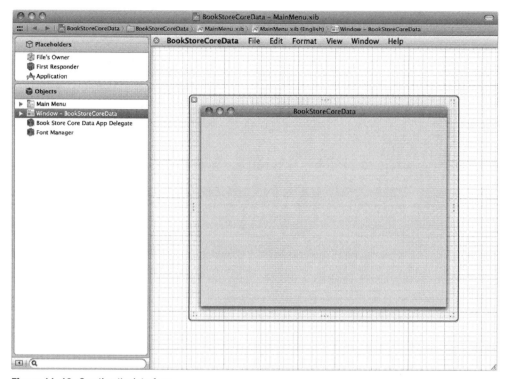

Figure 11–10. *Creating the interface.*

2. There should be a blank window. In order to add some functionality to our
    window, we are going to need to add some objects from the Object
    Library. To view the Object Library, select **View ➤ Utilities ➤ Object Library**.
    This Object Library will show you all of the objects you can add to your
    window. We are going to start by adding an Array Controller. In the Object
    Library, scroll down until you find the Array Controller. Drag it to your
    Objects pane on the left-hand side of the window. See Figure 11–11.

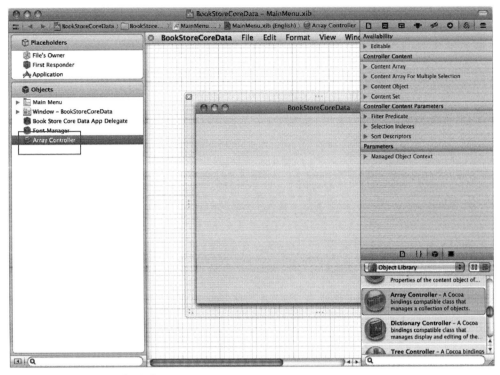

Figure 11–11. *New Array Controller.*

3. Double click on the Array Controller and type in the name, BookArray. Now select the Array Controller and look at the bindings for the object.

> **NOTE:** To view the bindings of any object, select **View ➤ Utilities ➤ Show Bindings Inspector**, or if you already have the utility window open, click on the circular symbol.

4. Under Parameters, if the managed object context portion is not expanded, click the arrow next to it. Now check the box next to Bind and select, Book Store Core Data App Delegate from the drop down menu.

5. In the Model Key Path, type managedObjectContext. This will bind our Array Controller to the default managedObjectContext of our application. This will allow us to add, modify, and save our books. See Figure 11–12.

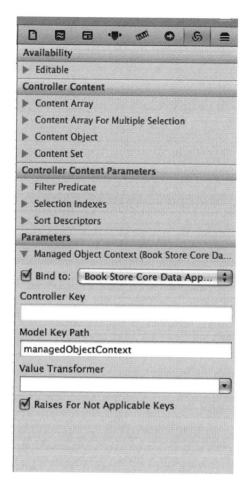

Figure 11–12. *The Array Bindings Inspector.*

6. Click on the icon that looks like a slider control (it is also referred to as a shield). Under the Object Controller heading, change the mode from Class to Entity Name. Type Book as the Entity Name.

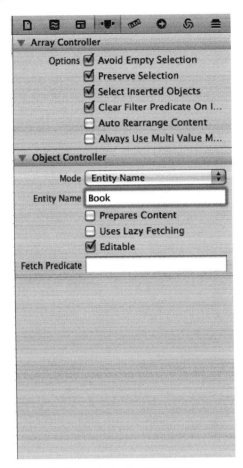

Figure 11–13. *Assigning the Entity Name.*

7. We need to set up our interface. In the Object Library, find a Table View object and drag it to your window. You can move it around and size it easily to fit your desired look.

8. Find two push buttons and drag them to your window. Change the text of one of the buttons to Add and the text of the other to Delete.

> **NOTE:** To change the text of a button and many other graphical objects, just double click on the object and you can type the replacement text.

Change the text of each of the two columns in the Table View. Double click on the column header and type Title in the first column and Price in the second column. Your window should now look something like Figure 11–14.

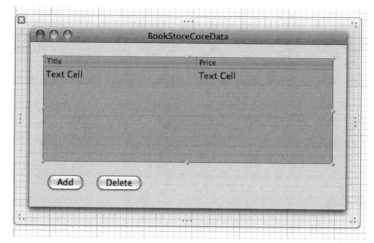

Figure 11–14. *The window layout.*

We now have a nice looking window, but none of the controls can do anything yet. In order to make the objects have a purpose, we will need to bind them to something.

> **NOTE:** Cocoa Bindings is a way to keep your views synchronized with your controller. They help to reduce the amount of code required for you to write.

To connect an object to a controller, you simple have to control click on an item and then drag to the item you will connect it to. Once you drag it to the item, you will be given a menu of the possible outlets available.

1. To start, control-click on your Array Controller and drag it to the table view. A little pop over window will appear with only one outlet selected. Select content. You are telling the table view that it will display the contents of the array controller. See Figure 11–15.

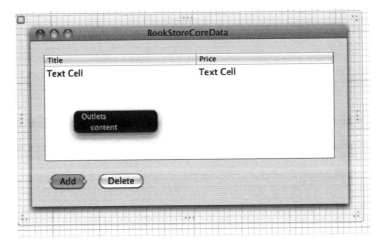

Figure 11–15. *Setting the bindings.*

2. Now control-drag from the Add button to the array controller and select Add. Control-drag from the Delete button to the array controller and select remove.

> **NOTE:** When an object is successfully connected it will blink twice to alert the programmer.

3. Most of our interface should be good now. We just have to tell each column in our Table View what to show. Double click on the first cell where the words Text Cell are located. This should select the column.

4. In the Bindings window, under Parameters, expand the Value title. Check the box next to Bind to and the Book Array should already be selected. Under Model Key Path, type the title (See Figure 11–16). Select the second column, and check Bind to, but type price in the Model Key Path.

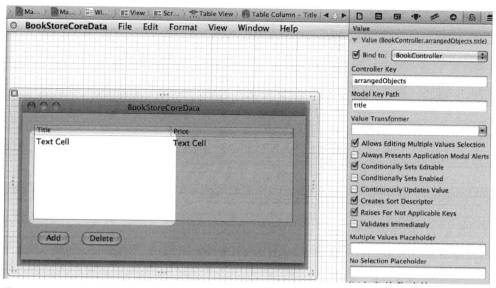

Figure 11–16. *Binding the columns.*

You should be done. Click on Run and you should be able to see your new application window. Click on Add and it should add a row to the Table View. Click in the Column cell and you can edit the Title and the Price. You will also notice that when you quit and relaunch your application, it will remember the values you stored in there before.

This is a very cursory introduction to Core Data for Mac OS X and IOS. Core Data is a very powerful API and can take a lot of time to master.

Summary

We've finally reached the end of the chapter. Here is a summary of the things that we covered.

- Preferences
  - You learned to use NSUserDefaults to save and read preferences from a file, both on the iPhone and a Mac OS X computer.
- Database
  - You learned what a database is and why using one can be preferable to saving information in a preferences file.
  - You learned about the database engine that Apple has integrated into the Mac and iPhone, and the advantages and limitations of this database engine.

- Core Data

    - Apple provided a framework for interfacing with the SQLite database. This framework makes the interface much easier to use.

- Book Store Application

    - You created a simple Core Data application.

    - You used Xcode to create a data model for your Book Store application. You learned how to create a relationship between two different Entities.

    - You used Xcode to create a simple interface for your Core Data model.

Exercises

- Add more fields to the Book entity. Try adding the publisher, pages, and an ISBN number.

- Change the layout of the Book tab. Reorder the columns.

- Add a default value to the author's first and last names.

Chapter **12**

Protocols and Delegates

Congratulations! You are acquiring the skills to become an iOS developer! However, there are two additional topics that iOS developers need to understand to be successful: protocols and delegates. It is not uncommon for new developers to get overwhelmed by these topics, so we thought it best to introduce the foundation topics of the Objective-C language first.

Multiple Inheritance

We discussed object inheritance in Chapter 1. In a nutshell, object inheritance means that a child can inherit all the characteristics of its parent. See Figure 12–1.

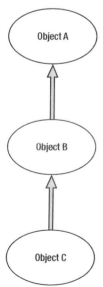

Figure 12–1. *Typical Objective-C inheritance*

C++, Perl, and Python each have a feature called multiple inheritance. **Multiple inheritance** enables a class to inherit behaviors and features from more than one parent. See Figure 12–2.

However, problems can arise with multiple inheritance because it allows for ambiguities to occur. Due to this, Objective-C does not implement multiple inheritances. Instead, it implements something called a **protocol**.

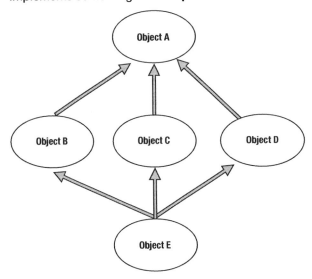

Figure 12–2. *Multiple inheritance*

Understanding Protocols

Apple defines a protocol simply as a list of methods declarations, unattached to a class definition. A protocol is very similar to a class interface with the exception that it is not defining a particular class. You must implement the methods listed for protocols. For example, the methods that report user actions for the mouse could be placed into a protocol. See the following example:

```
- (void)mouseDown:(NSEvent *)theEvent;
- (void)mouseDragged:(NSEvent *)theEvent;
- (void)mouseUp:(NSEvent *)theEvent;
```

Any class that wants to respond to mouse events could adopt the protocol and implement its methods. Protocols are very easy to use since they are not related to class hierarchy and any class can implement them.

Throughout the book, we have used the example of a bookstore. Previously, we discussed the fact that our bookstore may sell different types of media and have discussed how inheritance would help out in that situation. For the purpose of explaining protocols, let's say that our bookstore also sells gum and candy. We would want to create a class for those items. Call it EdibleItem. It would not make sense to have gum inherit the same methods as a book or magazine, but all of the items would need to be sold and the inventory would need to be tracked. In this case, it would make sense to add the methods to a protocol that could be shared by each of the items.

> **NOTE:** A protocol is much different than inheritance. When a class inherits from another class, it not only receives the method declarations, but it also receives the methods themselves. When using a protocol, the declarations are brought over, but the methods themselves need to be written.

Protocol Syntax

The interface example for a protocol is

```
@protocol InventoryItem

- (void)removeFromInventory;
- (void)addToInventory;

@end
```

The implementation file for this protocol example would be

```
@interface MyClass : SomeSuperClass < InventoryItem>
@end
```

Any object that wants to implement the `InventoryItem protocol` would include < `InventoryItem`> after the object definition.

For example, we could create the interface for the edible objects we sell.

```
@interface Edible : NSObject <InventoryItem>
{

}
```

It is not uncommon for iOS developers to have multiple protocols for their objects. This adds real power to your objects when needed. Additional protocols are placed after the first followed by a comma.

```
@interface EditbleItem : UITableViewController  <InventoryItem,SaleItem >
{

}
```

This example illustrates the power of delegates. `EditableItem` now has all of the method declarations from `InventoryItem` and `SaleItem`.

Methods that are defined for the object's delegate are called **delegates methods**.

Understanding Delegates

Delegates are helper objects. They enable us to control the behavior of our objects. The methods listed in the protocol become **helpers** to our `MyClass`.

> **NOTE:** The key to understanding delegates is to know that a delegate is a separate object consulted in order to augment the behavior of a host object. Thus, you can create an *application delegate* object that can affect the behavior of the iOS NSApplication object without subclassing or changing the NSApplication class. The object you create is the delegate object, and the messages that NSApplication will send your object are called *delegate methods*. These are typically defined in a protocol (<UIApplicationDelegate>) which your class must adopt. To work, a delegate object must be set as the delegate property of the host.

We can now use these methods in our object. For example, including the `<CLLocationManagerDelegate>` protocol in our `MyClass` interface definition enables our object to be notified by the iPhone's GPS of our new location. The following example shows the method that we will include and define inside our object's implementation file:

```
- (void)locationManager:(CLLocationManager *)manager didUpdateToLocation:(CLLocation
*)newLocation fromLocation:(CLLocation *)oldLocation
{
......
}
```

The `locationManager` delegate method automatically gets called as our GPS location changes, allowing your code to process the new and old coordinates. Listing 12–1 is an example of how to implement `didUpdateToLocation` and `didFailWithError` delegate methods from `CLLocationManagerDelegate` in our class `MyCoreLocationController`.

Listing 12–1. *Core location delegate example*

```
@implementation MyCoreLocationController //our own controller
@synthesize locationManager;

- (id) init {
    self = [super init];
    if (self != nil) {
        self.locationManager = [[CLLocationManager alloc] init];
        self.locationManager.delegate = self; // send location updates updates to myself
    }
    return self;
}

- (void)locationManager:(CLLocationManager *)manager
    didUpdateToLocation:(CLLocation *)newLocation
          fromLocation:(CLLocation *)oldLocation
{
    NSLog(@"Location: %@", [newLocation description]);
}
```

```
- (void)locationManager:(CLLocationManager *)manager
          didFailWithError:(NSError *)error
{
      NSLog(@"Error: %@", [error description]); //print error description
}

- (void)dealloc {
    [self.locationManager release];
    [super dealloc];
}
@end
```

Next Steps

You now have a great Objective-C foundation. After going through the last two chapters, "Memory, Addresses, and Pointer" along with "Debugging Programs with Xcode," you should be able to dive right into becoming a great iOS developer. Two great books that we recommend to students as they progress to becoming iOS developers are *Learn Objective-C on the Mac* by Mark Dalrymple and Scott Knaster, and *Beginning iOS 5 Development* by Dave Mark and Jeff LaMarche, both published by Apress.

You will be well prepared to read these books and begin writing your own iOS apps. Don't take time off—keep moving forward! Get started with these books and begin writing your apps. The faster you start using what you have learned, the better you will get. Whatever you do, don't stop now!

Summary

In this chapter we covered why multiple inheritance is not used in Objective-C and how protocols and delegates work.

There is still a lot to learn and know on your iOS journey. Keep it up and help others along their way.

You should be familiar with the following terms:

- Multiple Inheritance
- Protocol
- Delegate

Chapter 13

Memory, Addresses, and Pointers

Computers, just like you and me, need a place to work and store things. Think of computer memory like space on a desk, for example. Someone who needs to work on many projects at once needs to have enough desk space for all their papers and documents so they can be quickly and easily accessed. If the desk space is too small for the number of projects being juggled, some projects may have to be filed back into drawers so they can be quickly pulled back once there is more space on the desk. Making sure the desk space is used efficiently is also very important.

Dealing with a computer's memory is one of the more complicated areas of programming. Why is this the case? Surely these problems have been solved by now, right? Well, yes and no. Some languages have taken the approach to remove the need for programmers to manage memory at all. Some internal magic (and a little something called garbage collection) handles all the management of how memory is used and released when it is no longer being used. The negative side to this approach is that garbage collection does not give the programmer the ultimate say-so on how the memory should be used in all cases. Why is this important? Generally speaking, the issue is performance. With full control of memory management, the programmer also has full control over the performance (or lack thereof) of the program.

This chapter will introduce the ideas of working with the memory of a Mac, iPhone, or iPad. Working with memory on any device has its challenges. For example, the iPhone and iPad, being smaller devices, have less memory to work with, which means that it is important that their memory is used efficiently. Fortunately, Objective-C provides mechanisms that keep managing memory from being a chore. You will learn about how to allocate memory as well as about the new Automatic Reference Counting (ARC) feature of Xcode 4, which makes managing allocated memory much simpler than earlier releases of Xcode.

Understanding Memory

While many people may have associated computer memory with that of the human brain, I prefer to compare computer memory to physical space that you, as a person, have to work. You are like the computer's CPU, the part that actually processes information and does something with it. The more space you have to work, the easier it is to organize things and the quicker you can actually accomplish your tasks. Of course, we all reach that place where, no matter how much more space we get, we aren't able to work any faster.

To a computer, memory is the workspace where certain programs (or parts of programs) and data are stored. On the Mac, iPhone, and iPad, the most basic unit of memory is a **byte**. If you think of memory as nothing more than a grid of boxes, a byte would simply be a single box, as demonstrated in Figure 13–1.

Figure 13–1. *Bytes are like a row of boxes.*

Of course, there are generally billions of these boxes, or bytes, of memory in a typical modern computer. While it does seem like a vast, almost limitless amount, memory is the most important resource that a computer has at its disposal. Only programs that reside in memory can be executed and only data loaded from disk can be inspected or acted on. Also, on the iPhone or iPad, there is much less memory than on a typical PC or Mac computer. A certain degree of memory conservation is always a good practice.

Okay, so memory is like a grid of boxes that each holds a byte of information. What good is it at this point? How does the computer put each byte in its place and how does it pull it back out? Certainly, if my garage was full of unlabeled boxes, I would have a very difficult time figuring out where, for example, all of my old video games were stored. A computer has exactly the same problem, so it goes about solving that problem in a very organized way. Before we go into how the computer solves this problem, you need to understand the basics of units of memory and addresses.

Bits, Bytes, and Bases

In Figure 13–1, each box represents one byte, or memory space. Each byte can hold a total of 8 bits. A **bit** is simply a number that can be either a zero or a one—off or on. It is this sequence of zeros and ones that give the byte its value. These zeros and ones represent a **binary** numeral system; that is, each digit can have a maximum of two values, zero or one. This is sometimes referred to as base-2 numbering system (versus the base-10 or decimal numbering system that we all use in our everyday lives). Before we get into more specifics of memory, it's very important that you understand the numbering systems that are typically used on modern computer hardware.

> **NOTE:** Modern computers use 8 bits per byte. In the early days of computing, different manufacturers of computers sometimes had different byte sizes. For example, Control Data Corporation's CDC-6000 often used 12-bit bytes for display codes, and the DEC PDP-10 operated on bit fields, so a "byte" could be anything from 1 bit to 36 bits. IBM, with its popular System/360, set the standard on the 8-bit byte, as did the microprocessors of the 1970s.

Generally speaking, people use base-10 numbering for pretty much everything; from money to measurements, base-10 is the standard. However, in the realm of the modern computer, the base-10 system is rarely used. Instead, the computer typically uses base-2 (binary) or base-16 (hexadecimal).

> **NOTE:** Base-8, commonly referred to as octal, is also used but is not as common as hexadecimal.

Converting Base-10 (Decimal) to Base-2 (Binary)

A typical, everyday number may look like this: 1101. Now, most people would consider this number to be "one-thousand, one-hundred, and one." However in base-2 numbering, this number would represent the decimal number 13. Let's look at how this can be.

As shown in Figure 13–2, in base-10 numbering, each digit represents a power of 10; that is, each column increases by a power of 10 (10, 100, 1000, etc.), right-to-left. We add the 1000s column (10^3), 100s column, and the 1s column to get $1,101_{10}$ (the subscript means "base-10").

10^3	10^2	10^1	10^0
1	1	0	1

Figure 13–2. *Base-10 numbering system.*

Now, let's look at the same number in base 2, as shown in Figure 13–3.

2^3	2^2	2^1	2^0
1	1	0	1

Figure 13–3. *Base-2 numbering system.*

In base-2 numbering (shown in Figure 13–3), the columns all increase by a power of 2 (2, 4, 8, 16, 32, etc.), right-to-left. We add 8, 4, and 1 to reach a value of 13_{10} (in base-2 that is). Also note that a series of 4 bits, which represents half of a byte, is typically referred to as a **nibble**.

Of course, it was mentioned earlier that 8 bits (numbered 0 to 7) make up a byte. Figure 13–4 shows an example of an entire byte consisting of 8 bits. To get the value, add up all the columns as follows:

$128 + 16 + 8 + 4 + 1 = 157_{10}$

Bit 7				...			Bit 0
128	64	32	16	8	4	2	1
1	0	0	1	1	1	0	1

Figure 13–4. *An entire byte showing base-2 and base-10 values.*

Using Base-16 (Hexadecimal) Numbering

The last base that is worthy of mentioning, used quite ubiquitously in modern computers, is the base-16, or the **hexadecimal**, numbering system. In base-2, each digit can have one of two values, 0 and 1. In base-10, each digit can have one of ten values, 0–9. In base-16, each digit can have one of 16 values, 0–F. Yes, you read that correctly; the last value is **F**. To represent 16 values in a single column, it became necessary use letters to represent values. In the case of base-16, the numbering goes from 0 through 9 and A through F. It takes two hexadecimal (**hex** for short) digits to represent a single byte; each hex digit represents 4 bits, as shown in Figure 13–5.

Hex	Dec
0	0
1	1
2	2
3	3
4	4
5	5
6	6
7	7
8	8
9	9
A	10
B	11
C	12
D	13
E	14
F	15

Upper Nibble				*Lower Nibble*			
Bit 7				...			Bit 0
128	64	32	16	8	4	2	1
1	0	0	1	1	1	0	1
9				D			

Figure 13–5. *On the left, two nibbles make a byte. A simple hex to decimal conversion chart appears on the right.*

So the hex number 9D is equal to the binary number 10011101, which is equal to the decimal number 157. As shown in Figure 13–5, a byte can be any value between 0000 0000 and 1111 1111 (base-2), which is 0xFF in hex.

> **NOTE:** In "0xFF," the "0x" that precedes the "FF" is used in programming to indicate that the number is a hex number. While FF seems obvious, because there are only letters, a number like "10" is less clear, is it 10 or 16? Well, 0x10 makes it clear.

Hexadecimal takes some getting used to, but learning it is time well spent. This is because when dealing with memory, pretty much everything is expressed in hexadecimal. Just like in base-10, each numeric column is an exponentially larger than the previous, as shown in Figure 13–6.

0010	0001	1010	0010
16^3	16^2	16^1	16^0
2	1	A	2

Figure 13–6. *A 16-bit hexadecimal number.*

In base-10, each column is 1, 10, 100, 1000, and so on. In hexadecimal, the columns are base-16, so you have 1, 16, 256, 1024, and so on—each column is a multiple of 16. However, once you understand hexadecimal, you may want to express the number in decimal as well. Figure 13–7 is an example of how a 16-bit hexadecimal number is converted to a decimal one.

2	1	A	2
2×16^3	1×16^2	10×16^2	2
2 x 4096	1 x 256	10 x 16	2
8,192	256	160	2

Figure 13–7. *Converting a 16-bit hex number to decimal.*

If we add all our columns together, we will have our answer:

8,192 + 256 + 160 + 2 = 8,610
So 0x21A2 equals 8,610.

Figure 13–7 represents a 16-bit number. Calculating 32- and 64-bit numbers means simply increasing the columns to the left.

> **TIP:** If you find yourself calculating 32- and 64-bit values a lot, just use the calculator on the Mac (in the Programmer view), or a small investment will allow you to buy a scientific calculator that can work in hex.

We hope you haven't been scared off. Understanding computer memory at its lowest level is actually not that bad, and it's something that won't be necessary all the time. The important thing to remember is that when dealing with memory, it may be necessary to understand binary (Base-2), decimal (Base-10), and hexadecimal (base-16) values. This will become clearer when debugging an application, as discussed in Chapter 14.

Understanding Memory Address Basics

Like buildings on a street, memory has addresses, except that in some ways, memory addressing is much simpler. Earlier in this chapter, we mentioned that a computer could solve the problem of keeping track of boxes of old video games in a garage—virtually, of course. The first part of this process is to be able to keep track of certain locations in memory, called **addresses**. From a program's perspective, these addresses are stored into variables for later reference.

Memory in a computer is a linear set of bytes (or boxes) that store information. If you were to simply start labeling these boxes as 1, 2, 3, 4, and so on, you would have a set of boxes starting at 1 and ending with some very large number. These numbers are referred to as a **memory address**.

Figure 13–8 provides a simple example of addressing memory.

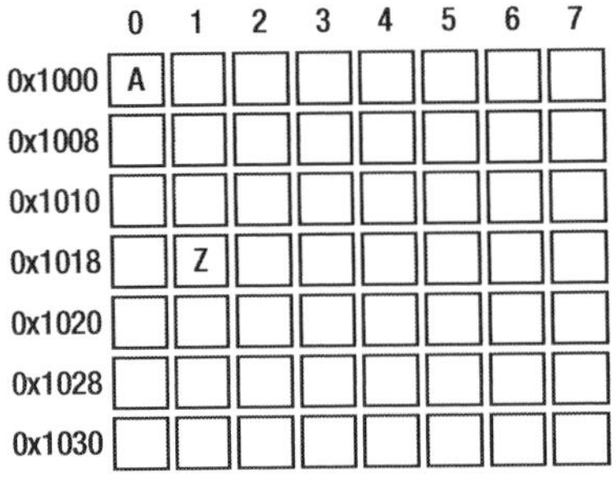

Figure 13–8. *A simple example of addressing.*

If each block is one byte, the first byte starts at address 0x1000 and ends at 0x1037. Remember that the "0x" that precedes the number indicates that the number, in this case, the address, is expressed in hexadecimal. So address 0x1000, for example, is really 4096 and not 1000. The number 0x1000 represents the start of our memory example. At this location is the letter "A." Also in the example is the letter "Z." The value of "Z" is located at the memory address of 0x1019. The address 0x1000 is an example of a simple 16-bit address. A 32-bit iPhone address would look like 0x03C06D80. A 64-bit address would be double the 32-bit size.

NOTE: If our program were given access to the memory in Figure 13–8, it would store the starting point of the memory, 0x1000, into a variable. This variable is commonly referred to as a **pointer**, since the value of the variable (the address 0x1000, which is just a number) points to the data we are interested in, like an arrow on a map.

Another way to think of this grid of memory is to consider it as an array. In this example, a variable has been declared as an array. The array size is 56 characters in length, the exact same size as our example in Figure 13–8. Whenever a variable is declared as an array, like myArray, the variable resolves to an address, or pointer. For argument's sake, let's assume that myArray has an address of 0x1000, just like our grid in Figure 13–8. If you were to look at the variable myArray, it would have a value of 0x1000. Remember, an array resolves to an address. So how do we access the memory in the array?

```
char myArray[56];
```

NOTE: In C and Objective-C, all arrays are **zero-based**. This means that the first element in the array is at element zero, not one. An array of 30 elements would start at element 0 and end at element 29. Element 30 is outside of the bounds of the array

Since C and Objective-C use zero-based arrays, if the program needs to access the first element in the array, it would be done as follows:

```
char letterA = myArray[0];
```

In this case, letter A would be set to the first element in the array, which would be the letter "A" (using **Figure 13–8** as the array). What's really happening under the hood is that the computer is simply using the array index and adding it to the address. Again, if the address is 0x1000, adding 0 result in a new address of 0x1000, which is where the letter "A" resides.

```
char letterZ = myArray[25];              // or myArray[0x19] if you are
                                         // getting into this hex thing!
```

In the preceding example, letter Z would be set to the value at element 25, which is the letter "Z." The computer adds 25 (0x19) to the base address of 0x1000, resulting in a value of 0x1019. This is where the letter "Z" is. Remember, arrays are zero-based, so "Z" is at element 25 because "A" started at element 0; "Z" is still the 26th element (using natural numbers, or counting numbers, that start at one).

Using the brackets ([ ]) after a pointer makes it very simple to access elements within that array of memory. There is a different way to do this that will yield the same result. This example will hopefully help the understanding of pointers and addresses even more.

Listing 13–1. *Using Pointers.*

```
1    int main(void)
2    {
3        char myArray[] = "ABCDEFGHIJKLMNOPQRSTUVWXYZ";
4        char *aPointer;
5        char letter;
6
7        aPointer = myArray;
8        letter = myArray[25];    // letter == 'Z'
9        letter = *(aPointer+2);  // letter == 'C'
10       letter = aPointer[3];    // letter == 'D'
11   }
```

In Listing 13–1, line 3 declares a new array. The brackets ([…]) are empty because we're assigning the array a value of the alphabet. In this case, since we provide the values, the compiler knows what size the array is going to be. So, our new array is just like **Figure** 13–8: the first value at element 0 is the letter "A," and the last value at element 25 (0x19) is the letter "Z." myArray is equivalent to a pointer in that it can be assigned directly to a pointer variable, as shown in line 7. It points to memory that has the alphabet in it.

Line 4 declares a variable that is a pointer. aPointer is a pointer to a char data type, if line 4 were int *aPointer, then aPointer would be a pointer to data of type int. In our case, we'll keep it as char. Remember, a pointer is just an address, and an address is just a number.

On line 5, the program is declaring a character variable. We'll be using this variable to store data from the array.

Line 7 looks a little strange, but what it's doing is assigning the aPointer variable, the value of myArray. As mentioned previously, a variable that is an array always resolves to a pointer. So, myArray is equivalent to a pointer, which is an address, which is just a number. That number is assigned to aPointer. The program does not copy the array to aPointer; it just sets the value of aPointer to what myArray is. At this point in the program, myArray and aPointer have the same value in that they both reference, or point to, the same area of memory.

Line 8 adds 25 to the address of myArray and returns the value that is 25 bytes into the array, which results in the letter "Z."

Line 9 adds 2 to the value of aPointer. Remember, aPointer is equal to myArray. aPointer + 2 now points to the letter "C." If this seems a little off mathematically, remember zero-based arrays:

- aPointer+0 points to "A"

- aPointer+1 points to "B"

- aPointer+2 points to "C"

Hopefully, you are getting used to zero-based arrays. Line 9 also makes use of the **dereference operator**, the asterisk (*); there is more about this in the next section.

Line 10 is equivalent to line 8. Both `myArray` and `aPointer` effectively point to the same memory, so the array operator works.

Using the Dereference Operator

Line 9 looked a little different from the other lines, so let's examine it a little closer:

```
letter = *(aPointer + 2);
```

First, let's consider what's inside the parentheses:

```
aPointer + 2
```

This should be pretty straightforward: we are adding 2 to the pointer `aPointer`. If `aPointer` is 0x1000, the resulting value would be 0x1002. The pointer now *points* to the letter "C." Using a pointer this way is very different from using the brackets in lines 8 or 10. We're manually adjusting the pointer so that it results in a new value. Next, we need to ask the computer, "What does the pointer point to?" With the array operator on lines 8 and 10 of Listing 13–1, that question is implied, and the program responds. But when we simply change an address by adding, subtracting, and so on, the program needs to explicitly ask this question. This is where the asterisk (*) comes into play.

Using an asterisk in front of a pointer *dereferences* the address and returns what value the pointer is pointing to. So, if our pointer is 0x1000 and the letter "A" is stored at 0x1000, we can get to the letter "A" by dereferencing the pointer. `*(0x1000)` would return the letter "A" if our example was pointing to real memory (don't actually do this because 0x1000 is not a real address, just an example is used to simplify the problem). Remember, a pointer is an address and an address is just a number. The asterisk asks the computer to return what's stored at the address rather than to return the address itself.

> **NOTE:** In most common programming, the programmer rarely gets to tell the system, for example, at location 0x1000 is our data. The reason for this is that memory is **virtualized**. Virtualized memory can allow more memory to be used than is physically present on the machine *(virtual memory is out of scope of this book)*. Because of this, the operating system manages where the data is stored. As a result, the computer tells the program where its memory is, rather than the program telling the computer. Regardless, the concept is the same.
>
> When developing software at the hardware or device driver level, using hard-coded addresses is much more common. Typical programs in Mac OS X or iOS will never use hard-coded addresses.

Allocating Memory

In modern operating systems, the program allocates memory, and the operating system complies by returning a pointer to the requested memory. In C and Objective-C, a **pointer** is declared by preceding the variable name with an asterisk (*), as shown in the following example:

```
char *theData;
NSString *theString;
```

Don't confused the asterisk here with the **_dereference operator_**. Only when declaring a variable does the asterisk identify the variable as a pointer.

Here are some more examples of requesting memory:

```
1.  char data1[100];
2.  char *data2 = malloc(100);
3.  NSString *myString = [[NSString alloc] init];
```

In example 1, memory is allocated in the form of an array declaration. The program now has an array (data1) that **points** to 100 bytes of memory. In C, it's easier to just remember that any variable that is declared as an array is _referenced_ as a pointer even though it's not declared as one.

Example 2 is a little more complex. data2 is declared as a pointer to a char data type. A pointer is declared using an asterisk preceding the file. The next part of the line is malloc(100), which is a standard C library function call. This function allocates the requested amount memory and returns a pointer to it. In our example, malloc is passed the value 100. This requests that 100 bytes be allocated. When the function returns, data2 contains a _pointer_ to the 100 bytes of memory.

Example 3 is a more traditional Objective-C type memory allocation. First, the program declares a pointer to an NSString class named myString. Next, the following code is executed: [[NSString alloc] init]. This will allocate the necessary memory for the object and return a _pointer_ to it.

In all these examples, memory is requested from the operating system and returned to the program via a pointer, even in example 1—except example 1 is just a little different from the rest.

Working with Automatic Variables and Pointers

Any variable created within a function or block is considered an **automatic variable**, or **auto-variable**. In our previous examples, example 1 allocates 100 characters as an array. It does so automatically since, as you learned, all variables are auto-variables by default. Because we define all the space up front via an array declaration, all this memory is managed automatically for us. Examples 2 and 3 are also auto-variables, but they allocate just enough space to hold a pointer to memory—that's all. Recall that a pointer is just a variable that holds an address to memory; it's not the memory itself. So, char* data2 and NSString *myString are really just variables that hold a number, which represents an address to memory.

> **TIP:** Think of pointers this way: a *pointer* is like a ticket to a concert and the allocated memory is like the seat. The ticket has the information on how to get to the seat. If the ticket is discarded (or lost), the ability to find the seat is also lost. However, the seat (allocated memory) still remains.

Examples 2 and 3 are auto-variables that hold the "ticket" to the memory, not the memory itself (see Figure 13–9). This means that, when the function exits and the variables go out of scope, the pointers to the memory will be lost; the "ticket" is lost. The problem with this is that the program needs to also release, or deallocate, the memory that the pointer points to before it is lost. The manually allocated memory does not go out of scope with the pointer; allocated memory is global to the program and doesn't get released until the program exits.

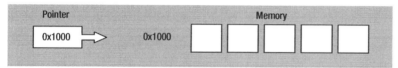

Figure 13–9. *A pointer is not the memory itself.*

What's very important to remember is that memory that is manually allocated must be deallocated at some point, depending on how the memory is used. Some memory might be allocated at the start of the program and doesn't have to be released until the program exits. However, the most common memory allocations happen many, many times throughout the life program, thus it is critical that the associated memory be deallocated as soon as the object is no longer being used. Memory that is allocated manually must be deallocated manually. Memory that is allocated automatically (i.e., char array[100];) is automatically deallocated.

Deallocating Memory

When a program allocates memory, it needs to ensure that it's released, or **deallocated**, once the program is finished using the memory. Using the examples again, example 2 allocates memory with the malloc command. When the program is finished with that memory, it needs to be deallocated. Failing to deallocate memory is a common programming mistake and goes by the descriptive name of **memory leak**.

To prevent memory leaks (which eventually lead to program crashes), allocated memory must be managed with care. Listing 13–2 shows how the code should look when properly deallocating memory for examples 2 and 3.

Listing 13–2. *Memory Allocation and Deallocation.*

```
1   int main(void)
2   {
3       char *data2 = malloc(100);
4       NSString *myString = [[NSString alloc] init];
5       … // standard "doing-stuff" ellipse
6       …
7       free(data2);  // Deallocate the 100 bytes
8       data2 = NULL;
9       [myString release];
10      myString = nil;
11  }
```

In Listing 13–2, data2 is allocated on line 3. This type of allocation is plain old standard C and is not typical in an Objective-C program, but it's still very important to know and understand.

Line 4 declares and allocates an Objective-C object, NSString.

Line 7 deallocates the block of memory allocated from line 3.

Line 8 sets the pointer to NULL. This is a good practice and will be explained in the next section.

Line 9 releases the object that was allocated on line 4. The release message is a request to deallocate the object. The reason that release message is a *request* to deallocate memory has to do with the mechanism of how memory is managed for Objective-C objects. This mechanism is referred to as the **retain/release model**, or sometimes as **reference counting**.

> **NOTE:** Prior to Xcode 4, the retain/release model was the only model to use for iOS development. Xcode 4.2 introduced an option called Automatic Reference Counting (ARC). ARC causes the compiler to automatically include the retain and release methods on your behalf. While ARC is optional, it defaults to being on for any new project started in Xcode 4.2. Opening older projects created before Xcode 4.2 will still compile fine and ARC will be disabled.
>
> While ARC is a nice feature, it's still very important to understand what is still happening under the covers. ARC doesn't remove calls to the retain and release methods, it just hides the implementation much like Objective-C properties hide getter and setter methods.

Reference counting makes using memory a little more efficient because it allows the objects to know when memory should be deallocated. It's a slightly better mechanism than completely managing memory manually.

Line 10 is equivalent to line 8. Objective-C pointers *can* be set to NULL but it's much better to set the pointer to nil. A nil object in Objective-C has a special meaning and can actually respond to a message. NULL does not have that same property.

Let's also look at how this listing would change if we were to be using ARC:

Listing 13–3. *Memory Allocation with ARC.*

```
1   int main(void)
2   {
3       char *data2 = malloc(100);
4       NSString *myString = [[NSString alloc] init];
5       ... // standard "doing-stuff" ellipse
6       ...
7       free(data2);  // Deallocate the 100 bytes
8       data2 = NULL;
9       myString = nil;
10  }
```

The major difference between Listing 13–2 and Listing 13–3 is the omission of [myString release]. Since ARC is being used, it handles the releasing of the memory.

Using Special Pointers

As you've learned, a pointer is just a number that represents an address to memory. There are two special pointers that are worth mentioning. They really aren't pointers per se, but they represent an empty pointer—a pointer that doesn't point to anything. These two pointers are NULL and nil. NULL is nothing more than zero, zilch, nada. Since pointers are just numbers that represent an address, an address of 0, or NULL, represents a pointer that logically points to nothing.

Using an address of zero is a convention that modern computers use; computers do not allow any program to store something at the address 0, which makes using NULL to represent an empty or unused piece of memory much more meaningful. This is important to know because if memory allocation fails, the resulting pointer returned is NULL. NULL is also useful to indicate that the pointer is no longer valid or is simply empty. This is true for all of standard C. Here's how NULL can be used to initialize a pointer:

```
char *data = NULL;
```

It should also be used in comparisons like the code fragment in Listing 13–4.

Listing 13–4. *Using NULL to Verify and Clear a Pointer.*

```
1   char *data = malloc(100);
2   if (data != NULL) {
3       // Do something with the memory.  It's valid.
4       free (data);   // Deallocate the memory, we're done with it.
5       data = NULL; // Set the pointer to NULL indicating that it's empty.
6   }
```

In Listing 13–4, line 2 checks to make sure that the malloc function worked by checking the pointer with NULL. If the pointer is not NULL, the allocation worked and the program can use the returned value. The memory is then deallocated on line 4 and set to NULL on line 5 to indicate that the pointer is no longer pointing to anything.

When we are dealing with Objective-C objects, the equivalent of NULL in Objective-C is nil. Like NULL, nil is a special pointer to nothing. However, in the case of Objective-C, nil is actually an empty object. Since Objective-C is heavy on sending messages to an object, an empty pointer should respond to message sent to it, even if that pointer is empty—the `nil` empty object fulfills this purpose. Listing 13–5 is a sample code fragment that is similar to the standard C version.

Listing 13–5. *Using a Property on a Possibly Nil Object.*

```
1  NSArray *bookList = [bookstore booksOnSale];
2  for (NSUinteger i=0 i<bookList.count; ++i) {
3      // If bookList is non-nil, this part of the for loop will run.
4      // If bookList is nil, then this part of the loop will be skipped.
5  }
```

> **TIP:** When using the ticket metaphor for deallocated memory, here is something to watch out for: If a ticket is a pointer to a seat in a theater, what happens when the show is over? Well, the ticket still points to that same seat, but it isn't valid anymore; the show is over. The same is true with memory. If the memory that a pointer points to is deallocated, that memory is now free to be used by another memory allocation. However, the pointer still points to that old memory. It's important to clear the pointer so it isn't mistakenly used. This is what is referred to as a dangling pointer. The practice of checking to see if the pointer is not NULL before using it paired with the practice of setting a pointer to NULL or nil when the object is deallocated is a "best practice" that should be strictly followed.

Managing Memory in Objective-C with ARC

As mentioned earlier, ARC is the new feature that Xcode 4.2 introduced that hides the need for the retain/release model. By default, ARC is enabled for any **new** project started in Xcode 4.2. Older projects have ARC disabled. To enable or disable ARC, simply look for **automatic reference counting** in the build settings of an Xcode 4.2 project, as shown in Figure 13–10.

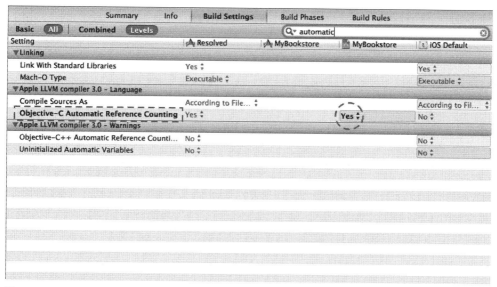

Figure 13–10. *Enabling or disabling ARC in an Xcode 4.2 project.*

We're going to examine how we can now manage memory in Objective-C, taking advantage of the new ARC feature.

First, retain/release and autorelease (discussed later) are no longer valid methods. Under ARC, these methods are deprecated. This also includes the `release` keyword in a property. Prior to Xcode 4.2, it was common to write a property like this

```
@property (nonatomic, retain) NSString *name;
```

Now with Xcode 4.2, this changes a little bit. The property is written as

```
@property (nonatomic, strong) NSString *name;
```

The `strong` keyword replaces `retain`; `strong` is used to tell the compiler that this object needs to be retained when assigned. Conversely, the compiler will know to also release this object when it's no longer being used or is re-assigned.

Here's another code example of how an implied `strong` variable is used:

Listing 13–6. *Using Automatic Reference Counting.*

```
1   - (id)init
2   {
3       self = [super init];
4       if (self) {
5           self.theBookStore = [[NSMutableArray alloc] init];
6           Book *newBook = [[Book alloc] init];
7           newBook.title = @"Objective-C for Absolute Beginners";
8           newBook.author = @"Bennett, Fisher and Lees";
9           newBook.description = @"iOS Programming made easy.";
10          [self.theBookStore addObject:newBook];
11
```

```
12          newBook = [[Book alloc] init];
13          newBook.title = @"A Farwell To Arms";
14          newBook.author = @"Ernest Hemingway";
15          newBook.description = @"The story of an affair between an English "
16                              "nurse and an American soldier "
17                              "on the Italian front "
18                              "during World War I.";
19          [self.theBookStore addObject:newBook];
20          newBook = nil;
21      }
22
23      return self;
24  }
```

If we look at Listing 13–6, we can clearly see that a new Book object is being allocated on line 6. However, where ARC comes in play is line 12. Here, we reassign the pointer by allocating a new Book object. Under the old rules of memory management, we would have had to release the old value first, otherwise there would be a memory leak. Under ARC, the compiler knows to perform a release on the pointer before it is reassigned. This is also the case with line 20. Line 20 is actually not needed since when the variable goes out of scope, ARC would have also auto-released it. Assigning it to nil is just a more direct way of doing the same thing.

Further inspection of this source file (*Bookstore.m* from the example in Chapter 8) reveals that there is no dealloc method. So, the self.theBookStore variable **without** ARC would have caused a memory leak. With ARC, the programmer doesn't have to worry about releasing the self.theBookStore variable because ARC does it automatically whenever the Bookstore class is no longer being used.

Managing Memory in Objective-C Without ARC

While it is recommended to use ARC when starting new projects, sometimes there is a need to manage an old project that is either earlier than iOS 4 or was built with the retain/release model in place. For these projects, Xcode 4 will not automatically convert them over to ARC. This section describes how to handle a program without ARC.

As mentioned earlier, Objective-C handles allocated memory in a slightly different way than most applications written in standard C. Recall that the Objective-C system uses something called the retain/release model. With this model, memory that has been allocated by an object gets counted every time the application that is interested in the memory sends a retain message to the object. At various stages of the application, the program indicates that it's finished using the memory and sends a release message. When the number of releases equal the number of retains, the memory associated with the object is finally deallocated. Let's see how this model looks like in practice. Listing 13–7 is a very basic example.

Listing 13–7. *Allocating an Objective-C Object.*

```
1   int main(void)
2   {
3       NSString* myString = [[NSString alloc] initWithUTF8String:"Hello World!"];
4       // Code to do something with the string...
5       [myString release];
6       myString = nil;
7   }
```

In this example, line 3 allocates a new string object using `alloc`. This line is actually very important in this situation; the reason will be explained in a bit. So line 3 created the new string. As it's created, the Objective-C system automatically sends a `retain` message to the object. At this point, the `myString` variable points to an object that has one `retain` so far.

Line 5 issues a `release` to the `myString` object. The release subtracts one from the current retain count (which is 1). As mentioned before, once the retain count reaches zero, the object is deallocated. So, once line 5 has finished, the `myString` variable points to deallocated memory.

Line 6 sets our original variable to `nil` to indicate that the pointer is empty.

Using the Retain/Release Model

The process of retaining and releasing memory is something that Objective-C uses extensively to manage memory. The alternate name of this process, reference counting, is a little more descriptive because the process of retaining and releasing memory is a way of counting how many times the memory has been retained rather than released. Note the term "memory" is used here generically. Memory management in Objective-C allocates memory for *objects* instead of just blocks of memory. The Objective-C base class `NSObject`, which most Objective-C objects are derived from, keeps track of the retain count.

> **NOTE:** If you are looking for exactness, the `NSObject` protocol group actually defines the reference counting messages. `NSObject` implements that protocol.

So far, things sound fairly simple: for every `retain`, there needs to eventually be a `release`. This doesn't sound too tricky, right? Well, it's not always straightforward to know when an object is retained. Consider the example in Listing 13–8.

Listing 13–8. *A Retain Count.*

```
1   NSMutableDictionary *dict = [[NSMutableDictionary alloc] init];   dict retainCount = 1
2   NSDate *today = [[NSDate alloc] init];                            today retainCount = 1
3
4   [dict setObject: today forKey: @"TODAY"];                         today retainCount = 2
5   [today release];                                                  today retainCount = 1
6   today = nil;
7   [dict removeObjectForKey: @"TODAY"];                              today deallocated
8   [dict release];                                                   dict deallocated
9
```

Looking at Listing 13–8, the retain counts of the dict and today objects are shown. The dict object looks pretty normal: it has a retain count of 1 whenever the object is created. The same is true for the today object on line 2.

In line 4, things look a little odd. For some reason, the today retain count is now 2. What happened? Well, if we look closely at the NSMutableDictionary documentation for the setObject: forKey: method, we see, in the documentation for the setObject:, part of the message that "the object receives a retain message before being added to the receiver."

According to the documentation, before an object is added to the dictionary, the object is sent a retain message. This is why today had a retain count of 2.

Why does the dictionary do this? Well, the answer is quite simple. If we add an object to the dictionary, the dictionary should then be responsible for it; we basically hand it over to that class. We can release any local variables to objects we add to the dictionary. The dictionary then becomes the owner of the objects. To ensure this, the NSMutableDictionary class sends all the data it stores a retain message so that the system knows that someone is using that object.

Since dict is managing the object, line 5 is used to release our object. The dictionary still has the same memory that the today object has; we've just told the system that we're finished with it. Had the dictionary object *not* sent a retain message, line 5 would have actually deallocated the message. The rule is pretty simple: Once the retain count of an object reaches zero by way of a release, the object is sent a dealloc message, and the memory to that object is actually deallocated.

Line 6 is a simple convention to indicate we're finished with the pointer.

Line 7 removes the object by way of the key TODAY. When an object is removed from a dictionary, the object is automatically sent a release message. At this point, the object that today used to point to is sent a release message. Since this now makes the retain count of the object zero, the object is also sent a dealloc message to deallocate its memory.

Line 8 simply sends a release message to the dict object. This will deallocate the memory of the object, since nowhere else is the object retained.

Working with Implied Retain Messages and Autorelease

How do we know which objects need to be released and which don't? The answer basically falls under the rule of object ownership. If an object is created that has alloc, copy, or new in the message name, you own the object, and it, therefore, needs to be released once the program is finished using it. There are other examples, but no hard and fast rules unfortunately. Properly deallocating memory takes an understanding of the objects and what messages result in an explicit retain.

While an object can be sent an explicit retain message, in the examples so far, there isn't one retain because there are automatic or implied retain messages. For example, whenever the message setObject: forKey: is sent to the dictionary object, the object we add is automatically sent a retain message. As mentioned previously, whenever we are allocating an object a retain is implied:

```
NSMutableDictionary *dict = [[NSMutableDictionary alloc] init];
```

Other calls are not so obvious, as seen in the following example:

```
NSDate* today = [NSDate date];
```

In the case above, the object was allocated but has in implied release—called autorelease. As mentioned above, anything with an alloc, copy, new requires that the program manually releases the object. For anything else, the object is released automatically.

The key is that the return value is a new date object. Because it's a new object, it receives a sort of implied retain message. But more importantly, it will automatically be released since the object wasn't created with an alloc/copy/new method. The program could just have also been written as follows:

```
NSDate* today = [[[NSDate alloc] init] autorelease];
```

This code would yield the exact same results. The difference is that, in the second example, we are explicitly allocating the memory but marking it as autorelease. The Objective-C run-time system will automatically release the memory. While using autorelease seems like the best way to handle releasing memory, it may not necessarily be what is needed. Variables that are marked as autoreleased don't stick around very long. All iOS and some Mac applications have something called a **run-loop**. Basically, an application for the most part just waits around for input. If you touch the screen, for example, the application will perform some function and then eventually go back to waiting for more input. Whenever the application goes back to wait for more input, all autorelease variables are released; this could easily be as short as 1/60th of a second. So, autorelease should be used with caution and only in an area where the need for a variable is within the span of the current run-loop. If the program needs to have an autorelease variable stick around for a while, then either don't use autorelease (use the standard alloc and init) or simply send a retain message to the object.

Listing 13–9. *Keeping an Autorelease Variable Available.*

```
1   - (NSDate *)getDate
2   {
3       return [NSDate date];
4   }
5
6   - (void)captureDate
7   {
8       // Capture the current date and store it in the class's iVar
9       currentDate = [[self getDate] retain];
10  }
11
12  - (void)dealloc
13  {
14      // Release the memory for the current_date.
15      [currentDate release];
16  }
```

Notice on line 9 that the `getDate` method is called and then we immediately send a `retain` message to the object. This is because `getDate` is set as autorelease. If the program didn't do this, the memory to `current_date` would have been autoreleased.

> **NOTE:** In any iOS application developed before Xcode 4.2, there is a line in the `main.m` file that looks as follows:
>
>   NSAutoreleasePool * pool = [[NSAutoreleasePool alloc] init];
>
> This is the mechanism the program uses to autorelease memory that has been sent an `autorelease` message when it was allocated, like our example above. The `[NSDate date]` returns memory that is automatically added to this autorelease pool and then automatically deallocated at the next run-loop.

Sending the dealloc Message

Under normal circumstances, your program should never send a `dealloc` message to another object. There are some exceptions. One of these is when handling the `dealloc` message itself. You will be dealing with the `dealloc` message only for objects you create. Listing 13–10 is a snippet of code that shows how a typical dealloc message is coded. Every object that you create should implement a `dealloc` message except when using ARC, garbage collection, or if there's nothing to release.

Listing 13–10. *A Typical dealloc Implementation.*

```
1   - (void)dealloc
2   {
3       self.iVar1 = nil;      // If we had iivars, make sure they are deallocated.
4                              // This instance variable was a property (Chapter 10)
5       [iVar2 release];       // Another example.  We release an instance variable
6                              // that we were using - it wasn't a property.
7       [super dealloc];       // We finally tell our parent to deallocate itself.
8                              // This is one of the few times dealloc will be called
```

```
9                              // explicitly.
10   }
```

Listing 13–10 is strictly an example, and the instance variable names are completely fabricated.

Line 3 sets an instance variable to `nil`. Not only is this common practice, but also, in our example, the instance variable is a property. If the property was created with the `retain` keyword like the code below setting the property to `nil` automatically sends a release message to whatever object `iVar1` was pointing to first.

```
@property(retain) NSDate* iVar1
```

It's a very clean way to release an object.

Line 5 shows how a nonproperty instance variable would be released. We've used this method in many of our examples so far.

Line 7 is the only case in which you would send a `dealloc` message to an object. In this case, the program is telling its parent (the superclass) to deallocate itself. The parent would end up doing the same, sending a `dealloc` to its parent and so on until the base object is finally deallocated. Also note that [`super dealloc`] is the last thing the method does—it's not a good idea to deallocate the parent class and then continue to do more things.

Dealing with the retain/release model will take some time to get used to but overall is a fairly straightforward system of managing memory. Here's a word of caution though: even though our examples talked about the `retainCount` method of an object, do not rely on this value. Since you have no idea what parts of the framework have an interest in your objects, the retain count could be higher than you expect. However, knowing about the `retainCount` is beneficial in troubleshooting a potential memory leak. Continue to practice working with the retain/release model, and make sure that you read the developer documentation when sending or receiving objects so that you know how the object in question is being handled.

If Things Go Wrong

Allocating memory either through the standard C mechanisms or the Objective-C object allocation methods works most of the time. However, the programmer cannot assume that allocating an object or allocating memory works *all* the time. When memory allocation fails, it's generally a sign that bigger problems are at hand, and the program may not be around too much longer (it will crash because of memory issues). However, even though the program may be getting into a bad state because it can't allocate memory, the program should not ignore the memory allocation failure signs. Here are some conventions that are used to test if memory allocation has failed:

```
1   int main(void)
2   {
3       char *data2 = malloc(100);
4       if (data2 == NULL) {// Malloc returns NULL (0x00000000) if allocation fails.
5           // Application has detected a major failure.
6       }
7   }
```

In this standard C example, if the `malloc` function fails, a NULL pointer is returned. Recall that NULL pointer is nothing more than a pointer that points to location 0x00000000. Memory never starts at this location, so NULL can be used to indicate a *bad* memory allocation.

In Objective-C, there are two main areas that we need to perform validity checks. Here's the first:

```
1   int main(void)
2   {
3       MyObject* obj = [[MyObject alloc] init];
4       if (obj == nil) {    // If the object is valid….
5           // Application has detected a major failure.
6   }
```

In this example, we try to create an object, but we check to see if the pointer returned is nil or not. Recall that a nil object is basically a default empty object used as a placeholder to mean "empty," or "nothing." Don't confuse this with an empty MyObject, because that it is not.

The second validity check only applies to objects we've created. This check is done in the init method of the class:

```
1   - init
2   {
3       self = [super init];
4       if (self != nil) {
5           // Do object initialization here on a valid self object.
6       }
7       return self;
8   }
```

In this example, in the object's init method, the program explicitly tests to see if self returns a value that is not nil. If self is not nil, things are OK, and the method can continue initializing the object. The method then returns self, which can be either nil or not. The important thing to note here is that we are testing to ensure that the call to [super init] works before proceeding to work on self.

A Note About ARC

While we covered a lot of the manual ways of handling memory if ARC isn't used, it is advisable to use ARC on any new project you create. What you learned here is that, while ARC hides how memory is retained and released, it is important to understand what's really happening under the covers.

Summary

We've covered quite a bit in this chapter. Hopefully, you now have a clearer understanding of how memory, addresses, and pointers work. In this chapter, we covered the following:

- Defining memory

- Using base-2, base-10, and base-16

- Defining and using memory addresses

- Defining and using pointers

- Defining and using the dereference operator

- Allocating memory

- Using auto-variables and watching out for pitfalls so as not to cause a memory leak

- Deallocating memory and preventing memory leaks, including using the `dealloc` method

- Using the special pointers NULL and `nil`

- Understanding memory management using ARC

- Managing memory using Objective-C and its retain/release model

- Detecting when things go wrong with memory allocation.

This chapter definitely covered a lot of ground, so congratulate yourself on making it through. Understanding how memory works on a Mac, iPhone, iPad, or any computing device is very important.

Exercises

- In the following memory space, how large is the memory block? What is the address of the very last byte in this block of memory?

```
         0   1   2   3   4   5   6   7
0x1000 [ A ][  ][  ][  ][  ][  ][  ][  ]
0x1008 [  ][  ][  ][  ][  ][  ][  ][  ]
0x1010 [  ][  ][  ][  ][  ][  ][  ][  ]
0x1018 [  ][ Z ][  ][  ][  ][  ][  ][  ]
0x1020 [  ][  ][  ][  ][  ][  ][  ][  ]
0x1028 [  ][  ][  ][  ][  ][  ][  ][  ]
0x1030 [  ][  ][  ][  ][  ][  ][  ][  ]
```

- Using the code from Listing 12-1, try to determine what these statements will do and why:

  - `*(aPointer + 2) = '1';`

  - `(aPointer + 2) = '1';`

- Look at the Apple developer documentation for the method `addObject` in the `NSMutableArray` class.

  - What differences are there between the `addObject:` method of the `NSMutableArray` class and the `NSMutableDictionary` class's `setObject:forKey:` method?

  - How would using an `NSMutableArray` change, if at all, the code in Listing 13–1?

Chapter 14

Introducing the Xcode Debugger

Xcode is fantastic! Not only is this tool provided free of charge on Apple's developer site, but it is actually really, really good! Aside from being able to create the next great Mac OS X, iPhone, or iPad app, Xcode has a fantastic debugger built right into the tool.

So, what exactly is a debugger? First of all, let's get something straight—programs do *exactly* what they are written to do. Sometimes, what is written isn't exactly what the program is really meant to do. Sometimes, this means the program crashes or just doesn't do something that is expected. Whatever the case, when a program doesn't work as planned, the program is said to have **bugs**. The process of going through the code and fixing these problems is called **debugging**.

There is still some debate as to the real origin of the term "bug," but one well-documented case from 1947 involved the late Rear Admiral Grace Hopper, a Naval reservist and programmer at the time. Hopper and her team were trying to solve a problem with the Harvard Mark II computer. One team member found a moth in the circuitry that was causing the problem with one of the relays. Hooper was later quoted as saying, "From then on, when anything went wrong with a computer, we said it had bugs in it."[1]

Regardless of the origin, the term stuck and programmers all over the world use debuggers, such as Xcode, to help find bugs in programs. People are the real debuggers; debugging tools merely help programmers locate problems. No debugger, whatever the name might imply, fixes problems all on its own.

This chapter will highlight some of the more important features of the Xcode debugger and will explain how to use them. Once you are finished this chapter, you should have a good enough understanding of the Xcode debugger and of the debugging process in general to allow you to search for and fix the majority of programming issues.

---

[1] Michael Moritz, Alexander L. Taylor III, and Peter Stoler, "The Wizard Inside the Machine," *Time,* Vol.123, no. 16: pp. 56–63

Getting Started with Debugging

If you've ever watched a movie in slow motion just so you can catch a detail you can't see when the movie is played at full speed, you've used a tool to do something a little like debugging. The idea that playing the movie frame by frame will reveal the detail you are looking for is the same sort of idea we apply when debugging a program. With a program, sometimes it becomes necessary to slow things down a bit to see what's happening. The debugger allows us to do this using two main features: setting a breakpoint and stepping through the program line by line—more on these two features in a bit. Let's first look at how to get to the debugger and what it looks like.

First, we need to load an existing program. Our examples in this chapter use the MyBookstore project from Chapter 8, so open Xcode and load the MyBookstore project.

Second, make sure the **Debug** configuration is chosen on the Run Scheme, as shown in Figure 14–1. To edit the current scheme, choose Product➤Edit Scheme from the main menu. **Debug** is the default selection, so you probably won't have to change this. This step is important because if the configuration is **Release**, debugging will not work at all!

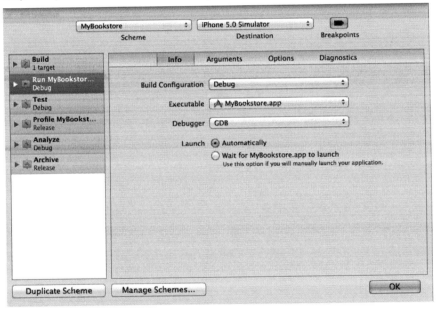

Figure 14–1. *Selecting the Debug Configuration.*

While we won't discuss Xcode Schemes in this book, just know that by default, Xcode provides both a **Release** and a **Debug** configuration option for any Mac OS X or iOS project you create. The main difference as it pertains to this chapter is that a release configuration doesn't add in any program information that is necessary for debugging an application, whereas the debug configuration does.

Setting Breakpoints

To see what's going on in a program, we need to make the program pause at certain points that we as programmers are interested in. A **breakpoint** allows us to do this. In Figure 14–2, we've set a breakpoint on line 25 of the program. To do this, simply place the cursor over the line number (not the program text, but the number 25 to the left of the program text) and click once.

If line numbers are not being displayed, simply choose Xcode ➤ Preference from the main menu and then click on the "Text Editing" Tab and check the "Line Numbers" checkbox.

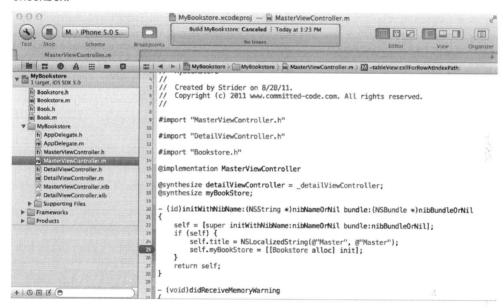

Figure 14–2. *Our first breakpoint*

We can also remove the breakpoint by simply dragging the breakpoint to the left or right of the line number column and then dropping it. In Figure 14–3, the breakpoint has been dragged to the left of the column. During the drag-and-drop process, the breakpoint will turn into a puff of smoke.

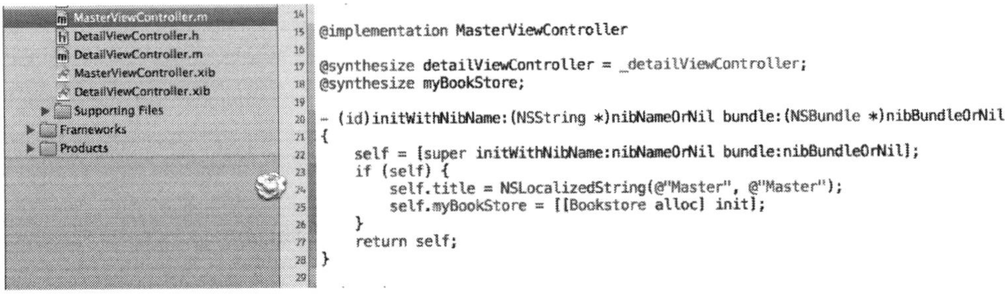

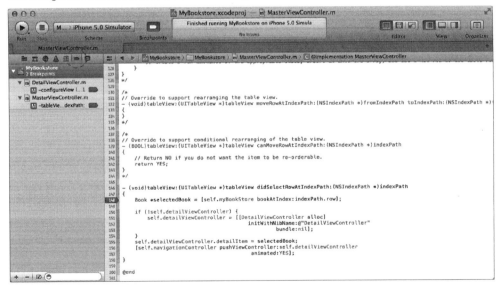

Figure 14–3. *The breakpoint disappears in a puff of smoke.*

Setting and deleting breakpoints are pretty straightforward tasks. There are other ways to delete breakpoints, but this way is the most entertaining!

Using the Breakpoint Navigator

With small projects, knowing where all the breakpoints are isn't necessarily hard. However, once a project gets larger than, say, our small MyBookstore application, managing all the breakpoints could be a little more difficult. Fortunately, Xcode 4 provides a simple method to list all the breakpoints in an application called the Breakpoint Navigator. This can be found by clicking on the Breakpoint Navigator icon in the navigation selection bar, as shown in Figure 14–4.

Figure 14–4. *Accessing the Breakpoint Navigator in Xcode 4*

Once clicked, it will list all the breakpoints currently defined in the application. From here, clicking on a breakpoint will take you to the source file with the breakpoint. You can also easily delete and disable breakpoints from here.

To disable/enable a breakpoint, simply click on the blue breakpoint icon in the list (or wherever it appears). Don't click on the line; it has to be the little blue icon, as shown in Figure 14–5.

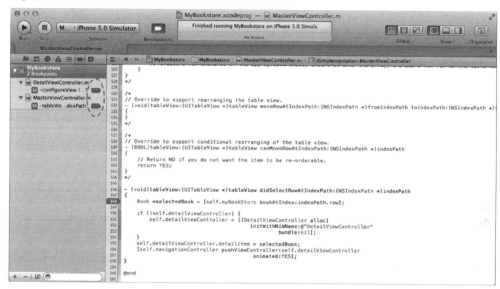

Figure 14–5. *Using the breakpoint navigator to enable/disable a breakpoint*

It is sometimes handy to disable a breakpoint instead of deleting it, especially if you plan to put the breakpoint back in the same place again. Disabling a breakpoint is actually quite simple. Just click the existing breakpoint and it will turn from a dark blue color to a very faded blue. The debugger will not stop on these faded breakpoints, but they remain in place so they can be conveniently enabled and act as a marker to an important area in the code.

It's also possible to delete breakpoints from the Breakpoint Navigator. Simply select one or more breakpoints and press the **delete** key. Make sure you select the correct breakpoints to delete since there is no undo feature.

It's also possible to select the file associated with the breakpoints. In this case, if you delete the file listed in the Breakpoint Navigator and press delete, all breakpoints in that file will be deleted.

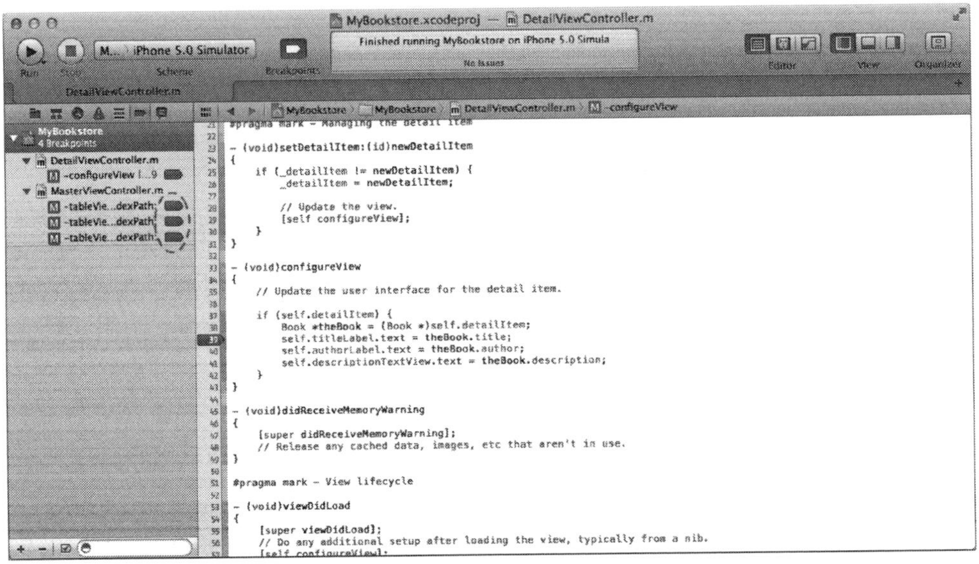

Figure 14–6. *A file with several breakpoints*

Please note that breakpoints are the lines with the small breakpoint icon, as shown in Figure 14–5. The file is outdented from the breakpoint; in Figure 14–5, the files are DetailViewController.m and MasterViewController.m. Figure 14–6 shows an example of what a file looks like with more than a single breakpoint.

Debugging Basics

Set a breakpoint on the statement shown in Figure 14–2. Next, as shown in Figure 14–7, click the **Run** button to compile the project and start running it within the Xcode debugger.

Figure 14–7. *The Build and Debug button in the Xcode toolbar*

Once the project builds, the debugger will start; the screen will show the debugging windows and the program will stop execution on the line statement, as shown in Figure 14–8.

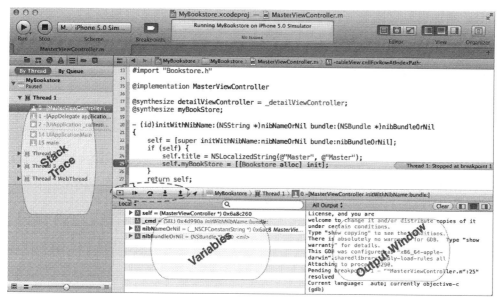

Figure 14–8. *The Debugger view with execution stopped on line 25*

The debugger view adds some additional windows. Let's go over the different parts of the debugger shown in Figure 14–8.

1. **Debugger controls**: (circled in red) The debugging controls can pause, continue, step over, step into, and step out of statements in the program. The stepping controls are used most often. The first button on the left is used to show or hide the Debug area. In Figure 14–8, the Debug area is shown.

2. **Variables:** The variables window displays the variables currently in scope. Clicking on the little triangle just to the left of a variable name will expand it.

3. **Output Window:** The output window will show very useful information in the event of a crash or exception. Also, any NSLog output goes here.

4. **Stack Trace:** The stack shows the object stack as well as all the threads currently active in the program. The stack is a hierarchical view of what methods are being called. For example, main calls UIApplication and UIApplication calls the AppDelegate class. These method calls "stack" up until they finally return, hence the name.

Working with the Debugger Controls

As mentioned previously, once the debugger starts, the view changes. What appears are the debugging controls (item B in Figure 14–8). The controls are fairly straightforward and are explained in Table 14–1.

Table 14–1. *Xcode debugging controls*

Control	Description
	Clicking the **Stop** button will stop the execution of the program. If the iPhone or iPad emulator is running the application, it will also stop as if the user clicked the Home button on the device. Clicking the **Run** button starts debugging. If the application is currently in debug mode, clicking the **Run** button again will restart debugging the application from the beginning; it's like stopping and then starting again.
	Clicking this causes the program to **Pause or Continue** execution. The program will continue running until it ends, the **Stop** button is clicked, or the program runs into another breakpoint.
	When the debugger stops on a breakpoint, clicking the **Step Over** button will cause the debugger to execute the current line of code and stop at the next line of code. If the debugger encounters a breakpoint while stepping over code, the debugger will go to the breakpoint instead of skipping over it. In Figure 14–5, clicking this icon will cause the debugger to go to the next line.
	Clicking the **Step Into** button will cause the debugger to go into the specified function or method. If we clicked this control, the debugger would go into the `init` method shown in Figure 14–5. This is very important if there is a need to follow code into specific methods or functions. Only methods for which the project has source code can be stepped into.
	The **Step Out** button will cause the current method to finish executing and the debugger will go back to the caller. Using Figure 14–5 as an example, if we were to step into line 25 and then immediately click Step Out, the `init` method would finish executing, and the debugger would then go back to line 25, effectively finishing the current method (`init`) and stepping back out.

Using the Step Controls

To practice using the step controls, let's step into a function. As the name implies, the **Step Into** button follows program execution into the method that is highlighted. Make sure there is a breakpoint set on the line statement shown in Figure 14–8 (Line 25 of the example; yours may be different) of the MasterViewController.m file and click the Run button. Your screen should look similar to Figure 14–9.

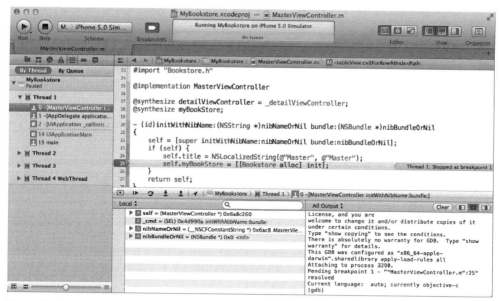

Figure 14–9. *The debugger stopped on line 25.*

Click the **Step Into** button 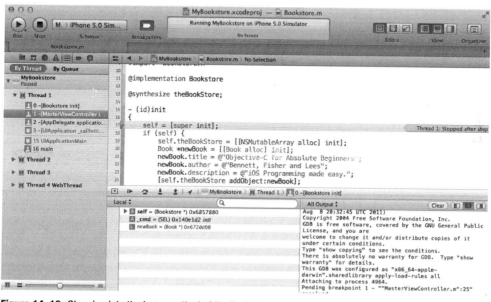; this will cause the debugger to go into the init method of the Bookstore object. The screen should look like Figure 14–10.

Figure 14–10. *Stepping into the init method of the Bookstore object*

It's important to note that not only is the debugger in the Bookstore object, but the debugger has also moved to the Bookstore.m file (it used to be in the MasterViewController.m file).

The control, **Step Over,** ⮌ continues execution of the program, but doesn't go into a method. It simply executes the method and continues to the next line. **Step Out,** ⬆ , is a little like the opposite of **Step Into**. If the **Step Out** button is clicked, the current method continues execution until it finishes. The debugger then returns back to the line before **Step Into** was clicked. For example, if the **Step Into** button is clicked on the line shown in Figure 14–9 and then the **Step Out** button is clicked, the debugger will return to the MasterViewController.m file on the statement shown in Figure 14–9 (line 25 in the example), the line where the **Step Into** was made.

Looking at the Thread Window and Call Stack

As mentioned earlier, the thread window displays the current thread (there is only one in our program). However, it also displays the **call stack**. If we look at the difference between Figures 14–9 and 14–10 as far as the thread window goes, we can see that Figure 14–10 now has the [Bookstore init] method listed because [MasterViewController initWithNibName:bundle:] calls the [Bookstore init] method.

Now, the call stack is not simply a list of functions that *have* been called; rather, it's a list of functions that are currently *being* called. That's a very important distinction. Once the init method is finished and returns (line 17), [Bookstore init] will no longer appear in the call stack. You can think of a call stack almost like a breadcrumb trail. The trail shows us how to get back to where we started.

Debugging Variables

It is possible to view some information about a variable (other than its memory address) by hovering over the variable. In our current example of the Bookstore, all the variables are synthesized properties. The problem is that they are not visible through the debugger. So, in order for the debugger to actually show these variables, we'll have to explicitly declare them. To do this, simply navigate to the Book.h header file and add an instance variable called title, as shown in Figure 14–11.

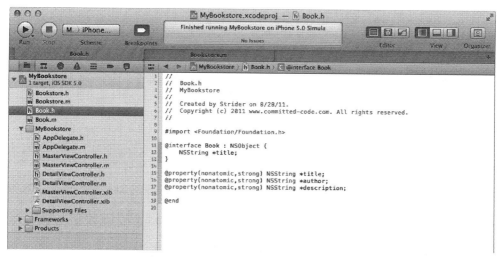

Figure 14–11. *Adding an explicit instance variable called title*

(If you are currently running the application, click on the STOP icon in the upper left corner before modifying the Book.h file). Next, run the application. The debugger should stop at the breakpoint we placed in Figure 14–9. Step into the statement; this will take the debugger to the Bookstore.m file. Next, step through the code using the step over command until the debugger is pointing to the "newBook.author = …" line.

Position the cursor over any place the newBook variable appears and open the Book object. You should see what is displayed in Figure 14–12.

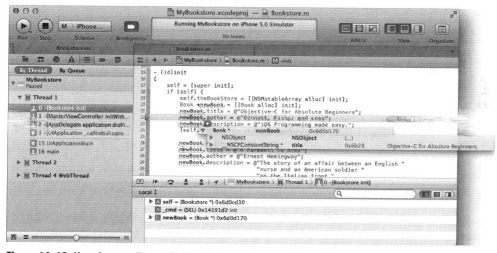

Figure 14–12. *Hovering over the newBook variable reveals some information*

Hovering over the newBook variable reveals its information. This variable is a local variable declared in this method. It can also be seen in the lower left Variable window. In

Figure 14–12, you can see the newBook variable expanded; it shows the same information we can see by hovering.

The pertinent information in the newBook variable is the NSCFConstantString variable. To simplify things, just know that NSCFConstantString (Core Foundation String) is still the NSString class we used in building the Book class. The "Core Foundation" is simply the base library of classes Apple provides programmers. The information to the far right (gray colored text in the debugger) is the actual value of the class' strings. When a variable's contents change, the debugger highlights the variable's new contents in blue italics, as you can see in the Variable window in Figure 14–13. Since these are new values to the newBook class, the values are blue and in italics. For values that are unchanged, the debugger leaves them colored gray and not italicized.

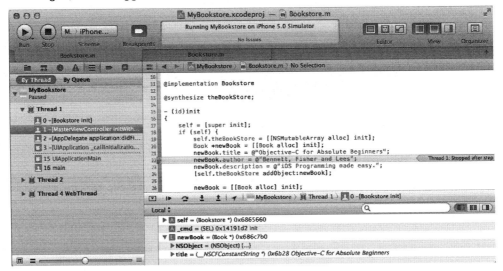

Figure 14–13. *Value changes are highlighted in blue italics in the variable window.*

Dealing with Code Errors and Warnings

While coding errors and warnings aren't really part of the Xcode 4 debugger, fixing them is part of the entire debugging process. Before a program can be run (with or without the debugger), all errors must be fixed. Warnings won't stop a program from building, but they could cause issues during program execution. It's best not to have warnings at all.

Let's take a look at a couple of different types of errors. To start, let's add an error to our code. On line #25 of the MasterViewController.m file, change

```
[[BookStore alloc] init]
```

to

```
[[BookStore alloc] initialize].
```

Save the changes and then build the project by pressing ⌘+B to build the program. There will be an error, as shown in Figure 14–14, that may show up immediately or after the build.

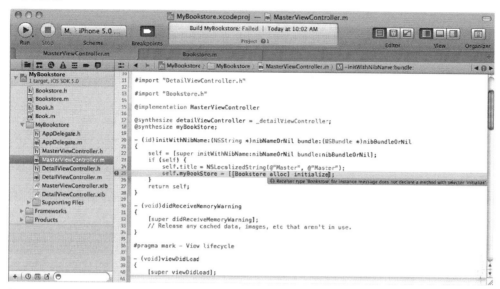

Figure 14–14. *Viewing the error in Xcode*

Next, let's move over to the Issue Navigator window, as shown in Figure 14–15, by clicking on the triangle with the exclamation point. This view shows all the errors and warnings currently in the program—not just the current file, MainViewController.m, but all files. Errors are displayed as a white exclamation point inside a red octagon. In our case, we simply have one error. Also, if the error doesn't fit on the screen or is hard to read, simply hover over the error on the Issue Navigation window and the full error will be displayed.

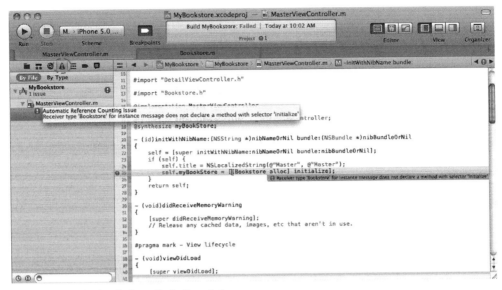

Figure 14–15. *Viewing the Issue Navigation window*

Generally, the error points to the real problem. In the case above, the BookStore object doesn't know about a method called 'initialize'.

> **TIP:** Encountering this error when building a project generally means the method name is misspelled or perhaps the proper header file hasn't been included to let the compiler know about this method. If you know the method exists, then check to see if the header is included. Otherwise, it might just be a typo.

OK, let's fix the error by changing the word 'initialize' to 'init'.

Warnings

Warnings indicate potential problems with the program. As mentioned above, warnings won't stop a program from building, but may cause issues during program execution. It's outside the scope of this book to cover those warnings that may or may not cause problems during program execution; however, it's good practice to eliminate all warnings from a program.

Comment out line with @synthesize MasterViewController (line 14 in the figure below; your line may be different) of the MasterViewContoller.m file by putting two slashes in front of the '@sythesize myBookStore', as is shown in Figure 14–16. Build the project by pressing ⌘+B to build the program.

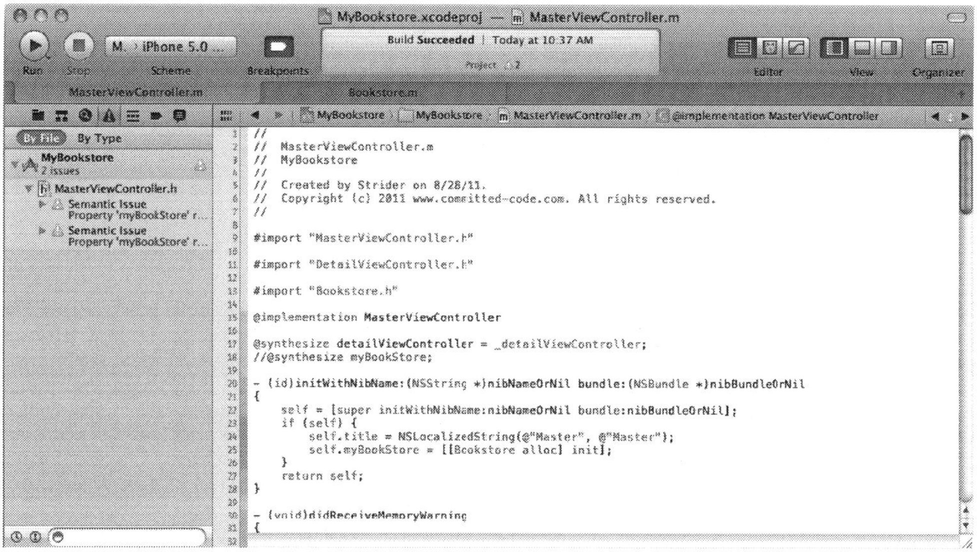

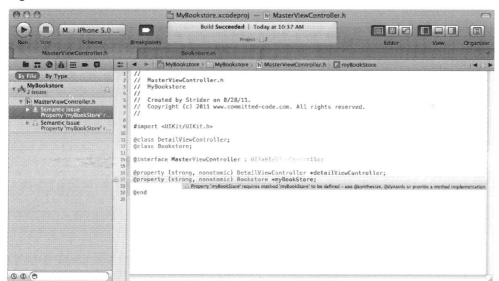

Figure 14–16. *Viewing the warnings in the Issue Navigator*

Unfortunately, the warning doesn't show in the MasterViewController.m file. Clicking on the first warning in the Issue Navigator will bring us to the first problem, as shown in Figure 14–17.

Figure 14–17. *Viewing our first warning*

In the main window, we can see the warning. In fact, this warning gives us some clue as to the problem with the code. The warning states:

"Property 'myBookStore' requires method 'myBookStore' to be defined – use @synthesize, @dynamic or provide a method implementation."

Our code has a @property, but because we commented it out, it doesn't have a @synthesize. The compiler considers this a warning because the method could be provided dynamically during runtime. In our case, however, we aren't doing this; we just didn't include the @synthesize keyword in the implementation file.

To fix this problem, simply navigate back to the MasterViewController.m file and remove the comments we just added on line 14. To navigate back to the file list, click on the *folder* icon, as shown Figure 14–18 (or simply click on the back button located at the top of the edit window).

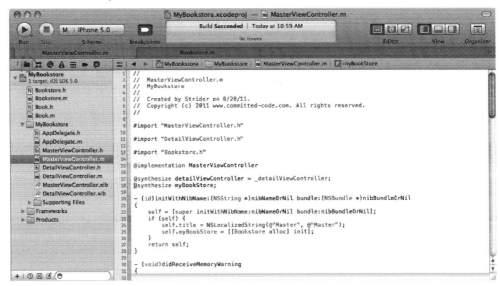

Figure 14–18. *Navigating back to the file list and fixing our warning problem*

Summary

In this chapter, we covered the high-level features of the free Apple Xcode debugger. Regardless of price, Xcode is an excellent debugger. Specifically, in this chapter, you learned the following:

- The origins of the term "bug" and what a debugger is;
- The high-level features of the Xcode debugger:
  - Breakpoints
  - Stepping through a program;

- How to use the debugging controls:
    - Tasks (stop sign),
    - Restart and continue (pause),
    - Step over,
    - Step into,
    - Step out;
- Working with the various debugger views:
    - Threads (call stack),
    - Variables,
    - Text editor, and
    - Output;
- Looking at program variables; and
- Dealing with errors and warnings.

Index

▓N